LOOK, MOM- I'M A CONGRESSMAN!

(And Other Shames I Brought On My Family)

JAMES ROGAN

SHENANDOAH
PRESS

Library of Congress Control Number:

Hardcover 978-1-956033-10-6
Paperback 978-1-956033-11-3
E-book 978-1-956033-12-0

Printed in the United States of America

For my siblings
Teri, Pat, Christie, and John
And for the truly unique Mother whom we shared

Contents

"Congressman James Rogan is absolutely one of the finest people serving in the U.S. House of Representatives and a man of impeccable personal reputation."

—SPEAKER OF THE HOUSE NEWT GINGRICH,
LARRY KING LIVE, CNN, APRIL 8, 1998

"James Rogan: You are an arrogant, offensive asshole. You must be a horrible individual in your personal life. I am ashamed you are my representative. I have no faith in your intelligence nor integrity. You are not a man of honor. Your serious, grave, overblown rants during your impeachment presentation had me actually laughing at my television. You are doing a piss-poor job as a congressman, so please resign. You are a damned hypocrite who has put the interests of the right wing above the interests of your nation. God damn you, sir."

—KEITH M. (CONSTITUENT),
PASADENA, CALIFORNIA, DECEMBER 1998

Prologue

When Alice Rogan wanted a cigarette, she wanted it now, and she didn't care what event it interrupted.

That principle applied even while watching her eldest son claim victory in his race for a seat in the United States Congress. I had eked out a 50.1 percent win in November 1996—a huge feat given that the top of my Republican ticket, Senator Bob Dole, lost the presidency handily to Bill Clinton. Poor Bob garnered an anemic 38 percent of the vote in Los Angeles County, where my congressional district encompassed a large chunk of the Hollywood entertainment community.

Bob Dole for President, Jack Kemp for Vice President, and James Rogan for Congress campaign button worn by supporters at my election night party, November 5, 1996. (Author's collection)

On that long-ago election night, I wrapped up my victory speech by thanking the huge crowd of jubilant supporters. When I climbed off the stage to greet well-wishers, I caught sight of my mother, who had slipped away, stood alone in a corner of the hotel ballroom, and lit up another smoke from the two-pack-a-day habit she indulged since her teens.

Mom puffed away as she surveyed the scene with much satisfaction over its unlikeliness. The youngest child of my dowdy grandmother and my longshoreman grandfather (a no-nonsense San Francisco dockworker for forty-five years), Mom took a cocktail waitress job out of high school, became pregnant out of wedlock by her bartender/soon-to-be-ex-boyfriend that dumped her when she refused his abortion demand, and then she gave birth to me in an era when unwed promiscuity invited neighborhood scandal and shame. She later married, divorced, and raised her four kids as a single working mom. Buying our groceries with food stamps, she did whatever she felt necessary to keep the family together, which included going to jail more than once for welfare and credit card fraud. With that pedigree it is no surprise that Mom was tough-as-nails, street savvy, possessed a raw vocabulary that could peel paint, loved a good time, was thoroughly irresponsible and irreverent, lied through her teeth when it suited her purpose, and—most of all—she didn't give a damn what you or anyone else thought about her.

Knowing Mom possessed an unfiltered mind and tongue, I gave her an unconditional directive before we departed my hotel suite for that election night party: "Mom, once we get downstairs, if any reporters approach you, don't talk to them. They're all liberals, and no matter how nice they pretend to be, they're not your friends. Do not speak to any of them. I mean it."

"Don't worry, Jimmy," she said with the deep conviction in her voice upon which I learned never to rely. "I won't talk to any of those bastards. I promise."

After my speech, and while posing for pictures with campaign volunteers, a grinning local reporter who had covered my congressional race approached. "Hey," she exclaimed, "I just interviewed your mother!"

"Of course," I grimaced.

"Yeah, she's great!" The reporter then related how, after pulling out her steno pad and approaching Mom, she said, "Well, Mrs. Rogan, you must be very proud of your son tonight."

"Which one?" came the reply. "I've got three of them."

Sensing my mother's lack of cooperation, the reporter pressed. "Well, of course, I'm talking about your son James. I mean, let's face it. Here you are, a former welfare mother and a convicted felon, and now he's elected to Congress. That's a remarkable story."

Mom never broke eye contact with her inquisitor as she drew a final puff from the stub pinched between her index and middle fingers. "Listen, honey" (Mom called everyone she didn't know *honey*), "my son Patty's an engineer. My son Johnny's an engineer. I'm a convicted felon, and now Jimmy's going to Congress." Flicking the expired cigarette butt on the floor, Mom concluded the interview with this summation: "Goddamn it, someone was bound to shame the family."

Chapter 1

Road Trip

Serving as majority leader in the California State Assembly while simultaneously running for Congress in the nation's number-one district targeted by the Democrats, I assumed there would be time to decompress from an intense and lengthy campaign after securing my narrow 1996 win.

Wrong.

Within days of victory, I left for Washington to attend a two-week cram session of orientation meetings and briefings. Upon returning, I closed my two state legislative offices, vacated my Sacramento apartment, staffed my new district and Washington congressional offices, and looked for a place to live in D.C.

Most congressmen maintain two residences: one in Washington and one back home. Some keep their families in the district, but my wife Christine and I decided to relocate back East with our twin four-year-old daughters Dana and Claire. They had remained in the district during my time in the state legislature. Typically, I kissed them goodbye on Sunday afternoon, flew to Sacramento, and remained there for the legislative week until returning home Thursday or Friday night. From then until Sunday (when the travel cycle started anew) the telephone and fax machine rang incessantly, and constituent, office, and campaign demands always crowded out my already limited family time. For our upcoming Washington experience, we chose a different model. I took Congressman Howard Berman's (D-CA) advice to move the family: "In Washington," he told me during orientation, "you can have breakfast or dinner with your wife and kids most days. When you fly home to California alone on the weekends, you can focus on constituent affairs and not feel guilty about missing so much family time. Don't split up your family over this job. It isn't worth it." I appreciated this bipartisan counsel.

Wanting to get settled before my new job started, and since hiring professional movers was beyond our budget, I rented a Ryder van to transport our belongings and decided to drive it myself from California to Washington. Christine and the girls would fly back and join me after I had arrived and unloaded the boxes. As it happened, I would not make the trek alone: Frank Ambrose, my old high school pal, offered to tag along and keep me company on the cross-country journey.

In my 2004 book, *Rough Edges,* I described my first impressions of meeting Frank the summer between eighth and ninth grade in 1971:

> Frank looked much more mature than fourteen. A year older than I, and light years ahead of me in street smarts, his leather biker wardrobe and expletive-laced vocabulary spoken in a Marlon Brando-*The Godfather* timbre added to his street punk mystique. I'm sure Frank knew how to fight, although I never saw him in one, because would-be troublemakers chose targets (like me) that appeared far less menacing. Under his sinister look was a guy who'd give a friend the shirt off his back. Frank had an old-world sense of honor when it came to family, and to be Frank's friend meant one had joined his family.

I took this photo of my hoodlum boyhood friends Frank Ambrose (at left) and Rocky Iaukea in 1971. More about Rocky shortly. (Author's collection)

By the time of my election, Frank (at age forty) retained that thug aura: a menacing and gravelly voice, deep-set pale blue eyes, a scar on his forehead, and a perpetual cigarette dangling from the corner of his mouth. Not much had changed over the years. He still looked more like a potential truck hijacker than a prospective truck passenger.

• • •

On Saturday, December 28, 1996, Frank and I braved the rain as we loaded the family possessions into a fifteen-foot rental van. I then strapped my car to the trailer. By nightfall we had finished the job dirty, soaked, and tired.

Standing outside the small, 1931-built Glendale house into which Christine and I moved the day we returned from our honeymoon in 1988, I kissed her and the girls goodbye. Neighbors began approaching. These were friends who watched me over the years go from a young lawyer to municipal court judge to state legislator, and now to Congress. With tears and hugs they came to say farewell. Although I would be back often, I had a melancholy sense that things would never be the same.

It was time to go. Frank and I climbed into the cab of the van, and he started the engine. As the truck lurched slowly down the dark, narrow, tree-lined street, I felt an unexpected and sudden pang of remorse. Three years earlier I traded the dignified, calm, and secure lifestyle of a trial court judge for the brutal and uncertain world of politics. Although my state legislative experience was rough, it would be child's play compared to what Washington promised. With this new career move I was upending our stability once again, only this time yanking my family three thousand miles from relatives, friends, church, and neighbors all for the pleasure of getting my brains beat out on a regular basis as a conservative Republican representing a liberal Democrat district. I leaned my head back and closed my eyes as a rare moment of doubt took hold. "Frank," I mumbled as I shook my head, "why the hell did I do this?"

Not one to suffer whining lightly, Frank cut me no slack. He pointed to my rearview side truck mirror. When I looked, I saw illuminated under a streetlight the dissipating silhouettes of Christine, Dana, and Claire waving goodbye as we turned the corner and pulled out of sight. "That's why you're doing this," he said coolly. I started to thank him for this much-needed perspective, but he brushed me off. "You know," he said, "this is going to be a long drive. Do I have to listen to you sniveling *Oh, what have I done?* all the way to Washington? Suck it up, crybaby." Frank took a final drag on his cigarette before tossing the butt out of my open passenger window. Turning to me, he asked: "Any questions?"

• • •

The notion of a young, idealistic, newly elected congressman driving across the United States on his way to serve in Washington has a certain romantic appeal. Soaking up the spacious skies, fruited plains, and amber waves of grain seemed an appropriate preface to my induction into office. As I contemplated this scenario before leaving, the road symbolized a great asphalt metaphor to the vastness of America. I approached this journey wanting to savor each mile while reflecting upon my forthcoming responsibilities. However, in crafting this high-minded daydream, I neglected to calculate Frank's lack of appreciation for melodrama. To him there was nothing remarkable about a cramped truck cab with no reclining seats, no car radio, and mounds of ill-stacked and ill-tied boxes tumbling on us whenever he applied the brakes too swiftly. Frank did not see the road as poetry. He saw our destination as quarry that he must bag as quickly as possible.

"You need to know," he announced from his power position behind the wheel a few minutes into our trip, "that I've decided we're driving nonstop to Washington. We'll eat along the way as we drive. Motels and restaurants are a waste of time, so we won't be doing any of that."

"Oh, really? What about taking a shower? Brushing our teeth? Changing clothes?"

"We did all that this morning." Then, pulling age rank on me, he proclaimed, "I'm the oldest and I'm driving. That makes me captain of this ship. You may be the congressman when we get there, but while I'm behind the wheel, I'm the Big Daddy of the truck."

And so it was to be. Other than hitting gas stations every 150 miles or so, gobbling down fast food from inside the truck cab while driving, and making occasional pit stops at public restrooms or deserted roadsides, Big Daddy drove nonstop. No matter how much I entreated, Frank would neither rest nor surrender the truck's ignition key to a new driver. As he continued articulating his numbing vision of travel protocol, I knew I had made a profound mistake before we left Glendale in agreeing to his cheery, "Hey, why don't I drive the first leg?" offer.

• • •

That first night we traversed California through to Kingman and Flagstaff. The darkness was rarely broken by oncoming headlights. We saw almost no traffic in either direction as we slowly wended through the black night. By late morning we neared Albuquerque. The majestic flat-topped red mountains almost looked painted against the pastel sky. It was a beautiful, desolate sight. Meanwhile, we freshened up with the tiny packaged moist towelettes that Frank snagged at an Arizona chicken-and-waffle mini-mart, where we had luxuriated in a rare break at a restroom with cold and hot running water.

And then we kept driving.

"How about stopping for a real meal?" I suggested to Frank as the morning wore on.

"No need. I picked up breakfast for us at that mini mart the last time we stopped for gas." He reached down to the floorboard, pulled up a brown paper bag, and tossed its contents onto the middle of the cab's bench seat: pretzels, beef jerky, and a box of red licorice.

"Here's breakfast," he said.

"Did you at least get us some bottled water?"

"No. I found something better than water." Frank handed me a second bag. Inside were small cartons of warm Nestlé's Strawberry Flavored Milk, each with a little child-sized straw taped to the box. "I bought plenty of these," Frank reassured me. "Enough to last us all the way to Washington." With apologies to the Nestle Corporation (headquartered in my congressional district, coincidentally), I hated strawberry flavored milk even as a boy. Frank, on the other hand, couldn't get enough of it. "This stuff is hard to find," he told me as he slurped down the contents with great satisfaction. "That's why I bought up all they had."

• • •

Our nation is blessed with endless miles of rolling plains, hills, and mountain ranges. To those who experience such wonders from the comfort of an air-conditioned or heated sedan, these monuments are breathless reminders of nature's awesomeness. However, to a captive inside a crawling and rickety moving van, they became a curse. Unlike the cars skimming these elevations at freeway speeds, our truck climbed those mountain ranges at fifteen miles an hour. Also, each time we ascended one, the gas gauge needle rocketed toward "E," more boxes fell over, and Frank smoked another cigarette with his window rolled up.

I came to hate America's rolling hills.

True, I did see a great deal of our scenic country during the drive, but not always by choice. It proved impossible to get any sleep in the cab. The horrible vibration of the old truck caused my head to bounce against the window and door frame whenever I closed my eyes and leaned against them. Frank also made sleep elusive by enforcing his newfound credo: "If I don't sleep, nobody sleeps."

• • •

Many motorists find the drive across the Texas panhandle bleak and boring. To me it provided a welcomed blessing: flatland. No hills meant higher speeds and fewer stops to refill the unquenchable gas tank.

When we took a ten-minute break at a near-deserted truck stop outside Amarillo, my stomach was at near-revolt from our junk food diet. I went inside to find whatever nourishment was available. In this, the Truck Stop from Hell, the proprietor had stocked his shelves with the locals' four basic food groups: Pretzels, beef jerky, red licorice, and small cartons of Nestlé's Strawberry Milk.

• • •

Exactly twenty-four hours after leaving Glendale, I called Christine and the girls. "Where do you think we are?" I asked. Expecting the slow, lumbering truck would not fare well speed-wise, Christine guessed we were somewhere in Arizona. I scoffed. "We're in Oklahoma City!" Thanks to Frank's obsessiveness, we had covered twelve hundred miles the first day.

Sometime after midnight on the second day we rolled into Arkansas. The weather was terrible, and a thick pea-soup fog engulfed the road. Sleep deprivation now gripped me in extremis, so in desperation I climbed into the small compartment above the truck cab to curl up and take a real nap. The fact that a thundering, frigid rain leaked through a crack and dripped all over me didn't matter. Neither was I dissuaded by the large sticker affixed to the wall above my head warning that this narrow compartment was not meant for human occupation, and that a serious case of squashing would result in the event of a rollover. By now even death had a compelling aspect: a cadaver gets to stretch out flat and close its eyes.

Frank did not sanction my relocation. He cursed me for leaving him to drive alone and for not doing my part to help keep him awake. When invective failed to coax me down from the overhead space, he displayed his continued disapproval by making feigned emergency swerves across multiple traffic lanes on the wet freeway. Down came more boxes as my body thrashed against the upper compartment walls.

I climbed back into the passenger seat.

• • •

When we crossed the river into Tennessee, I made a firm demand. I had never been to Nashville, and since it was on our direct route, I told Frank I wanted to see it. After all, I reasoned, an hour or so delay would not preclude a timely Washington arrival. "Sure," he replied. "No problem." As we hit Nashville's city limits, instead of pulling off the freeway, Frank punched the accelerator pedal. "You want to see Nashville?" he asked while pointing out the window toward the vaporizing skyline. "There. You saw it."

• • •

After commemorating the forty-eight-hour mark of our trip in Knoxville, Tennessee, we rounded the Great Smoky Mountains, and then traveled northeast along the Appalachians. As the sun arose Tuesday morning, we entered the final leg. The Virginia countryside epitomized serenity with its low fog spilling across the Shenandoah Valley. There was a bonus aspect to this home-stretch segment: After two days behind the wheel, an exhausted Frank finally surrendered the truck keys.

As the truck's new Big Daddy, I bided my time to exact revenge for his dictatorial control. That opportunity came near Fredericksburg when Frank yawned, stretched, and then he mumbled, "Pull over, dude. I need to take a leak."

"Sorry, but you'll have to wait. We need to get to Washington, remember? *No stopping.* That was your rule. We'll need to keep driving."

As the minutes clicked by, and Frank alternated between begging and threatening, I remained resolute. After an hour, and with Frank's anxiety escalating, he finally sought the mercy I awaited. "Come on, man!" he cried. "Stop the truck! I'll do anything—"

Now the coiled serpent struck, and I knew where to pierce him to make it really hurt. But first I must digress to explain the back story. As I mentioned earlier, Frank grew up as a street-tough kid. He was also a very proud guy, and he was especially proud of his oft-proclaimed cultural superiority over everyone who did not share his Italian ancestry. Back in the old neighborhood, we had a Hawaiian friend, Curtis "Rocky" Iaukea, who was part Chinese. One day while in high school, Frank started mocking the inferiority of Rocky's Chinese heritage compared to his own Italian breeding. Growing tired of it, Rocky (a big, bull-strong kid who became a professional WWF wrestler in adulthood) grabbed Frank and slapped on him a submission chokehold, which he refused to release until Frank gave in to Rocky's demand to, "Say the magic words!"

After a barrage of gagged vulgarities, Frank realized the futility of struggling. "What are the magic words?" he gasped.

"Say *Chinese are better than Ambrose.*"

"NO!"

"Say it, you bastard: *Chinese are better than Ambrose!* Say it!"

"NO!"

Rocky tightened the vice, and Frank's face turned various shades of purple before he finally conceded the ancestral point. Decades later, nothing got under Frank's skin faster than reminding him of his coerced admission that not only were the Chinese superior over all Italians generally, but that the Chi-Coms were better than every ancestor and future member of the Ambrose family lineage.

With that explanation, we now return to our moving van narrative and to Frank begging for relief. I dragged out his misery a while longer, and then I relented. "Okay, Frank," I told him. "The joke's gone on long enough. I'll stop the truck. All you have to do is say the magic words."

"All right. *Please* stop the car."

"Actually, those aren't the magic words. I'll stop as soon as you say *Chinese are better than Ambrose.*"

Not since Generals Lee and Burnside engaged each other in that same valley 135 years earlier had such sizzling profanities littered this serene landscape. Eventually I pulled over for Frank, but only after he unzipped his fly and appeared ready to perpetrate a tremendous indignity upon my pant leg.

"Just remember," I shouted out the window as Frank, with britches now tumbling below his knees, ran to a nearby cluster of bushes along the roadside, "who's the *Big Daddy* of this truck now!"

• • •

Making our final stop at a small grocery store an hour outside of Washington, we waited in line behind a careworn young woman. She wore no wedding ring and looked fatigued as she tried keeping in tow her four runny-nosed children dressed in old clothes. A look of embarrassment crossed her face as she made her purchase with food stamps. Frank said nothing about the scene until we returned to the truck.

"That looked familiar," he said with a tinge of sadness.

It did. A quarter century earlier, when we lived next door to each other, both of our mothers were single, on welfare, buying groceries with food stamps, and he and I left high school in the tenth grade to take jobs. Long ago we walked in that family's shoes, and now I had been given the rare privilege of being in a position to help needy people like that young mother. I did not want the memory forgotten nor the opportunity wasted.

• • •

At noon on New Year's Eve, the Washington Monument adorned the horizon. We drove a victory lap around the Capitol, and then we parked the van and trailer on a side street under the shadow of the great dome. I turned off the engine and we sat in silence looking at that magnificent symbol of liberty.

The sound of rapping on glass interrupted our private reverie. A Capitol policeman motioned for me to roll down the window. "Hey, you bums," he barked. "Move this truck."

We hadn't showered or shaved in three days; our hair was matted to our heads, our clothes were dirty, and mud covered our truck and trailer. Frank and I looked at each other, and then we laughed. "Officer, you got it all wrong," Frank assured him. "I'm a taxpayer and a veteran of the Vietnam War era." Then pointing to me, Frank added, "This guy's a new member of Congress. He's the bum, not me." After producing my identification, the cop apologized, wished me luck, and drove away.

Frank smiled. "Well, Jimmy," he said, "you've come a long way." The tears welling in his eyes told me that he wasn't just talking about our just-completed 2,717-mile marathon drive.

"No, Frank. *We've* come a long way. And there's nobody on earth with whom I'd have rather made this trip." We toasted the moment with our two remaining cartons of warm Nestlé's Strawberry Milk.

"By God," I thought, "right now, nothing ever tasted quite so good."

Frank Ambrose (at left) and the congressman-elect after a shower, shave, and wardrobe change, New Year's Eve 1996. (Author's collection)

Chapter 2

The Whirlwind

When one wins a seat in Congress, it doesn't take long for friends to come a-callin'.

On Election Day morning, I gathered my staff together and told them that win or lose, I expected everyone to report for work the next day. Since I remained a member of the state legislature until my term expired the following month, I didn't want my constituents to think I had walked off of the field. We owed them our best until I hit either Washington or the unemployment line. The following morning, when we reunited in our district office, we remained exuberant over our squeaker victory in what proved to be an otherwise slaughter of Los Angeles County Republican candidates. I hadn't been there an hour when one of the very senior members of my campaign finance committee (I'll call him Paul—not his real name) arrived with his teenage son to offer felicitations. Paul had proved tireless in helping us raise the money we needed to beat back my Democrat challenger—an opponent who self-financed a large amount of his congressional race from the trust fund left to him by a billionaire relative.

"Boy, we sure pulled that win out of the hat!" Paul exuded as he pumped my hand. "Every time I made fundraising calls on your behalf to reel in those high dollar checks so that we could send you to Congress, I kept telling myself that all this hard work I'm doing for you is worth it because we need you in Washington. No effort was too big when it came to helping you." Hiding my growing discomfort over his continued expressions of self-sacrifice, I waited for Paul to get to his point. It didn't take long: "I'd like you to meet my son, Paul Junior, who's always dreamed of going to one of the military academies—West Point would be nice, by the way. Did you know that, as a congressman, you get to directly appoint young people to each of the military academies? It becomes a four-year tuition-free college education for a deserving young man who then gets an officer's commission at graduation. Anyway, no pressure. Here's Paul Junior's resume." He handed me a single page document. When I glanced at it, the first item catching my attention was Paul Junior's 1.9 high school grade point average.

"No rush on this!" Paul said as he turned to leave. "Get settled into your new job, and then let me know if you can help Paul Junior. Well, we'd better go. Come along, Paul Junior!"

My office manager, Denise Milinkovich, had overheard the conversation. She knew how important Paul had been to our campaign. After father and son had left, she asked me, "What are you going to do? That kid's a loser."

I called a staff meeting, "Listen," I told everyone, "we're in politics. And in politics, sometimes we have to do favors for friends. But there are two places we don't do favors. One is in judicial recommendations, because having been a judge I know how critical it is to get the right people on the bench. The second place is in appointments to the military academies. In fact, if I *have* to do a favor in one of those two areas, I'll do it for a judgeship before I'll do it for an academy appointment. If some dumbbell becomes a judge, the appellate courts can fix their mistakes. If someone's moron kid slips through the cracks and winds up as a commissioned officer because of me, he could lead soldiers straight to the graveyard. We need to establish a system to protect against this."

My chief of staff, Greg Mitchell, contacted the local veterans' organizations in our county and put together a volunteer committee of retired military officers holding the rank of captain or higher from each of the branches. From my first to last day in Congress, no academy application ever made it to my desk for final review unless our committee gave the applicant a unanimous recommendation. The young men and women we sent to the academies were the best of the best. Paul Junior was not among them.

And, last I heard, Paul Senior was finance chairman emeritus for www.DefundTheMilitary.com.

• • •

The volume of congratulatory messages became so great that we had to bring in volunteers to help. Besides responding to them (and deflecting major donor requests to inflict their idiot kids on the United States Armed Forces), the press calls flooding my office the day after our victory also proved overwhelming. As a deputy district attorney, county judge, and state legislator, I had handled media inquiries often. Usually, they came from the local newspapers: *Glendale News Press, Burbank Leader, Pasadena Star News, San Marino Tribune,* and occasionally the *Los Angeles Times.* Now calls came into my office from the networks (CBS, ABC, NBC, CNN, Fox News) and the major dailies (*New York Times, Washington Post, Wall Street Journal*). Even the BBC called for an interview. As we fielded these calls, I started developing a sense of heightened importance.

Late that afternoon, my press secretary Staci Turner entered my office and interrupted a telephone conversation with my mother: "Excuse me," Staci said, "but *Time* magazine is calling. They're on line two."

Time magazine calling? That substantiated my prominence.

"Sorry, Mom, but I gotta go," I told her. "*Time* magazine is on the phone. They need to interview your son." If you must hang up on your mother, you might as well impress her along the way.

I dropped Mom and took the incoming call. Giving it my best Edward R. Murrow imitation voice, I announced in a bold manner, "This is James Rogan."

"Mr. Rogan, good afternoon. This is Ray Jones from *Time* magazine. Thank you for taking my call."

"It's my pleasure," I replied. "What can I do for you?"

"It's not what you can do for me. It's what I can do for you. If you subscribe today...."

• • •

A week after my victory, the House leadership summoned all newly elected members to Washington for a biennial rite of passage: Freshman Congressman Orientation Week. This tradition is something of a death march of photo ops, policy briefings, press availabilities, new staff interviews and hires, classes on everything from parliamentary procedure to introducing bills to setting up an office, lobbyist meet and greets, and jockeying—lots of jockeying. Obtaining an appointment to a key committee, winning a freshman class officer position, finagling interviews with the crème of the Washington press corps, and other indicia touting one's arrival are best not left to chance. The Darwinian competition among new members, though masked by nonchalance, existed. We all knew without being told that the senior House members and D.C. powerbrokers would be watching for the smoke signals designating who among our group were the future "comers."

A day or so after I arrived in Washington, I had my first big interview request. A producer from CNN News called and invited me, as a freshman Republican, to appear live in studio with freshman Democrat Darlene Hooley of Colorado for a segment regarding our mutual impressions of this orientation whirlwind. I agreed to do it.

"Sir," the producer advised, "we'll send a car for you. After you arrive at the studio, you'll be escorted to our makeup room. Then, after you're made up, you and Ms. Hooley will wait in the green-room until we go live for your interview."

"That all sounds fine," I said, "but I'll skip the makeup. I don't wear it."

"Well, uh, the studio lights are pretty harsh. I know you're a Southern Californian, but even with a tan you'll look washed out. I strongly suggest you wear makeup."

"I appreciate your concern, but I'll pass. I don't wear makeup. Thanks anyway."

"Okay, sir. It's your call."

When I told my chief of staff Greg Mitchell about the CNN interview and my rejection of their makeup offer, he urged me to do as the producer suggested. I dug in my heels: "I've never worn makeup before and I'm not starting now. Anyway, I have to go. They said the car would be outside in a few minutes." Once I left, Greg placed a frantic call to my senior campaign manager in Sacramento, Jim Nygren. He told Jim about my upcoming live interview on a national broadcast and my makeup intransigence.

While on the way to CNN, the limousine car phone rang. The driver answered it, and then he handed me the receiver. "It's for you," he said. "A Mr. Nygren on the line."

I took the phone. "Hi, Jim," I said as the car pulled up to the CNN studio entrance. "How's it going?"

"I'm only going to say this once," he replied. "In 1960, Kennedy wore makeup. Nixon didn't. Put on the makeup." Then he hung up.

The producer awaited my arrival in the lobby. After shaking hands and introducing myself, I asked her to please lead me to the makeup.

I followed her up the elevator and through several doors. We entered a room with side-by-side barber chairs stationed in front of large lighted mirrors and a counter filled with assorted brushes, talcums, pastes, combs, sprays, and other things found in a salon. A pleasant woman introduced herself as the makeup artist. She tied a bib around my neck, reclined my chair, and then she went to work. I don't think I squirmed so much when receiving my first boyhood haircut as I did under her application of pencils and powders. "Please sit still," she entreated as I fidgeted and griped during the ordeal.

When she finished, I felt as if she had transformed me into Emmett Kelly.

With this humiliating effeminate torment over, an escort brought me to the studio, where Congresswoman-elect Hooley and I broadcast our segment. As soon as it ended, I rushed back to the makeup room to get all the goop removed ASAP.

An uncomplaining man undergoing a second makeup artist's powdery and penciled transformation reclined in the barbershop chair adjoining the one into which I had scampered. I paid little attention to him, because getting my own puss scrubbed clean remained my sole priority.

"I've been doing this for many years," my makeup lady said as she took wet wipes to my face. "I've never seen anyone in the chair complain and wiggle as much as you. You're like a little kid. What's the big deal about getting makeup?"

"Listen," I told her, "my grandfather raised me. He was a long-shoreman on the San Francisco dockyards for forty-five years. I'm his namesake. He was a tough, old-school kind of guy. He's been my hero and role model of manhood for my entire life. If Grandpa knew that I ever wore makeup, he'd spin in his grave, and I don't want to listen to him chewing me out for eternity when we're reunited in Heaven."

"But it's just a little makeup!"

"It doesn't matter how little," I replied. "It's still makeup. And makeup's for women and sissies."

I was somewhere between the words *women* and *sissies* when I happened to glance over at the man in the adjoining chair. With his now-fully made-up face completed, he sat upright after listening to my conversation. Our eyes met, and then an awkward silence followed. Clearing my throat, I volunteered the opening salvo:

"However, may I say that on you, General Haig—"

Alexander M. Haig, the U.S. Army four-star general, former supreme allied commander of all European military forces, White House chief of staff to Presidents Richard Nixon and Gerald Ford, Secretary of State under Ronald Reagan, and a former presidential candidate, continued staring as I groped for words to extricate myself from this unfortunate dilemma: "—On you, General Haig, no, seriously, it looks great! Very masculine. In fact, perhaps your makeup lady could fix me up just like you. Miss, can you give me the General Haig Look before I leave? That would be wonderful." To my relief, the general had a sense of humor.

Following that first makeup capitulation at CNN, in every subsequent in-studio television interview I ever did, when faced with the choice of either wearing sissy makeup or going without and reflecting masculine virtue, I never again flinched. Thereafter, whenever the studio makeup artist approached me in the greenroom, I told her firmly: "Ma'am, for my base foundation, let's cocktail some Max Factor Formula 15 with a temperamental sienna rouge. Then, with your stippling brush, try to give my eyes a halo contour...."

• • •

Seniority determines office selections for members of Congress. After the returning senior members trade up for better digs in the days preceding the start of orientation, a lottery for the leftovers is held for the freshmen.

There are three House office buildings across the street from the Capitol, with each named for a former Speaker: Joseph Cannon, Nicholas Longworth, and Sam Rayburn. Senior members prefer the Rayburn Building because it is the newest (opened in 1965), it houses many of the committee rooms, and it has a subway connecting it to the Capitol for easy House chamber access when the clanging bells signal a vote. Longworth (opened in 1933) is the second-most preferred, and Cannon (the oldest, opened in 1909) tends to quarter the more junior members. The freshmen office lottery scuttlebutt was to forget about getting into Rayburn until one's third or fourth term: aim for Longworth, but if one must get stuck in Cannon, choose any office that isn't on the top (fifth) floor. "We call Fifth-Floor Cannon 'Freshman Ghetto,'" one senior staffer warned me:

> The elevators don't run to the fifth floor because that was used for storage when they built Cannon. Plus, the building has a copper roof, so you'll bake to death in the summer because the air conditioning system is so antiquated. Also, those offices don't have majestic high ceilings like the rest of the offices on the lower floors. Fifth-Floor Cannon has the 'dog' offices of Capitol Hill, so avoid them at all costs.

I rejected this counsel. The day before the lottery, I toured the available office space and found that I preferred the bright and elegant Cannon Building over the dark and charmless Longworth. Also, Fifth Floor Cannon was anything but a ghetto. So what if the ceilings weren't as high as those downstairs? They were high enough, and the HVAC system appeared to function (at least it did on the day of my visit). Because no elevator traffic ran to that floor, it proved quieter than the bustling lower levels. Mostly, history drew me to Fifth Floor Cannon. My inquiry to the Library of Congress revealed that in the 1940s Congressmen John F. Kennedy, Lyndon B. Johnson, Richard Nixon, and Gerald Ford all occupied offices on Fifth Floor Cannon. Quiet charm, coupled with possible executive branch upward mobility, clinched for me the decision to try for Fifth Floor Cannon.

On lottery day, I drew a low number, which gave me many choices from which to select. Members and staff assembled for the sweepstakes guffawed when I bypassed all of the available Longworth and lower-level Cannon spaces to claim 502 Cannon. "The poor dumb bastard," I overheard someone say. "Fifth Floor Cannon! That's what happens when you don't know what the hell you're doing at these things." I knew what I was doing. I had inspected Room 502 previously. It was more than satisfactory, and it also happened to be the office that Congressman Lyndon Johnson had once occupied (according to the LBJ Library records). For me it proved ideal—right down to the copper roof.

Inhabiting LBJ's former suite tested my devotion to constituent services when a class of fifth graders on a cross-country field trip from Glendale, California, visited me in Washington. When I gave them a tour of my Cannon quarters, I mentioned the LBJ connection. One boy's voice filled with excitement as he told me, "I just did a report on Lyndon B. Johnson! I got an A on it! I learned all about him. Was this really Lyndon B. Johnson's official office?"

Yes, I told him, LBJ had occupied it from 1943 until he won election to the U.S. Senate in 1948.

"Wow! Now I can tell everyone that I stood in Lyndon B. Johnson's official office!" Looking around, he pointed to one of two closed doors. "What's in there?" he asked.

"The closet."

"Was that Lyndon B. Johnson's official closet?"

"Yes."

"Can I look inside?"

"Sure."

He opened the door and stepped inside. Housing nothing but my overcoat and umbrella, the otherwise bare closet did not diminish his interest. "Oh, boy!" he exclaimed. "Now I can tell everyone that I stood in Lyndon B. Johnson's official closet!"

Pointing to the other door, he asked, "What's in there?"

"It's the bathroom."

"Was that Lyndon B. Johnson's official bathroom?"

"Yes."

"Can I look inside?"

Knowing the bathroom remained clean thanks to the building's efficient janitorial staff, I told him to go ahead. He opened the door and studied the unimpressive inner chamber after entering it. "Now I can tell everyone that I stood inside Lyndon B. Johnson's official bathroom! Hey, was that Lyndon B. Johnson's official sink?"

"It's an old porcelain sink, so I guess it was here back then."

"Can I wash my hands in it?"

"Help yourself." He ran his hands under the running tap: "Now I can tell everyone that I washed my hands in Lyndon B. Johnson's official sink!" After drying them, he pointed to the commode. "Was that Lyndon B. Johnson's official toilet?"

"Yes." By now, I had detected a predictable pattern. The boy's next question matched my anticipation:

"Can I pee in it?"

During Freshman Orientation Week, none of the classes we took that covered effective constituent services quite prepared me for this request, so I improvised. "Before answering, I have a question for you," I told him. "When you get home to Glendale, what do you plan to tell your parents about meeting me in Washington?"

The boy's face radiated enthusiasm as he replied, "I'll tell them that you're a great congressman and a great guy, and that they should vote for you!"

"That's fine. And one more thing, kid. After you close the door behind you—

"—don't forget to lift Lyndon B. Johnson's official toilet seat."

• • •

Swearing-in day for the 105th Congress of the United States fell on January 7, 1997.

On the first day of a new Congress, it's easy to spot the rookies from the veterans. While the old-timers await the start of the session looking indifferent or bored, the freshmen are filled with excitement. On swearing-in day, the chamber is far more crowded than usual. Between the crush of bodies and the hot television lights, it becomes stuffy very quickly. Still, at my first oath-taking, I was too energized to pay attention to discomforts. Since age ten, my goal was to serve in Congress, and now I sat in the mighty chamber moments away from becoming one of its members. My young twin daughters Dana and Claire sat on my lap, and my wife Christine (in the gallery above) smiled and watched with pride. It was a family moment to remember.

My daughter Dana, perched on my lap alongside her twin sister Claire, looks up at the House photographer as the newly elected members of the 105th Congress await their swearing in, January 7, 1997. On my left is Congressman-elect Kevin Brady (R-TX); at right is pro-football Hall of Famer and second-term Congressman Steve Largent (R-OK). (House of Representatives photograph)

A few minutes past noon, House Clerk Robin Carle banged the gavel, called to order the newly constituted 105th Congress, and proceeded to the first agenda item: electing a Speaker. After each party nominated their caucus choice, a lengthy individual roll call vote delivered a second term to Speaker Newt Gingrich (R-GA), who took his oath from the dean of the House, John Dingell (D-MI).

Speaker Gingrich delivered brief remarks, and then the moment had arrived. He instructed the members-elect to rise for the administration of the oath of office. Along with the others, I stood, scooped my daughters into my arms, and then I raised my right hand.

What goes through a person's mind at the culmination of one's lifetime ambition? For me, I felt overwhelmed by history. While in law school, I bartended on Hollywood's Sunset Strip and in nightclubs with predecessors named Chee-Chee, Zoot, and No-Thumbs Mike. Now I prepared to begin a job with predecessors named Jefferson, Madison, Lincoln, and Webster. My emotions remain indescribable.

As Speaker Gingrich began reciting the prescribed oath, an unexpected intrusion interrupted my contemplation. Claire whispered six words in my ear:

" Daddy, I have to go potty."

Oh, God.

"Sweetheart," I whispered, "Daddy's being sworn in. Just wait a minute."

"Daddy," she repeated, "I have to go potty. Now. "

I took another shot at explaining to my four-year-old that we would find a potty momentarily. Claire associated my lack of immediate action with a hearing deficiency. "DADDY," she shouted. "I **NEED** TO GO POTTY. DADDY—**NOW!** DADDY!"

Speaker Newt Gingrich (lower left) administers the oath of office to the new members of the 105th Congress. The circled area of the photo (top right) depicts me with my oath-taking hand raised and twin girls under my arms—the very moment that Claire shared with me her sudden urgency. (House of Representatives photograph)

Members with raised hands standing nearby started chuckling. Because of Claire's escalating volume, reporters in the overhead press gallery also joined in the laughter. Even Speaker Gingrich, at mid-oath, glanced over to determine the source of disruption.

Thankfully, nature deferred to constitutional process. After uttering the final words of the oath, "So help me God," I became an official member of the United States House of Representatives. There was no time to savor the moment. I finished taking the oath at 2:42:00 p.m.; at 2:42:01 p.m., Capitol tourists caught sight of a disoriented and frantic new congressman barreling down marble corridors while carrying cackling girls under each arm, and all while playing an apparent new game called Who Hid the Bathroom?

It wasn't exactly a Madisonian moment, but it would do.

Chapter 3

Prime Time

few weeks after my induction into Congress, I received an unexpected telephone call from one of Speaker Gingrich's senior aides.

"So, Mr. Rogan," he asked, "are you ready for prime time?" He told me that Speaker Gingrich had invited me to preside over the House of Representatives during three hours of debate that evening. "Are you interested?"

Was I interested? Until 1995, no Republican congressman had presided over the House throughout their forty consecutive years in the minority. Now, after only a few weeks in office, Gingrich offered me an honor that had eluded most of my Republican predecessors over the last half century. My euphoria heightened when the aide told me that I would preside during that night's "special orders." I didn't know what that meant, but its very title connoted gravity. "The Speaker doesn't need me for *ordinary* orders," I thought. "He needs me for the *special* orders." With a sense of destiny calling, I accepted.

I could hardly contain my excitement when I called my mother in California and told her to watch C-Span from 7 to 10 p.m.

Washington time (4 to 7 p.m. on the West Coast) and see her son take his place on the national stage. With typical enthusiasm, Mom hung up and started calling every family member for whom she had a phone number.

• • •

As each hour brought me closer to the designated moment, my initial exhilaration morphed into second-thought jitters. I didn't know the House rules of procedure, and my few weeks on the job showed me that a gigantic learning curve awaited. My mind raced: "What if I foul this up? I'll look foolish in front of millions of viewers. I could hurt the Republican agenda by making rookie mistakes, all while my family in California is watching. I'm not ready for this." After lamenting my impulsive acceptance, I resigned myself to the obligation. Speaker Gingrich needed me in the chair tonight, and it was too late to turn back. I must answer duty's call.

• • •

Following the directions given me, at a few minutes before seven o'clock I arrived in the Speaker's Lobby, which is an ornate hall just outside the House chamber. The walls are adorned with eighteenth-, nineteenth-, and twentieth-century paintings of the men who once wielded the gavel just a few feet from where I stood. I paced the now-empty lobby nervously while wondering what it would be like to ease myself into the large brown leather chair atop the platform. This was the same chair that Speakers and vice presidents used during joint sessions of Congress. Previous squatters in that prestigious seat were future presidents Truman, Coolidge, Johnson, Nixon, Ford, and Bush, along with legendary Speakers such as Rayburn, John Nance Garner, Tip O'Neill, Newt Gingrich, and now, only moments away and of zero legendary standing, me. For the next three hours, for better or worse, I would be "Mr. Speaker," and as such I meant to do the People's Business.

House Parliamentarian Charlie Johnson interrupted my mental gyrations when he pushed open the door separating the House floor from the Speaker's Lobby. "Good evening, Mr. Rogan," he intoned. "It's time." I nodded, took a deep breath, and then strode with great purpose into the chamber.

Expectations of grandiosity deflated upon entering the holy of holies, which stood deserted save for a lone congressman reading his speech to an audience of one—the Speaker pro tem, whom I was about to replace.

"Hey," a staffer from the Speaker's office called over to me, "let's go. You're on." At his direction I mounted the platform, where a Florida Republican who had presided for the preceding three hours occupied the Chair of History. He sat slumped, slack-jawed, and with eyes glazed as he fingered through a copy of yesterday's *USA Today* newspaper.

"Who let this guy preside?" I thought. "He looks comatose. What an embarrassing image to project to Americans watching these proceedings on live TV." I concluded that it was a good thing I showed up to replace him, otherwise his slovenly appearance might diminish respect for our Republican majority.

With more than a hint of condescension in my voice, I advised him, "I'm here to relieve you." With that news, the Floridian corpse came to life. He greeted me with the passion of a liberated prisoner of war.

"Have fun!" he called out as he dashed for the exit. "I left you the newspaper."

For now, I chose to forego sitting in the ceremonial chair. Unlike my unworthy predecessor, I wanted America's new Speaker of the House to look dignified and make a good impression on those television viewers watching democracy in action. I stood behind the desk, posture erect, and I maintained my grip on the polished Speaker's gavel in case I had to move into rapid action.

Shortly after assuming my duties, Charlie Johnson joined me

at the desk to brief me on the proceedings. "You'll be presiding for three hours over special orders," he said.

"I know," I replied. "By the way, what are special orders?"

"At the end of all legislative business, Democrat and Republican members may sign up to speak for an hour in alternating blocks of time. During their hour they can talk about anything they want."

"Anything?"

"Yes, anything."

"That doesn't sound very special. And how come nobody's in the chamber now?"

"Since there is no legislative business left on the calendar, most members have gone home. They don't want to sit around listening to other members talk for hours about whatever they feel like."

"What am I supposed to do during all of these special order speeches?"

"You preside."

"Yes, I know, but what do I *do* for the next three hours?"

Charlie's eyes drifted to the *USA Today* left by my predecessor, which now sat atop a nearby wastebasket. "Well," he asked, "have you read the newspaper yet?"

• • •

Forty-five minutes later, with me "presiding" but without any speaking lines as yet, I conceded propriety to comfort and settled into the large brown leather chair. My eyes studied the details of the chamber, which looked surprisingly small and intimate from this perspective. On the Speaker's desk was an ornate silver triple inkwell stand that once belonged to Speaker Henry Clay (1777–1852). To my right was the historic Mace, a large baton symbolizing House order and in use since the days of Webster and Lincoln. Behind me hung an American flag flanked by marble pillars. Encircling the room were the sculpted heads of mankind's great lawgivers such as Hammurabi and Solon; staring down at me from his place above the center clock was Moses. Semicircular wood and leather pews with over four hundred fixed (and now empty) seats faced me. Directly in front and a few feet away was the lower lectern used by presidents of the United States to deliver their speeches to joint sessions of Congress, including those seeking two war declarations earlier in the century (President Woodrow Wilson, 1917; President Franklin D. Roosevelt, 1941).

Without warning, an assistant parliamentarian rushed to my side. (Charlie, the head man, by now had also gone home.) "Get ready, sir," the assistant told me. "We're about to get some movement here."

"This is it," I thought. My heart raced as I stood and picked up the gavel. All my training and instincts as a former prosecutor, judge, and state legislator were about to be tested. I watched as the assistant parliamentarian scrawled a hurried note, and then shoved it into my hand.

"Read this—now!" he directed. After clearing my throat, I followed his direction:

"The gentleman from Minnesota is recognized for the balance of the hour."

With that, the Republican who had been giving his speech walked out of the chamber, while another Republican stepped to the microphone and started talking.

"What just happened?" I asked the assistant parliamentarian.

"The congressman giving the speech wanted to go home," he replied, "so he found someone to finish it for him."

• • •

It had now been an hour since I had assumed the Speaker's chair, and thus far I had read one sentence. Just then I spied two Democrats stalk into the chamber and take seats on their side of the room. They appeared agitated as they huddled in a private but animated conversation. I suspected that the Republican orator had struck a nerve, and they came to challenge him in debate. Things were about to heat up.

Bingo! One of the Democrats stood at the microphone and sought recognition. The assistant parliamentarian began scribbling modifications on the same note he had given me earlier. "Hurry!" he said. "Read this."

"The gentleman from Minnesota's time has expired. The gentleman from New York is recognized for one hour."

There was no confrontation. For the next hour, the two Democrats tag-teamed on a speech in which they paid a birthday tribute to an old man who had shuffled into a seat in the overhead visitors' gallery.

I was hungry. In the excitement of being asked to preside earlier, I had neglected to eat lunch or dinner. I opened the drawer to the Speaker's desk looking for abandoned breath mints or a leftover roll of Life Savers. I found only paper clips and unsharpened pencils.

• • •

Two hours into my tenure, the birthday speeches ended and both Democrats, along with the celebrant, left. The assistant parliamentarian placed before me another piece of paper to read. After giving it a quick glance, I waved it away and improvised: "The *distinguished* gentleman from Maryland is recognized for one hour."

I derived a sense of professional satisfaction knowing that at the start of my third hour in the chair, I needed no amateur prompting and knew my line cold. However, one unexpected problem arose. When I looked up after recognizing the gentleman from Maryland (whose name came from the prearranged list of people on the Speaker's desk), I discovered that the gentleman had apparently changed his mind. Nobody was on the House floor or in the gallery. I stood at the Speaker's platform staring at the assistant parliamentarian awaiting a cue that didn't come. All he did was shrug his shoulders. After a seemingly interminable period, I leaned over the desk and asked him, "Hey, are those goddamn C-Span cameras still on?"

Yes, he advised me, the goddamn C-Span cameras were still on—along with their goddamn microphone, which was "hot" and carrying everything I had just said to the worldwide television audience. He neglected to mention that I should have pressed the "mute" button before offering collateral chatter.

Oops.

There was no time to meditate on my faux pas. The rear doors of the chamber flew open. The gentleman from Maryland rushed down the center aisle and took his place at the microphone. He had not gone home; he had fallen asleep in his office watching the previous special order speeches and had missed his cue. "Mr. Speaker," he intoned, and another hour-long monologue was underway.

Settling back in my chair, I noticed on the schedule that three additional hours of speeches remained after my shift concluded. "Lord Jesus," I prayed silently, "now might be a good time for the Rapture."

• • •

My replacement (another excited freshman) arrived a few minutes before his start time of 10:00 p.m. He found me slumped in the big chair, flipping through the leftover copy of *USA Today*, and oblivious to the distinguished gentleman from Maryland's braying. I grunted a goodnight to my successor and handed over the gavel. As I shuffled out of the chamber, I heard the new Speaker pro tem intone with great solemnity, "The gentleman from Oregon is recognized for one hour."

It was almost midnight when I returned to my Arlington townhouse. Since my usual carpool partner had departed hours earlier and the buses had stopped running, I had to fork over twenty-five bucks for the cab ride home.

I called my mother in California and asked if she had seen me preside over Congress tonight. "No, honey," she told me. "I was

watching, but I never saw you. I fell asleep in front of the TV. Sorry."
Later, I learned that relatives called her to complain. "We watched
that boring show and never saw him" was the consensus gripe.

• • •

The next morning, I discussed the experience with my congressional
staff, each of whom agreed that presiding over the House during
special orders was a waste of time and that I should never do it again.
They registered shock when I told them that I had already volunteered for another round. When pressed for a reason, I reminded
them that in show business, there are no small parts—

—Only small actors.

Chapter 4

Rules Are Rules

Despite my staff's consensus that presiding over the House was a waste of time, during my first year in Congress, I did it occasionally. After developing some experience at the task, the front office invited me to chair occasional legislative floor debates. One memorable opportunity came in 1997 when Speaker Newt Gingrich turned over the gavel to me so that he could address the House, and a national television and radio audience, on what his office billed as a special order speech of national importance.

• • •

A few minutes before session began that morning, I met with House parliamentarian Charlie Johnson in his office just off of the chamber. He told me that in his decades-long congressional experience, this was the first time a Speaker turned over the gavel so that he could deliver a major policy address as a special order speech. Accentuating the rarity of the upcoming event, he congratulated me on my selection as the pro tem Speaker to preside over it.

"Why doesn't Newt just address the chamber from the Speaker's desk?" I asked.

"That goes against tradition," Charlie replied. "Typically, the Speaker avoids parliamentary debate. However, if the Speaker wishes to address the body, by tradition he turns over the gavel for another member to preside. Keep in mind that when the Speaker hands you the gavel this morning, you become the Speaker of the House, and he becomes the gentleman from Georgia. Don't call him 'Mr. Speaker.' That's what he will call you. You refer to him as the gentleman from Georgia."

"Got it. Why does he want to address the House?"

"His staff told me that he will announce to the American people the Republican congressional agenda for the 105th Congress, which makes this speech doubly important. Speaker Gingrich will be setting forth the majority party's policy vision for the next two years."

For the first time since I came to Washington, it looked like a "special order" speech was indeed special.

• • •

Shortly after 10 a.m. Speaker Gingrich arrived in the chamber and called the House to order. After the chaplain's prayer, Newt asked me to lead the Pledge of Allegiance and to handle pro forma legislative housekeeping matters. Then he called me forward. As he handed me his gavel, I dropped on the Speaker's desk a thick folder. He motioned at my files and looked at me quizzically. I smiled and whispered, "It's my reading material. That's in case you start boring me. I've presided over special orders before."

Newt chuckled. "I'll try not to bore you," he said, and then he descended the platform and walked to the microphone stationed at the Republican side on the House floor.

I rapped the gavel on the sounding block and then looked down at Newt standing below me. "For what purpose does the gentleman from Georgia seek recognition?" I asked.

"Mr. Speaker," he replied, "I ask unanimous consent to address the House for one hour."

"Without objection, the gentleman from Georgia is recognized for one hour." With that, Newt began talking and I settled into the chair.

• • •

In my book, *Catching Our Flag: Behind the Scenes of a Presidential Impeachment*, I wrote this observation about my friend and former colleague Newt Gingrich—perhaps the most consequential member of the House of Representatives who served during my lifetime:

> House Republicans used to joke that Speaker Gingrich suffered from attention deficit disorder (truthfully, when they said it, not everyone was joking). The synapses of his brain fired at too high a rate, making it hard for him to focus on any single topic for too long, and harder for his troops to follow him into multi-front battles. By the time we absorbed his newest powerful idea, Newt was off on ten new topics, all brilliant and all worthy of immediate focus. The practical problem was that the rest of us could not keep up with the most peripatetic mind in Washington.

Presiding over Newt's special order this day might have been the incident that gave me this insight. Had I been drafting his "Agenda for the 105th Congress" speech, I would have focused on two or three key points. Fifty minutes into his hour-long speech, Newt was riffing on something like his seventeenth point (I had stopped counting), and he still had a large stack of unread pages to go.

As we neared the end of the hour, I rolled back my chair, stood, picked up the gavel, and started rubbing its head into my palm, which was my signal to whomever was talking that time was about to expire and to wrap up the speech. The assistant parliamentarian stationed at my side walked over and asked me what I was doing. I told him that I wanted to let Newt know that his time was about up. The assistant parliamentarian gave me a look of grave concern mixed with incredulity. "You certainly don't intend to gavel down the Speaker, do you?" he asked.

"He's not the Speaker," I replied. "I'm the Speaker. He's the gentleman from Georgia. Charlie Johnson told me so. I recognized the gentleman from Georgia for an hour, and he has about three minutes left."

"You're kidding, right?"

"No."

"Excuse me," he said, and then he rushed out of the chamber.

Moments later, Charlie Johnson appeared. He climbed the few steps up to the Speaker's dais and sidled alongside me as I remained standing and tapping the gavel in my palm. Looking away from me and across the chamber, and in a nonchalant manner, he asked, "So, Mr. Rogan, how's it going?"

"Fine, Charlie. How's it going with you?"

"Fine, thank you."

Clearing his throat, he continued. "You know, as I said earlier, I've been here about thirty years, and this is the first time I have ever seen an incumbent Speaker present a one-hour special order speech."

"You did mention that, Charlie."

"This is a very rare event."

"Yes, rare."

He looked at his watch. "And it looks like his hour is just about up," he noted.

"Just about."

"And he doesn't appear to be finished."

"No, he doesn't."

Charlie's voice adopted a grave tone. "So, if he does go a little bit over, I think we need to let the Speaker finish."

"He's not the Speaker. I'm the Speaker, remember? You told me that when he handed me the gavel, I became the Speaker of the

House, and he became the gentleman from Georgia."

"Yes, I did say that, and that is all true, but—"

"And didn't the Speaker—me—recognize the gentleman from Georgia—him—for one hour?"

"Yes, you did, but—"

"And isn't it true that the gentleman from Georgia has now used up about fifty-eight and a half of his sixty minutes?

"Yes, but—"

"Thanks, Charlie. I was just checking. If you want to go back to your office now, it might be better if you weren't standing next to me ninety seconds from now."

As an aside, I want to assure the reader that I wasn't trying to be officious or troublesome. It was a matter of fairness. When I was a trial court judge, if I gave each side a certain amount of time to present their case to the jury, I held each side to it. I never favored one side over the other in the courtroom, so I didn't feel it appropriate to do so in the House chamber. Newt had requested and had been granted an hour, and the next scheduled speaker, Patsy Mink (D-HI), was at the minority party's table awaiting her scheduled turn.

Rules are rules.

Anyway, back to the story: as Charlie stepped off the dais, he made frantic hand signals to catch the attention of Jay Pierson, Newt's floor aide who sat in front of Newt and out of camera range. Jay caught sight of Charlie pointing to Newt and me, and then Charlie drew his finger back and forth across his throat in a slashing motion. Jay looked over and saw me standing, checking my wristwatch, and tapping the gavel head into my palm. Jay waved his hands at his boss until he drew Newt's attention, and then he signaled for Newt to look back at me.

When Newt glanced up, I smiled and nodded, looked at my wristwatch again, and then, while keeping my eyes on my watch, I raised the gavel and held it aloft as if about to bang it on the sounding block. With more than a hint of irritation in his voice, Newt said, "Mr. Speaker, I ask unanimous consent to revise and extend my remarks."

"Without objection, it is so ordered," I replied. "The gentleman from Georgia's time has expired."

Bang! Down came the gavel.

Newt scooped up his speech notes, dropped them into the clerk's basket on the desk (for later printing in the *Congressional Record*), and then stalked off the floor with several aides following in his wake. I then recognized Congresswoman Mink, who began her one-hour speech.

A few minutes later, Charlie Johnson reentered the chamber, followed by a procession of all of his assistant parliamentarians. They formed a line behind Charlie, and then each one walked up to the dais and shook my hand. After I greeted the last one, I asked Charlie if this was an expression of their respect for a Speaker pro tem who followed the rules without fear or favor.

"Actually, no," he replied. "We just wanted to say that it's been nice working with you—and goodbye, because you won't ever be back presiding."

• • •

As it turned out, and to my gratitude, Newt never held it against me for enforcing the rules. In fact, I think he admired my gumption. Two months later, the Republican leadership brought before the House for debate and vote one of the Republican leadership's key legislative priorities, H.Con.Res. 84, which was a resolution to balance the federal budget. As the House considered that contentious measure, Newt called me up to the dais, handed me his gavel, and asked me to preside over the remainder of the historic debate. The measure passed, and that year the Republican Congress, with President Bill Clinton's signature, gave America her first balanced budget in thirty years.

Later that evening, Newt inscribed and signed the gavel that he and I had used to preside over H.Con.Res. 84, and then he gave it to me. That treasure remains on display in my office to this day.

The lesson: you can score some pretty nifty swag when you follow the rules.

Gavel used by Speaker Newt Gingrich and Speaker Pro Tempore James Rogan during the debate and vote on H.Con.Res. 84, May 21, 1997—the first federal balanced budget since 1969. (Author's collection)

Chapter 5

Gold Fever

Members of Congress are a very generous lot. They love to give things away, and I'm not talking about gift baskets or flowers. Their generosity extends well beyond a Trader Joe's wine sampler. "Members" (as they call each other and as insiders call them) give away money—lots of it. And, lest anyone overlook their largesse, an array of government-funded press secretaries, staffers, and "franked" (i.e., free) mail churns out a PR onslaught to the folks back home to ensure proper credit attends the doer of good deeds. Being a "generous" member is easy, because congressmen have an inexhaustible supply of other people's money with which to extend their generosity. Where else but in Congress can a benefactor get 100 percent of the credit for showering happiness upon a fortunate recipient (and future grateful voter) while only having to foot 1/330 millionth of the actual cost? Imagine getting a similar return at your local bank: deposit a buck, get $330 million credited to your account. Sign me up.

One would think that with so much money on the table begging to be spent, it would strain the members' creativity on whom or on what to spend it. After all, there are only so many destitute people to feed, so many highways to pave, and so many private contractual arrangements in which to meddle. What to do with the rest? Fortunately, members are blessed with unlimited genius for making sure taxes collected don't go unspent. *Reader's Digest* published a few recent examples of such inspired outlays:

- The Pentagon paid $28 million in licensing fees to Afghanistan to copy the Afghan Army's military uniforms. Why? Because the Afghan Army came up with a camouflage pattern that stands out more readily. In other words, the U.S. military chiefs paid $28 million for camo that is easier to see (readers may need to think about this for a moment to grasp the irony);

- Paying pre-identified "hip people" $5 million to not smoke in the expectation that this will make smoking look, and I quote, "uncool";

- $518,000 to study how cocaine affects the sex habits of Japanese quail;

- $3 million to study what makes hamsters angry;

- $1.7 billion (that's with a *b*) to study how not to use 770,000 vacant government-owned buildings;

- $500,000 to build an IHOP restaurant in Washington, D.C.

Every now and then a tiny handful of fiscal spoilsports express outrage over wasteful spending such as those above, not to mention the oft-cited government-purchased $800 toilet seat and $2,000 basic screwdriver. Still, even the most vigilant budget hawks might be surprised by the proliferation of congressional generosity in an area that is so discreet that virtually all but the sharpest fiscal watchdogs miss it:

Members of Congress love giving away gold.

And no, I am not speaking metaphorically. I mean gold—as in the stuff locked away at Fort Knox. To be more precise, members of Congress give away solid gold medals. These trinkets, known as (you guessed it) the Congressional Gold Medal, do not come cheaply. Depending on exchange rates, a single medal costs the taxpayers more than $30,000 to mint.

In a subliminal attempt to divert attention from who is really behind the giveaway, Congress presents these twenty-four-karat trophies "on behalf of a grateful nation," which, in Congress-speak, means that you, and not they, gave away the gold. Without knowing it, you have been expressing such gratitude repeatedly, and for a very long time. According to the House of Representatives' History, Art and Archives office:

> Since the American Revolution, Congress has commissioned gold medals as its highest expression of national appreciation for distinguished achievements and contributions. Each medal honors a particular individual, institution, or event. Although the first recipients included citizens who participated in the American Revolution, the War of 1812 and the Mexican War, Congress broadened the scope of the medal to include actors, authors, entertainers, musicians, pioneers in aeronautics and space, explorers, lifesavers, notables in science and medicine, athletes, humanitarians, public servants, and foreign recipients.

Ah, I'll bet you missed the key phrase in that official description. Go back and read that paragraph again. You still missed it? Okay, I'll help you out. Congress used to give these medals to war heroes defending our shores in times of national peril. Later, Congress "broadened the scope of the medal…".

Do you see where this is going?

We used to give gold medals to people like General Washington for leading our troops to victory in the American Revolution; to General Jackson for leading our troops to victory during the War of 1812; to General Grant for leading our troops to victory during the Civil War; and to General Pershing for leading our troops to victory during World War I. Now, thanks to Congress "broadening the scope," through them you have bestowed gold medals on various members' favorite movie stars, cartoonists, baseball sluggers, golfers, and pop singers. Thanks to Congress, you gave out gold medals to two guys who rode a balloon across the ocean. You gave a medal to a swing band leader who, in his spare time, patented an improved kitchen blender; a short-timer congressman known more for media stunts than legislative accomplishments received one posthumously for going to some cult hellhole (where he shouldn't have gone) and getting murdered there. When President Carter ordered the entire U.S. Olympic team to boycott the 1980 summer games in protest of the Soviet Union's Afghanistan invasion, and to ease the athletes' disappointment for missing the games, you gave a medal to every U.S. team member—all 650 of them. In an exemplary showing of restraint, these Olympics freebie medals were merely gold-plated; giving out that many solid gold versions might have led to a major depletion of our reserves and an international market crash.

What's going on here? The answer is that the medals have gone from recognizing rare acts of valor to recognizing some congressman's personal celebrity pick. Have you always wanted to meet your favorite movie star? It's easy: a) get elected to Congress; b) sponsor a resolution giving him or her a gold medal. If it passes, the luminary comes to Washington to claim the medal at a formal ceremony. As the sponsoring member, you get to sit on stage next to the honoree. Talk about the ultimate photo op.

How prevalent have these medal ceremonies become? During the first 100 years of our Republic, and not counting medals awarded for gallantry during wartime, Congress authorized eight non-war-related gold medals to distinguished citizens. Back up and consider that again: Congress awarded a total of eight gold medals in a 100-year period. Fast-forward to my stint in the House of Representatives (1997–2001): During that brief four-year span, Congress awarded *fifty-one* solid gold medals, and that is not counting all of the solid silver medals we also gave away—in your name, of course.

Oh, hell, I don't remember, but I probably voted for all of them.

After all, what sane politician from Los Angeles wanted to be the guy telling civil rights icon Rosa Parks to get lost? If I voted no on giving a gold medal to Pope John Paul II, he'd probably default to Christian forgiveness. If I voted no on Frank Sinatra's gold medal, I might get a midnight visit from some guy named Carmine.

There was one party-pooper in the House who told all those medal recipients to go pound sand: he voted no on each of them. Members (myself included at the time) looked upon him as an eccentric tightwad uncle that the family hid in the attic before company arrived. He didn't just vote against congressional gold medals. He voted against almost every other federal expenditure, earning him the nickname "Dr. No" among his bemused colleagues. Still, his constituents kept sending Ron Paul (R-TX) back to Washington. A three-time presidential candidate, Ron was perhaps the most consistent anti-Big Government congressman who ever served. He analyzed every bill through a simple filter: did Article I Section 8 of the U.S. Constitution grant Congress the power to do that which was proposed? The answer to that question was often no, so Ron voted accordingly. Like our other colleagues, I viewed Ron as a quirky purist who was dealt out of all deal-making discussions because he voted for almost nothing.

Despite Ron being the most tight-fisted overseer of federal dollars that I ever encountered during my public life, in him I also discovered the perfect example of the expression "All things are relative." During one late night House session in 1998, and with the primary season approaching, I sat in the chamber alongside my fellow freshman, Congressman Kevin Brady, a member of Ron's Texas GOP delegation. Kevin showed me several brutal direct mail hit pieces on Ron that his Republican primary opponent had just sent to every registered Republican voter in Ron's district.

"Ron has a primary?" I asked in amazement.

"Yeah, a big one," Kevin replied. "His opponent has some serious money. Here, look at these," and he handed me the samples of attack ads leveled at Ron. Emblazoned across them were eye-popping charges: "Defeat Ron Paul—Big Spending Liberal", and "Ron Paul—Wasting Your Tax Dollars in Washington."

"Is this a gag?" I asked. "This can't be serious, Kevin. Where'd you get this stuff?"

"From his district. This is real hit mail."

"How can anyone call Ron Paul, of all people, a big spending liberal?"

In his gentle drawl, Kevin replied with great seriousness: "You need to understand, Jim. In Texas, there is always someone more conservative than you."

• • •

I remember the day I started taking Ron Paul seriously. I only wish the moment had come at the front end of my congressional service instead of at the end.

It was near the conclusion of the 106th Congress, which was the last of my four years in the House. I cannot remember the legislation before us, but it was something popular, noncontroversial, and it was the kind of bill that would earn members who voted for it plaudits back home. As I entered the chamber and pulled out my electronic voting card, I recall thinking to myself, "I'll bet this is a measure where even Ron Paul will vote yes."

I was wrong. When the Speaker closed the roll, a green light illuminated next to every members' name on the huge tally boards except for one. There was a lone red light alongside Ron's. Standing around with a few colleagues, we saw Ron seated nearby and alone. We teased him about his solo vote. "Hey," I chimed in, "Ron even voted against giving Mother Teresa the Congressional Gold Medal!" Ho, ho, ho.

As the other members dispersed, I sat next to Ron and assured him that I was just ribbing him. "But I have to tell you, Ron, I've always been amazed that you voted no on giving Mother Teresa the medal. If ever you could have voted yes on a matter, I thought that would be it."

"Did you listen to my speech that day on why I voted no?" Ron asked. I had not, so he promised to send me a copy.

It arrived the next day. It was brief, and it shattered my hubris about my own good works in Congress as much as it shamed me for my conceit over Ron's cheapness with public funds. Because I think it should be required reading for every legislator now and in the future, I reprint it in full here:

Mr. Speaker, I rise today in opposition to H.R. 1650. At the same time, I rise in total support of, and with complete respect for, the work of Mother Teresa, the Missionaries of Charity organization, and each of Mother Teresa's Nobel Peace Prize-winning humanitarian efforts. I oppose the Gold Medal for Mother Teresa Act because appropriating $30,000 of taxpayer money is neither constitutional nor, in the spirit of Mother Teresa who dedicated her entire life to voluntary, charitable work, particularly humanitarian.

Because of my continuing and uncompromising opposition to appropriations not authorized within the enumerated powers of the Constitution, several of my colleagues found it amusing to question me personally as to whether, on this issue, I would maintain my resolve and commitment to the Constitution—a Constitution which only months ago each member of Congress swore to uphold. In each of these instances, I offered to do a little more than uphold my constitutional oath.

In fact, as a means of demonstrating my personal regard and enthusiasm for the work of Mother Teresa, I invited each of these colleagues to match my private, personal contribution of $100 which, if accepted by the 435 members of the House of Representatives, would more than satisfy the $30,000 cost necessary to mint and award a gold medal to the well-deserving Mother Teresa. To me, it seemed a particularly good opportunity to demonstrate one's genuine convictions by spending one's own money rather than that of the taxpayers who remain free to contribute, at their own discretion, to the work of Mother Teresa and have consistently done so.

The next day I sought out Ron and apologized—not just for teasing him, but for all the votes I had cast as a member of Congress and now wished that I could take back. Had I thought about the issue from a genuine constitutional perspective, I would have been the second red light on the tally board alongside his name on that day in 1997, and many, many other times thereafter.

What I never told Ron is that his simple speech, unread by me until almost four years after he delivered it, not only changed my opinion on giving out gold medals, but it had a profound and jarring impact on my entire legislative outlook. Ron's speech caused me to rethink and challenge every assumption I had carried throughout my life on the role of legislators. It humbled me to see how often I had fallen for the mirage. Ron's little speech was, for me, the cockcrow of daybreak: when government takes by compulsion money from wage earners, and then doles it out for extraconstitutional purposes to favored targets, it is not benevolence. It is plunder, and the people-pleasing politicians like me who jostled for compassion credit were conspirators against, not benefactors of, the public welfare.

Ron Paul's lesson took root, and it has remained with me throughout the many years since my separation from legislative office. I am embarrassed to confess that I never truly appreciated the fragility of a constitutional republic, or the threat to each of its virtues from an ever-expanding government acting outside the consent of the governed, until I was no longer positioned to help defend properly our Founders' gift to their heirs.

Perhaps I missed it because I was too busy chuckling at Ron Paul instead of standing with him.

Chapter 6

Triple Whammy

Before Ron Paul shamed me over voting for gold medal giveaways, in late 1999 I introduced House Resolution 2815, which was my only self-initiated attempt to award one. Actually, my resolution was a taxpayer-funded triple whammy: it sought to present the Congressional Gold Medal to the first men on the Moon: Apollo 11 astronauts Neil Armstrong, Buzz Aldrin, and Michael Collins.

As an eleven-year-old boy, I watched the live television broadcast of Apollo 11 and that first lunar landing with my great-aunt Della Glover on her old black-and-white Magnavox that required a "rabbit ears" antenna to pick up an analog TV signal. To me, the achievements of the astronauts appeared to be science fiction come to life. For Aunt Della, born before the Wright Brothers conquered gravity at Kitty Hawk, their milestone remained a feat too staggering to comprehend.

From that day forward, one of my great ambitions was to meet Neil Armstrong—the Christopher Columbus of our time. My dream proved elusive. A notorious recluse after retiring from NASA in 1971 to teach aerospace engineering in Ohio, he wrote no books, he avoided speeches and NASA reunions, and he kept such a low profile over the ensuing decades that the *Washington Post*, on his mission's silver anniversary, called him, "The world's most private famous person." Over those three decades between his flight and my election to Congress, I sought opportunities to meet him, but all my efforts proved fruitless.

During my first year in Washington, our GOP congressional leadership pushed for a series of federal budget cuts. Among their targets was NASA's Jet Propulsion Laboratory (JPL), which was located in my district. Aside from threatening critical research and development jobs, the intended cuts to JPL put on the chopping block projects ranging from the space station to the Mars terrain rover.

I saved JPL from the budgetary scalpel, but my win did not come from brilliant legislative prowess. Once I learned of the planned cuts, I visited with all of the Republican House chieftains, including the chairmen on the various committees and subcommittees of jurisdiction, and gave them this simple pitch: Each of you holds your powerful position by the thread of our slender GOP majority. My district will be a top Democrat target in the next election. Follow through with these cuts to JPL, and you will hurt me back home. If my seat flips to the Dems, we could lose our majority and you will lose your leadership slot.

Poof! All the money for JPL went back into the budget plus a little bump. Naturally, my staff cranked out torrents of press releases giving me full credit for the save. Everyone from the Speaker to the committee chairmen provided news quotes about my incredible leadership for consumption by my voters back home. With the money restored, I returned to the district and made a victory lap visit to JPL, where they cheered and feted their funding hero.

If people only knew how it really works in D.C.

Soon after my JPL success, NASA Director Dan Goldin came to see me. He pumped my hand and slapped me on the back.

"Congressman," he gushed, "you did it! NASA owes you big time. What can we do for you? You want me to send some astronauts to visit your district? You want something named for you at JPL? Are you interested in going up on the Space Shuttle? That last one's a tougher deliverable, but we have had a couple of congressmen go up in the past. They were committee chairmen, of course, and not a freshman like you, but if you're interested, I could at least look into it for you. You just tell me what you want."

I smiled. "I'll make it easy for you," I replied. "You don't need to name anything after me, send astronauts to my district, or launch me into space. I just want one thing. I want to shake hands with Neil Armstrong."

Goldin's face went blank. "Anything but that," he replied. "Armstrong doesn't come to NASA functions no matter how often we invite him. The guy's a hermit. It would be easier for us to send you up on the Space Shuttle." Goldin looked pensive as he scratched his chin, and then he brightened. "Come to think of it," he added, "maybe a Shuttle ride wouldn't be such a hard sell after all. Tell me—do you suffer from severe motion sickness?"

• • •

The year 1999 marked the thirtieth anniversary of Apollo 11's Moon landing, which renewed my fascination with the mission. As it turned out, and to my everlasting delight, I had the chance to meet Armstrong when he made a rare appearance in the D.C. area in time for the mission's anniversary.

This motivated me to poke around in the records. To my astonishment, I learned that Congress had never awarded its gold medal to the Apollo 11 crew. I resolved to correct the oversight by introducing House Resolution 2815, which authorized the Congressional Gold Medal for the three astronauts. Additionally, when I learned that NASA had broken ground on an office complex in Washington, I began drafting a separate bill to name the new edifice the Neil A. Armstrong NASA Center.

Seeking to award a Congressional Gold Medal involves time-consuming elbow grease. The rules of Congress required that I round up at least two-thirds of the members of the House of Representatives to cosponsor the resolution. In other words, find 290 or more congressmen to sign my petition. Even if I accomplished this, then I had to obtain the approval of the House Committee on Financial Services Subcommittee on Domestic Policy and Technology before the legislation could go to the House floor for a vote. Assuming I cleared those hurdles, I had to go over to the Senate and replicate the same drill: get at least 67 of the 100 senators to sign on as cosponsors and then obtain the approval of the Senate Banking, Housing and Urban Affairs Committee before the full Senate would vote on final passage. It proved a lot of work, but giving proper recognition to the Apollo 11 astronauts made the exertion worth it.

A month or so later, and after many expended hours button-holing colleagues individually, I had collected over three hundred House members' signatures on my petition (for reasons outlined in the previous chapter, I didn't bother asking Ron Paul to sign it). After the House committee gave its approval, the Speaker scheduled my legislation for a floor vote. With no opposition to the measure, I was almost halfway home.

I was working at my office in the Cannon Building a few days later when one of my staffers interrupted to tell me that I had an important phone call on Line 1.

"Who is it?" I asked.

"It's Neil Armstrong. He's calling from Ohio. I checked it out. It's really him."

I looked down at the phone resting on my desk. A lone button with a blinking light beckoned. Given our pleasant meeting some months earlier, I assumed that he had heard about my efforts to get him the medal and to name the new NASA facility for him, and he was following up to thank me. Maybe this would crack open the door of a friendship opportunity or, at least, getting to know him better. My mind raced back to that day thirty years earlier as I sat transfixed before Aunt Della's TV watching the grainy image of his momentous achievement. All I had to do was push a button to have a private conversation with my boyhood hero and bask in his heartfelt appreciation for my efforts. Moments like this don't come often.

I asked the staffer to step outside and close the door. Catching my breath, and trying to quell my excitement, I punched the blinking button and answered the phone.

"Congressman," he said, "this is Neil Armstrong."

And then it all went south.

"I wish I could say that it's nice to be making this call, but it isn't," he told me. "I just heard that you're trying to give the Apollo 11 astronauts a gold medal for our mission, and that you're also trying to name the new NASA building after me. I didn't authorize either of these proposals, and I don't want them." I listened to an uninterrupted blast as he went on and complained that the medal would inflate his crew's importance over all the aviation and space pioneers who went before them. He repeated that I should have cleared all of this with him in advance, and that I had no right to proceed without consulting him. When he finished dressing me down, he demanded that I withdraw my bills and put an immediate halt to these efforts.

Holy cow.

During Armstrong's stern monologue, I remained silent—partly out of shock, but mostly trying to get a grip on this unexpected development. To date, it remains three of the longest and most painful minutes of my life.

After he finished his harangue, an awkward silence followed. He left it to me to make the next move. Well, as they say, When in Rome…

"Mr. Armstrong," I asked, "are you through?"

"Yes."

"I understand your position completely. Now, let me tell you something. Who the hell are you to call a member of Congress and tell him what bill he can or cannot introduce? I'll introduce any goddamn bill that I please, and I don't need your permission or anyone else's to do it." As I spoke, my rising voice sounded angry, but I wasn't. Overwhelmed (or maybe hyperventilating) might be the more appropriate verb to describe my inner emotion. The more I roared about a congressman's independent legislative prerogative, the more I kept thinking to myself, *I can't believe I'm yelling at Neil Armstrong.*

"By the way," I growled as I wound down my reply, "did you even bother to read my statement on the medal resolution before calling and bitching to me?"

"Well, uh, no. I just heard—"

I cut him off. "Oh—you just heard. Listen, I don't care what you just heard. Maybe if you had read it, you'd know that I took great pains to pay tribute to all the pioneers of flight, and how your crew represented the collected efforts of the brave men and women who came before Apollo 11." In truth, as I barked out those words, I couldn't recall if I had actually included such tribute language in the resolution. Maybe I had, but, hey, life gets busy in Congress. I might have overlooked it. Still, this was not a moment to bog down in details, and Neil Armstrong was definitely not the man with whom I wanted to show self-doubt.

"I didn't know that," he said. "They—they didn't tell me." His voice grew friendly. "I'm really sorry. As you've described it, I think the medal would be a nice tribute. I'm sure it's fine. Could I impose on you to send me a copy of the resolution?"

"It will be my pleasure." While making that pledge, I jotted a hurried note onto my to-do list: "Tell Myron to amend Apollo 11 res. ASAP if necessary—add tribute language if not in there!!!"

"I really appreciate all that you've done on this," Armstrong continued. "I'm sure it was a tremendous effort. But I do have a small favor to ask. I really prefer not to have that NASA building named for me. It's your call, of course, but I'd be grateful if you'd cancel that gesture."

"Consider it done, Neil. I'll withdraw the bill."

"Thanks, Jim. Let me give you my personal email and phone number so we can stay in touch."

And with that, a relationship began that I cherished to the end of Neil Armstrong's life.

• • •

Before closing this chapter, there are a couple of postscripts to the story.

Neil Armstrong was not the only astronaut who contacted me over my proposed gold medal resolution. Apollo 11 command module pilot Michael Collins called one afternoon and thanked me for introducing it. Around the same time, my office received a call from his crewmate Buzz Aldrin, the lunar module pilot and the second man on the Moon. Aldrin said he would be in Washington later that week, and he wanted to come by and talk to me about the resolution. Since I was scheduled to be in California that day, he met with one of my legislative assistants.

Aldrin arrived with two aides. My aide escorted them into my private office. As Armstrong had done earlier, Aldrin complained about my medal resolution. He said it should cover every astronaut, and not just the Apollo 11 crew, to avoid jealousy among the other astronauts. Then he went a step further and suggested that I "improve" the resolution by dropping the medal idea altogether and replacing it with legislation providing for astronaut military promotions and retirement benefits. He ended by insisting that Armstrong, Collins, and he didn't need nor want another medal. "Inventing a medal for us is a bad idea," he said.

I had briefed my staff previously about my Armstrong telephone call, so my assistant knew what to say when talking to Aldrin (albeit without yelling). He told Aldrin that the resolution did not "invent" a medal for Apollo 11; he explained that the medal had a two-hundred-year tradition, that its first recipient had been George Washington, and that over the last two centuries its honorees included luminaries such as John Paul Jones, the Wright Brothers, and Winston Churchill. It was the highest award Congress bestowed, but regrettably, it could not include retirement benefits or promotions. "Although all the astronauts are heroes," he conceded to Aldrin, "your work in landing first on the Moon was a hallmark of world civilization. Congressman Rogan thinks that this great American accomplishment deserves special recognition. That's why he introduced the resolution to honor the Apollo 11 crew with the Congressional Gold Medal."

A guy in Aldrin's entourage chimed in. "We still don't like the bill," he said.

Aldrin cut him off. "Yes, we do," the Moon walker snapped. "We like it fine. We especially like it now that we understand it." Aldrin said to thank me, and to let me know that he wanted to come to my district and campaign for me in my next reelection bid—an unexpected but welcomed bonus. "Oh," he added as he rose to leave, "I do have two final questions:

"How much is the medal worth, and when do I get it?"

• • •

With months of legwork behind me, on June 20, 2000, the House passed my Apollo 11 gold medal resolution unanimously. The Speaker pro tem must have waited for Ron Paul to go to the restroom before calling up the measure for a vote.

Following House passage, and whenever I had spare time between votes, I hung around the Senate chamber to collect the signatures of the necessary cosponsors. Because the two-year 106th Congress would adjourn forever in less than six months, there was no time to waste in getting the required signatures needed for a Senate hearing and floor vote. If the Senate failed to approve it before Congress adjourned at year's end, the resolution would die and my work on it would be wasted.

Every senator I asked to cosponsor the bill did so eagerly, and soon I had collected the vast bulk of the necessary sixty-seven signatures. While working on completing the task, Senator Mike DeWine (R-OH) approached and asked if I would let him take over as Senate sponsor. He told me that since Neil Armstrong was his constituent, moving this resolution would bring him positive press in his upcoming tight reelection race. "If you'll let me be your Senate sponsor, I'll collect the rest of the signatures for you and get the resolution moving quickly," he promised.

"Of course, Mike," I replied. "I'm happy to turn this over to you. And, if it helps you back home, then all the better. I already have most of the signatures. You'll just need to collect a dozen or so. But you'll have to move fast. I've checked the Senate's calendar for the rest of the year. You guys are out most of July, all of August, half of September and October, and most of November and December. If we don't get this passed before year's end, it's dead, so time is of the essence."

"No worries. I'll get right on it. Thanks so much." I gave DeWine my signed Senate cosponsor petitions.

A few weeks went by. When I didn't hear back from DeWine, I tracked him down. "Oh, I'm so sorry," he told me. "I got busy. I'll get on this and take care of it." A couple days went by, and then a couple weeks. I called and he gave me the same excuse along with the same promise. Still later, when he had not introduced the resolution with the completed signatures, I called several times and left increasingly agitated messages. He never returned my calls until early October: "You know," he told me in a condescending tone, "we senators have a very busy agenda over here. I can't waste time collecting signatures to give away a medal. My constituents expect me to keep my focus on big issues. Why, if they found out I was wasting time getting a medal approved instead of doing the People's Business, they'd be furious at me. I can't help you with this." I didn't bother reminding DeWine that he had begged me to let him handle it.

I also didn't bother telling him where he could shove his very busy agenda.

My resolution to honor the Apollo 11 astronauts died with the 106th Congress' adjournment sine die on December 15, 2000. Almost a dozen years after I left the House, Congress finally awarded their gold medal to the Apollo 11 astronauts, but Senator DeWine wasn't there to take credit for passage: during the intervening period, he had been beaten for reelection.

• • •

Neil Armstrong suffered a fatal heart attack at age eighty-two on August 25, 2012.

After leaving NASA, Apollo 11 command module pilot Michael Collins served as President Nixon's Assistant Secretary of State for Public Affairs. Later he became director of the Smithsonian Institution's National Air and Space Museum; he opened a consulting firm, wrote several books, and took up painting. He died of cancer at age ninety on April 28, 2021.

Retiring from the Air Force in 1972, Buzz Aldrin wrote books and spent the next half century advocating for continued space exploration.

After losing his Senate seat, Mike DeWine enjoyed a comeback. After twice winning races for Ohio state attorney general, voters elected him governor in 2018. He won reelection in 2022. Congratulations, Mike. I trust that you're doing more for your current constituents than you did for Neil Armstrong.

H.R. 2815—My Apollo 11 Congressional Gold Medal Resolution, and the petitions in support of it signed by a bipartisan collection of over 300 House members. (Author's collection)

Chapter 7

Pedigrees

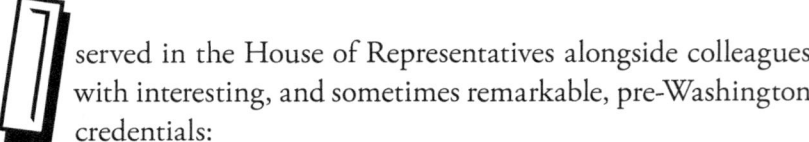served in the House of Representatives alongside colleagues with interesting, and sometimes remarkable, pre-Washington credentials:

- Sonny Bono (R-CA) was an international celebrity long before he came to Washington. Back in the 1960s, as a singer and song-writer, he teamed up with his girlfriend and future wife. *Sonny and Cher* went on to score ten gold records with 80 million sales worldwide. After conquering the music industry, they starred in a television variety show that remained a network hit for five years. When he and Cher divorced, and then his entertainment career peaked, he transitioned to successful restaurateur, Palm Springs mayor, and then won a congressional race in 1994.

- Sam Johnson (R-TX), a fighter pilot during the Korean and Vietnam Wars, spent almost seven years as a North Vietnam prisoner of war and endured unending and brutal physical torture that left him with permanent crippling injuries.

- John Lewis (D-GA) was one of the 1960s civil rights movement's "Freedom Riders." Arrested and beaten for participating in anti-segregation demonstrations, he suffered a fractured skull on Bloody Sunday while leading a nonviolent protest across Selma's Edmund Pettus Bridge.

- Mike Castle (R-DE) had served as his state's governor.

- Ron Paul (R-TX) was the Libertarian Party's 1988 presidential nominee.

- Amo Houghton (R-NY) was president of Corning Glass Works, a company founded by his great-great-grandfather in the 1850s. I saw Amo on the House floor the day the press had declared him to be the first confirmed billionaire to serve in Congress. As colleagues surrounded and offered congratulations, Harlem's flamboyant black congressman, Charlie Rangel, sidled alongside Amo. Wrapping his arm around the new billionaire's shoulder, Charlie drew closer as he bellowed in his gravelly voice, "You know, Amo, that *Houghton* was my slave name!"

- Rod Frelinghuysen (R-NJ), an heir to the Proctor and Gamble fortune, was the latest member of the Frelinghuysen political dynasty to serve in Congress—a lineage dating back to the Revolutionary War.

- Henry Hyde (R-IL) served as an OSS spy during World War II.

- Randy "Duke" Cunningham (R-CA) was America's first naval ace fighter pilot of the Vietnam War. His exploits were the inspiration for Tom Cruise's character in the 1986 motion picture, "Top Gun."

- Jim Ryun (R-KS), a silver medalist at the 1968 Summer Olympics, once held the world record for running a mile in under four minutes.

- Speaker Dennis Hastert (R-IL), a former championship wrestling coach, was an inductee into the National Wrestling Hall of Fame.

- Ellen Tauscher (D-CA) was the youngest person (age twenty-five), and one of the first women, to hold a seat on the New York Stock Exchange.

- In the late 1960s, Bobby Rush (D-IL) co-founded the Illinois chapter of the Black Panther Party. He served as Chicago's defense minister, and in that capacity, he urged "offensive violence" against the "power structure." (Growing up in San Francisco during this time, I remember the Oakland Black Panthers' form of power structure resistance: shootouts with police.) I found it hard to reconcile this background with the Congressman Bobby Rush that I knew: soft-spoken, kind, and a Christian pastor. He once told me that his salvation and faith in Jesus is what got him through each day, and it probably saved his life from his earlier days of militancy. In 2000, Bobby and I talked occasionally about our respective tough reelection campaigns that year. I drew a challenger in California flogging me for my role in the Clinton impeachment; back in Chicago, Bobby faced a primary challenger—a Democrat legislator decrying Bobby as a relic of the past who was "unable to build bridges" with white officials and "get things done." Bobby and I exchanged intermittent reports on our respective races back home. Ultimately, I lost my reelection that year, but Bobby prevailed over his upstart primary challenger: a young and ambitious Illinois state senator named Barack Obama.

Of course, not all of the colleagues with whom I served ended up with enviable resumes, including two mentioned above. Duke Cunningham and Dennis Hastert later went to federal prison. Duke pleaded guilty to various charges surrounding his acceptance of over $2 million in bribes from defense contractors; Denny pleaded guilty to financial irregularities after paying out millions of dollars in hush money to former students he once coached that came forward with claims that he had molested them decades earlier. After his conviction, Denny earned the ignominious distinction of being the only National Wrestling Hall of Fame inductee to be de-inducted.

Sadly, Duke and Denny weren't my only congressional colleagues who later faced the business end of the criminal justice system. According to Wikipedia's "List of American Federal Politicians Convicted of Crimes," this grouping also included others with whom I served:

- Jay Kim (R-CA) for accepting $250,000 in illegal campaign contributions. A judge sentenced him to two months of house arrest, and he lost his next bid for reelection.

- Jim Traficant (D-OH) for corruption. After a judge sentenced him to eight years in prison and he refused to resign, the House expelled him.

- Bob Ney (R-OH) for conspiracy and making false statements to the FBI over accepting trips from a lobbyist in exchange for legislative favors. He received a 30-month prison sentence.

- Bill Jefferson (D-LA) for bribery and fraud. When police raided his home, they found $90,000 cash in marked bills wrapped in tinfoil and stashed in food containers inside the kitchen freezer. In 2009, he received a thirteen-year prison sentence; in 2016, a judge dismissed seven of the ten counts based on a trial procedural error. The next year the court reduced Jefferson's sentence to time served, which was five years and five months in prison.

- Jesse Jackson Jr. (D-IL) for wire and mail fraud in connection with misusing $750,000 in campaign funds. He received a two-and-a-half-year prison sentence.

- Rod Blagojevich (D-IL) and I won election together in 1996, and we ended up as next-door neighbors on the Cannon House Office Building's fifth floor *Freshman Ghetto*. Rod and I became close friends, and I was delighted when he won election as Illinois governor in 2002. During his second term, FBI agents arrested him on multiple corruption charges. In 2009, the Illinois legislature impeached and removed him from office. After a jury convicted him, a judge sentenced him to fourteen years in prison. In 2020, President Donald Trump commuted the sentence after Rod had spent over eight years behind bars.

- Anthony Weiner (D-NY) for sending sexually explicit photographs of himself to a minor. He received a twenty-one-month prison sentence (later reduced to eighteen months), and he was required to register as a sex offender.

- Chaka Fattah (D-PA) for twenty-three counts of racketeering, fraud, and corruption. He received a ten-year prison sentence.

- Corrine Brown (D-FL) for diverting funds from a fake charity to a personal slush fund. She received a five-year prison sentence. Later, an appellate court reversed the conviction, finding that the trial court improperly excused a juror. To avoid a new trial, she pleaded guilty to one count and received a thirty-two-month federal prison sentence.

- Robin Hayes (R-NC) pleaded guilty in 2019 to making a false statement to the FBI in connection with an investigation into the attempted bribery of an elected state official. On President Trump's last day in office, he pardoned Hayes.

Whew!

When I went to Congress, my twin daughters were four years old. Back then, the House leadership scheduled a few noncontroversial votes on Monday nights at 6:00 p.m. The purpose was to get members back to Washington on Monday nights so we'd be in town for Tuesday morning committee hearings. I used to bring my girls to the Capitol for these Monday votes: these were our Daddy-Daughter Date Nights. Sometimes I took pictures of the girls with my congressional pals while we hung out in the cloakroom in between votes. A few years after I left Congress, Dana found one of the photo albums I had kept for her. She opened the album, leafed through the pages, and asked me to identify some of the people in the pictures with her. "Who's the man holding me on his lap?" she asked.

"Oh, honey, that's my good friend Jimmy. He always wore a funny-looking toupee to work. He's a great guy. I really like him a lot."

"Is he still a congressman?"

"Well, no. He got in trouble. He's in jail now."

A momentary look of horror crossed her face. Saying nothing, she turned the page. "Who's he?" she asked while pointing to a photo depicting her eating an ice cream cone purchased by the smiling man standing at her side.

"Oh, that's my good friend Duke. He came to California to do a campaign event for me. He's a well-known war hero."

"Is he still a congressman?"

"Well, no. He got in trouble, too. He's in jail."

Silently, she turned the page, pointed to the next picture depicting her and a stranger. "What about him?"

"That's you with my friend Bob. He was the chairman of the committee who oversaw everything that happened inside the Capitol. After I left Congress, he arranged for me to buy my congressional desk—the big one in my den upstairs. He's a great guy."

"Is he still a congressman?"

I cleared my throat. "No," I told her. "He got in trouble, too. He went to jail—but, hey—he's out now!"

Dana closed the photo album, handed it back to me, and left the room.

• • •

Not all of my former colleagues who landed underneath law enforcement's microscope ended up in the pokey.

In 1981, prosecutors charged a Democrat federal judge, Alcee Hastings of Florida, with perjury and accepting a $150,000 bribe. At his trial, when the government's main witness unexpectedly refused to testify, the jury acquitted him. However, the acquittal did not assuage Congress. A Democrat-controlled House impeached him, and a Democrat-controlled Senate convicted him and removed him from office. In previous judicial impeachment proceedings, Congress routinely included in the vote an order barring the disgraced official from ever again holding federal office. In Hastings' case, the committee staff accidentally omitted that standard language from the charging document. Because of this oversight, three years after the Senate had bounced Hastings from the bench, he ran for a seat in the U.S. House of Representatives—the same body that had impeached him—and won. He went on to win reelection every two years until his death in 2021.

Congressman Gary Condit (D-CA) was having a secret affair with a young intern working in his office when she disappeared mysteriously. Authorities located her corpse a year later. Although no evidence showed him culpable for Chandra Levy's murder, thanks to tabloid hysteria and public fixation over the scandal, many believed otherwise. The rumors accelerated when the press reported that police had searched his home and questioned him several times. He lost his reelection bid. Almost a decade after Miss Levy's disappearance, police arrested a suspect in her killing. A jury convicted him of her murder, but an appeals court reversed the conviction and prosecutors declined to retry him. As of this writing, her murder remains unsolved.

• • •

Despite these varied backgrounds and outcomes, I served with two House colleagues who earned serious pre-Congress bragging rights. Both had played in professional sports and had reached the pinnacle of recognition: Congressman Steve Largent (R-OK) was a member of the Pro Football Hall of Fame, and Congressman Jim Bunning (R-KY) was a member of the National Baseball Hall of Fame.

Steve played fourteen seasons as a wide receiver with the Seattle Seahawks. He retired from football in 1989 holding every major NFL receiving record, and the *Sporting News* named him one of the hundred greatest football players of all time. The Football Hall of Fame inducted him in 1995, the same year he entered Congress.

I knew Steve—not well, but I liked and respected him. As fellow evangelical Christians, we also shared a common faith. In 2002, the year he resigned from Congress to run for Oklahoma governor, his state's GOP invited me to keynote their annual convention, so I had the chance to make a campaign plug for him during that visit.

By 2004, both of us were out of government: Steve headed CTIA, the national cellular telephone association. I worked as an attorney at Venable, Baetjer, Howard, and Civiletti, a large Baltimore-based law firm. When my partners learned that CTIA was looking for a new lobbyist, and since I knew Steve, they chose me to pitch our firm to him and try to secure their contract.

Steve was on the road when I called his office, so I made an appointment with his secretary to take him to lunch. I asked where he liked to eat; she told me he'd eat anything and that I should take him wherever I preferred. "I really want to go to a place he likes," I said. "This is a client pitch and my firm's paying for it, so my partners will want him to be happy wherever we go."

"Steve's very easy," she assured me. "What would make him most happy is for you to take him where you like to eat. He's that kind of a guy."

On the appointed day, my firm's managing partner, Jim Shea, dropped by my office and handed me Venable's unlimited-expense credit card. "Where are you taking Largent for lunch?" he asked.

"I've lined it up with his secretary. I'm taking him to where she said he'd be most happy."

Jim smiled. "Go get 'em," he urged. "Spend all you want. Order the best of everything. Just remember to bring back the receipt with the credit card. We'll need it for bookkeeping."

I picked up Steve at his office, and we walked to my favorite D.C. restaurant. We caught up on family and politics for a couple of hours before we talked business. He promised to discuss my firm's proposal with his people and let me know when CTIA made a decision.

When I returned to my law firm, Jim Shea and a couple other senior partners were waiting in my office. "How did it go?" Jim asked excitedly.

"It went great," I told them. "He only had me on his schedule for an hour, but we spent three hours together. Steve said he'd let us know as soon as possible." As Jim and the other partners nodded with approval and congratulated me, I said, "Oh, I almost forgot these." I reached into my pocket and returned to Jim the firm's credit card and the restaurant receipt. Jim took the card, looked at the receipt, did a double take, and then he laughed.

"You gave me the wrong receipt," he said.

"Oh, sorry." I fished around for another piece of paper, but my pockets were empty. "Let me see that receipt," I said, and he handed back the slip of paper. I looked at it and then returned it. "That's the receipt," I said. "That's where I took him."

"This is a joke, right?"

"No. He said that he wanted to go wherever I like to eat. Since I like to eat at Quiznos, that's where I took him."

Jim and the partners looked dumbfounded. "Are you telling us," one of them choked out, "that with the firm's unlimited expense credit card, you took him for a lousy eight-dollar sandwich at a counter-service chain?"

I didn't like his tone of voice. "Well," I replied defensively, "if you had bothered to look at the itemized receipt, you'd see that I didn't just buy him a sandwich. I bought him the combo meal. The sandwich came with a refillable large soda and a bag of potato chips."

Ultimately, the law firm of Venable, Baetjer, Howard, and Civiletti didn't get the CTIA lobbying contract. I learned of their rejection second-hand, because by the time CTIA had selected their new lobbyist—

I was already employed at a different law firm.

• • •

Jim Bunning pitched in the Major Leagues for sixteen seasons (1955 to 1971). In 1964, he pitched the seventh perfect game in MLB history. When he retired in 1971, only Hall of Famer Walter Johnson had earned more career strikeouts. In 1996, nine years after voters sent him to the House of Representatives, the Baseball Hall of Fame inducted him as a member.

Jim struck me as a loner. He always appeared angry about something, and this attitude helped him maintain a privacy zone while on the House floor. I wasn't the only congressman who had that impression. Once I listened to a few colleagues talking about Jim's perpetual grouchiness. "What the hell does he have to be so mad about?" one of them asked. "He's in the Hall of Fame, he's a congressman, and he walks on water with his constituents back home."

"He was angry when he played baseball," another replied. "I followed his career back in the old days. I remember him as a beanball pitcher. If he didn't like a batter, which was most of them, he'd throw the ball at his head."

Despite this off-putting reputation, whenever I found myself seated alongside Jim, I'd ask about his baseball career, and he'd answer my questions politely. I can't say he was overly warm, but we got along fine, and he never shooed me away. In time, as our conversations continued, I felt insulated from his crabby reputation.

One afternoon, as I exited the House chamber after a vote, I ran into a lobbyist friend who also raised money for my campaigns. He appeared dismayed about something, so I asked what was up. "I've been a serious collector of baseball autographs since I was a boy," he told me. "I've been carrying this baseball in my briefcase for months hoping to get Jim Bunning to sign it."

"Why don't you just ask him?" I suggested. "He's in there right now. You can probably catch him when he comes out."

"I don't have the nerve," he replied. "I've been around him many times, but I'm afraid to ask. He always looks pissed off at the world. I just can't bring myself to do it."

Feeling that I had cracked through Bunning's forbidding persona, and wanting to show I was a can-do congressman for a loyal supporter, I bragged about my good relationship with him. "Give me the ball," I volunteered. "I'll get it signed for you."

"Really?"

"Sure. He'll do it for me. We're buddies. I talk baseball with him all the time."

"Thank you! But do you think he'll really do it?"

"Listen, I've got this covered. Jim and I are colleagues. I know the guy. Just give me the ball, wait here, and I'll go in and get it signed for you right now." I took the ball, went back into the House chamber, and I slid into a vacant seat next to Jim.

"Big Jim!" I said cheerily. "How's it going, Jimbo?" After he grunted a reply, I produced the ball and told him my purpose: "Hey, Jimmy, listen. I've got this lobbyist friend who's a huge baseball col-

lector. He's standing outside right now. He's been carrying this ball
around for months trying to get up the nerve to ask you to sign it!
He's afraid of you! He thinks you're a grouch! Hahaha! Isn't that a
scream?! Anyway, I told him I'd get it signed. I knew you wouldn't
mind. Whaddya say, Jimmy B.?"

At first, Jim said nothing, but had he stared at me with any
greater intensity, the heat generated by his popping eyeballs might
have fractured his contact lenses. After a painful silence, he snatched
the ball from my hand and scrawled his name on it, but not without
commentary: "Why the hell should I do this for a guy who won't
even ask for himself?" he growled. "This is bullshit. I shouldn't even
do this. You got a lot of nerve asking for that cowardly bastard."
He even stopped signing mid-signature to jab his index finger in
my face while he vented about how he didn't appreciate me doing
someone else's dirty work, what I should tell the guy when next I
see him, and on and on. He was still chewing on me after handing
back the ball and the ink on it had dried.

I slinked off the House floor, walked down the hall, and
approached the lobbyist waiting with wide-eyed expectation. I
handed back the treasure. When he saw the blue-inked signature
across the ball's sweet spot, he let out a joyful whoop. "You did it!
Oh, man, this is great! You came through for me!"

"You're welcome."

"Hey," he asked, "what did Bunning say when you asked him
to sign it?"

"It's not what he said to me that's important," I replied. "It's
what I'm saying to you now that you need to remember:

"Don't you ever [expletive] ask me to do that again."

• • •

A few months later, Christine, Dana, Claire, and I visited a Northern
Virginia shopping mall. While they browsed in a clothing store, I
killed some time by wandering into a nearby sports memorabilia

shop. On the top shelf of the sale display case rested an old Steve Largent football card and an even older Jim Bunning baseball card. "Wow, what a coincidence," I thought. "Here are their cards side by side, and I serve with both of them in Congress." I thought about buying them to get Steve's and Jim's autograph, but then I balked when recalling my previous Bunning signing encounter.

"Well," I decided, "this is different. Bunning was mad because I asked for a guy who was afraid to ask for himself. I'll tell him this is for me. Besides, we're both congressmen and colleagues. I can't believe he'll turn me down." I asked the proprietor how much for both, he gave me his price, and I handed him the money.

I saw Jim a few days later in the House chamber, as usual, seated alone in the back row. I sat beside him, showed him both cards, and I told him about the coincidental Bunning-Largent display in the store's case. "Now look, Jim," I told him, "I remember you were mad the last time I asked you to sign something because I was asking for someone else. I bought this card for myself, and I'd like you to sign it for me—your colleague—and not for some third party. What do you say?"

"Sure, I'll sign it for you," he replied.

"That's more like it," I thought as I handed him the card and a pen. As he wrote his name on it, he asked me a question: "How much did you pay for the cards?"

"I got a deal on them because I bought both."

"That's great. How much did you pay?"

Without giving his inquiry any thought, I answered truthfully: "That's the beauty of it. I asked the guy how much for the Largent card. He told me ten bucks. Then I asked him how much for the Bunning card. He told me, 'I tell you what—give me ten bucks for Largent, and I'll toss in Bunning for free.'"

If any of you are under the impression that honesty is always the best policy, then you never told the truth to Jim Bunning.

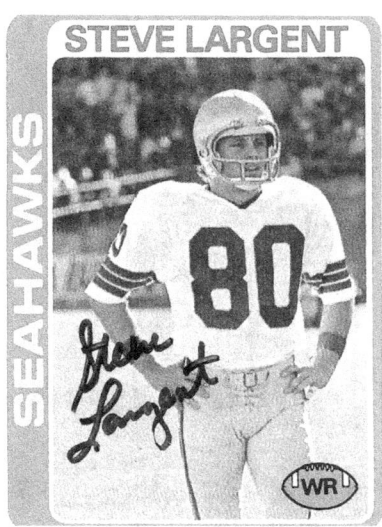

Above is my bargain-basement Steve Largent card that he autographed for me a day or so after I bought it. Where, you might ask, is my signed Jim Bunning card? It's gone. Believe it or not, when I told Bunning his card was a freebie thrown in with a purchased Largent card, the Bunning card burst into flames in his hand. No, seriously, I'm telling you—the card actually self-combusted! Its ashes landed all over the House chamber floor. You had to be there.

• • •

Steve Largent served in the House of Representatives from 1994 to 2002. After losing a race for Oklahoma governor in 2002, he headed the CTIA until he retired in 2014.

Following his six terms in the House of Representatives, Jim Bunning won election to the U.S. Senate in 1998. He served two terms and then declined to run for reelection in 2010. He died on May 26, 2017, at age eighty-five of complications following a stroke.

Chapter 8

Traditional Family Values (And Other Nuisances)

You don't hear much these days of Republican candidates for Congress making support for traditional family values a key plank in their promises portfolio. In my day, things were different: either Republican officeholders pledged support for traditional family values, or they risked drawing a primary challenger who did.

This topic never became the big deal to Democrats that it did to our team. I don't indict the Democrats by that statement. In fact, among the members of Congress with whom I served, the Republicans far outnumbered the Democrats in public sex scandals and broken marriages. The GOP became the torchbearers for the issue after evangelical Christians organized and became a key constituency in Ronald Reagan's 1980 victory. Conservative Republican candidates thereafter courted those voters, while the Democrats shifted leftward on evolving social issues: abortion, feminism, gay marriage, racial and other quotas, and the "welfare rights" movements (among others).

A case that best illustrates the family values toleration variances of the two parties is the House Page Scandal.

For almost two hundred years (until the program ended in 2011), the House of Representatives appointed high school students to page positions. During congressional sessions, the young pages worked in the House chamber serving as messengers or running errands. In 1983, the House voted to censure two congressmen, Republican Dan Crane of Illinois and Democrat Gerry Studds of Massachusetts, for having sexual relationships with underage House pages. Crane had sex with a seventeen-year-old female page. Studds had sex with a seventeen-year-old male page, and he did it in an era when physicians still viewed homosexuality as a mental disorder and when most voters of all stripes found the practice ghastly.

What happened at the next election? Crane's Republican district bounced him out of office; Studds' Democrat district returned him to Congress in a landslide and reelected him six more times until he retired in 1997.

• • •

By my count, member of Congress was the twenty-fourth job I had held. My pre-lawyer resume included a variety of livelihoods: stock boy, radial truck tire stacker, door-to-door vacuum cleaner salesman, telemarketer (back in the days of mimeographed lists and rotary dial phones), janitor, pizza cook, dishwasher, sandwich maker, warehouse worker, stripper club bartender, and (for a week) ticket-taker and bouncer at a Los Angeles porn theater. Of them all, *congressman* was by far the least family friendly. The hours are brutal, the travel incessant, and the pressure to be everywhere, both in the district and in Washington, is overwhelming. Members are almost never home, and when they are home, their limited family time competes with the accumulated demands of district events. Speaking invitations fill every breakfast, lunch, and dinner hour, and always from some local group claiming it is their biggest annual event—and it will offend their members deeply if you fail to come

("By the way, congressman, did I mention that your election opponent already RSVP'd his/her acceptance?"). There is the care and feeding of donors (large and small) and campaign volunteers, regularly scheduled meetings with (and pitches for federal dollar grants from) community and business leaders, and face time with elected officials ranging from dogcatchers to governors.

Once home, the congressman is occupied with preventing political wildfires and snuffing out the ones already ignited. There are the unending attendances at ribbon cuttings, awards presentations, service club mixers, bar mitzvahs, Eagle Scout Courts of Honor, school awards ceremonies, retirements, christenings, and burials. There are the commencement speeches (at every elementary and secondary school and college), press calls, editorial board inquisitions, staff infighting, hirings and firings, throwing out the first pitch at every Little League opening day, riding in parades in every district city on every patriotic holiday, speeches before every local organization irrespective of size, and thousands of other big and small issues that land in the congressman's lap—and all while he tries to carve out family time during this highly compressed weekend or recess before boarding the Sunday midnight flight back to Washington to start the week's cycle anew. No wonder the divorce rates in Congress are off the charts. Far worse, several of my colleagues had teenage children commit suicide, while others had to post bail for their rebelling offspring.

And then, if the above list of distractions isn't enough to split apart the seams of a congressman's home life, there are the girls (or, as the case may be, the boys).

Lots of them.

My family joined me in Washington for my 1996 freshman congressman orientation. While I endured meetings and briefings, Marilyn Quayle, the wife of former Vice President Dan Quayle, invited the new GOP House members' spouses to an intimate lunch. My wife, Christine, looked forward to meeting Mrs. Quayle, who remains a woman she admires. When I came home that night,

Christine looked shell-shocked. I asked her if anything went wrong at lunch. "It was wonderful," she reported, "and Mrs. Quayle is a delight. She gave me her home phone number and told me to call her anytime if I had any questions or just needed to talk to someone about family life in Congress."

"So what's the problem?"

"After lunch, she got up to speak to us. I expected her to talk about scheduling, babysitting options, organizations for congressional wives, finding a place to live, and so forth. Mrs. Quayle didn't talk about any of those things. Her speech was about eight seconds long, and it hit me pretty hard."

"What could she say in eight seconds that left you so rattled?"

"She said, 'Ladies, you need to understand one thing. Each day you will kiss your husband goodbye, and then send him to work in a building with twenty thousand young blonde vipers who will look for opportunities to destroy your marriage and your family. Be on your guard.'"

• • •

The congressional lifestyle proved to be so anti-family that I got the heebie-jeebies whenever I heard one of my Republican colleagues holding forth a little too piously as a defender of virtue, because too often they ended up as passengers on the family values train wreck. In my four years there, I served with many fellow Republicans who had pledged to stand for family values only to have that pledge crammed down their throats publicly for some now-disclosed past or present inconsistent behavior:

- During his first year in Congress, police caught Ken Calvert (R-CA) in his car receiving oral sex from a prostitute. Although he initially denied the allegation, he later apologized and cited the personal stress of his recent divorce and a family suicide for his lapse in judgment.

- A few days after Congresswoman Helen Chenoweth (R-ID) demanded that President Clinton resign for having an affair with a White House intern, the press revealed that she had an affair with a married man when she was single.

- During the Clinton impeachment trial, the press revealed the previous extramarital affairs of two House impeachment managers. After being confronted with the story, Congressman Henry Hyde (R-IL), the House Judiciary Committee chairman, admitted to an infidelity that occurred three decades earlier. Meanwhile, pornography magnate Larry Flynt published an affidavit from Congressman Bob Barr's (R-GA) ex-wife in which she claimed he had an affair during their marriage, and that after their divorce he married his paramour. A third House manager admitted to me privately that his wife had discovered his extramarital dalliance; the affair never became public.

- Demanding Clinton's resignation, Congressman Dan Burton (R-IN) had declared, "No one, regardless of what party they serve, no one, regardless of what branch of government they serve, should be allowed to get away with these alleged sexual improprieties." Soon thereafter it came out that he had an extramarital affair and had fathered an out of wedlock child with his mistress.

- After leaving Congress, Newt Gingrich (R-GA) admitted to engaging in an ongoing extramarital affair with a congressional staffer while he was Speaker. They later married after his divorce became final.

- The House GOP Conference selected Bob Livingston (R-LA) as their choice to replace Gingrich as Speaker. Before the full

House ratified that choice, Livingston admitted to having an extramarital affair after the press outed him. He stepped down as a candidate for Speaker and soon thereafter resigned from Congress.

- A former high school wrestling coach in the 1960s and 1970s, the man elected to replace Gingrich as Speaker in 1999, Dennis Hastert (R-IL), retired from Congress and the speakership in 2007 and became a lobbyist. He later pleaded guilty to financial irregularities relating to paying hush money to his former high school students who accused him of molestation. At his sentencing hearing, he never admitted directly that he had molested them, but he apologized "to the boys I mistreated when I was their coach.... What I did was wrong, and I regret it. They looked up to me and I took advantage of them." Unpersuaded by Hastert's vague statement of contrition, the judge sentenced him to fifteen months in prison and called him a "serial child molester."

- Senator Pete Domenici (R-NM) had an extramarital affair with and impregnated the daughter of a fellow GOP senator. Domenici managed to keep the affair and paternity a secret until after he retired from politics.

- Senator Strom Thurmond (R-SC), an avowed segregationist during his earlier political career, fathered a child out of wedlock with his family's sixteen-year-old black servant girl when he was a young man. The relationship did not become public until after Thurmond's death in 2003.

- Congressman Don Sherwood (R-PA) lost his reelection bid after his mistress revealed their extramarital affair and accused him of physical abuse.

- Congressman Mark Foley (R-FL) resigned his House seat following the revelation that he had sent sexually explicit text messages to various current and former male House pages.

- During the 2000 Republican National Convention in Philadelphia, Christine and I attended a Phillies baseball game with some of my House colleagues. Congressman Tom Davis (R-VA) brought as his guest a female member of the Virginia House of Delegates whom he introduced as a good friend. Later, Davis divorced his wife and married his good friend.

- While in the midst of his campaign for Nevada governor, a waitress accused Congressman Jim Gibbons (R-NV) of following her outside a restaurant and assaulting her sexually. He paid $50,000 to settle her lawsuit against him. After winning his statewide race, he divorced his wife of twenty-three years and petitioned the family law judge to decide which of them was entitled to live in the governor's mansion.

- Investigators found Senator David Vitter's (R-SC) name and contact information in the address book of a madam running a notorious Washington brothel. According to the *Washington Post*, he later admitted his patronage of the prostitution ring.

- Police arrested Senator Larry Craig (R-ID) for lewd conduct with an undercover vice officer in an airport men's restroom. He later pleaded guilty to disorderly conduct and announced he would resign from the Senate. After the heat died down over the criminal plea, he changed his mind about resigning and finished out his term.

- Congressman Vito Fossella's (R-NY) drunk driving arrest led investigators to discover that he had fathered a child with his mistress and maintained a secret second family with her. According to press reports, he and his mistress kept house in one city while he lived with his wife and their three children in another city. After these revelations became public, he chose not to seek reelection.

- Senator John Ensign (R-NV) had an extramarital affair with his senior aide's wife. Once the affair became public, the Senate Ethics Committee and the FBI investigated allegations that Ensign engaged in a cover-up by obtaining a high-paying lobbyist job for his mistress' spouse, and by having Ensign's parents pay the cuckolded husband over $90,000 in hush money. Ensign admitted his infidelity and resigned his Senate seat.

- Leisha Pickering, Congressman Chip Pickering's (R-MS) wife of twenty years and the mother of his five young sons, filed a lawsuit against Pickering's alleged mistress for alienation of affection. Her suit claimed that the alleged mistress' affair with her husband destroyed their marriage. Pickering, a former Christian missionary, filed for divorce and declined to seek reelection.

- Congressman Mark Souder (R-IN) resigned his seat after admitting to an extramarital affair with a staffer.

- Congressman Joe Barton (R-TX) apologized to his constituents after nude "selfie" photos surfaced that he had taken of himself and sent to women. Barton admitted that he did so during consensual sexual relationships with the women while separated from his wife. When the story became public, other women came forward and claimed that they also had engaged in extramarital affairs with Barton. He chose not to seek reelection.

- During Senator Tim Hutchinson's (R-AR) campaign for reelection in 2000, the *New York Times* reported that Hutchinson (a Southern Baptist pastor) "is identifying himself as a conservative, family-values Republican. The problem is that in 1999 Mr. Hutchinson, now 52, divorced his wife of 29 years, Donna, with whom he had three sons, and shortly afterward married a former member of his office staff, Randi Fredholm, now 39." He lost his reelection bid.

- Congressman Mark Sanford (R-SC) later won election as South Carolina governor. During his statehouse tenure, he told his staff he was leaving for a solo vacation to hike the Appalachian Trail. Instead, he slipped away to Argentina and rendezvoused with his mistress. When caught, he admitted to the extramarital affair and called the girlfriend his "soulmate." His wife of twenty-one years divorced him, and the South Carolina House of Representatives censured him. Sanford later became engaged to his soulmate girlfriend, but the relationship fizzled out short of the altar.

- During his fourth House term, Congressman (later Senator) Roy Blunt (R-MO) divorced his wife of thirty-six years and married a Philip Morris tobacco lobbyist. CBS News later reported that during Blunt's courtship with the lobbyist, he was caught trying to sneak language into an anti-terrorism bill that aided Philip Morris—after the company and its employees contributed over $140,000 to Blunt, and while his son also worked for Philip Morris as a lobbyist.

- During his third term in the House, Congressman Joe Scarborough divorced his wife (the mother of his two young children). A few months into his next term, he resigned from Congress unexpectedly in 2001, stating he wanted to spend more time with his children. A month later, he married a staffer for Florida Governor Jeb Bush. They had two children but divorced in 2013. In 2017, Scarborough quit the Republican Party, and the following year he married the Democrat co-host of his cable television show.

- As details of Congressman Duke Cunningham's (R-CA) bribery scandal became public, the press reported that one of the defendants who pleaded guilty to bribing Cunningham, Mitchell Wade, claimed that he and fellow defendant Brent Wilkes maintained hotel suites for Cunningham's use, and that they provided prostitutes for the disgraced congressman. Cunningham later pleaded guilty to conspiracy and tax evasion related to the government's multiple bribery allegations. He served over eight years in prison.

- Congressman Steve LaTourette (R-OH) had an extramarital affair with his chief of staff, and then he divorced his wife of twenty-one years and married the staffer. The former Mrs. LaTourette said her husband blindsided her one day with a telephone call telling her that he now had a girlfriend, and that he wanted a divorce. She later reflected on the experience: "Washington corrupts people," she said. "He was a wonderful husband and father, the best I ever saw, until he went [to Washington]. I told him I was trying to get him out of the dark side—all that power and greed and people kissing up to them all the time. Now he's one of them. All they care about is getting reelected."

Yikes.

By the way, that's just a list of the Republicans with whom I served whose marriages crumbled or whose infidelities and scandalous behaviors exploded across the headlines. The above recitation did not include the publicized sex scandals of my Democrat colleagues, and some of those were doozies, too.

- Congressman Barney Frank (D-MA) hired a gay prostitute for sex, and later employed him with personal funds as an aide. The House reprimanded Frank (but declined to censure him) for using his congressional influence to have thirty-three parking tickets dismissed that the prostitute accumulated while driving Frank's car. None of this impacted Frank's political longevity: his Boston area constituents reelected him eleven more times until his retirement in 2013.

- Senator John Edwards (D-NC) self-destructed his 2008 presidential campaign after he had an extramarital affair with a campaign worker and impregnated her. When the press caught on to the story, an Edwards aide came forward and claimed responsibility for paternity. Later, the aide admitted that he took the blame at Edwards' urging to cover up the scandal. Edwards initially denied the affair and paternity, but later he admitted that he had fathered the child. His cancer-stricken wife of thirty-three years left him; she died later that year.

- Congressman Anthony Weiner (D-NY) sent sexually explicit photographs of himself to various women for several years while in Congress. When the scandal became public, he resigned his seat. Two years later he revived his political career by entering the New York mayoral race, but during that campaign authorities discovered he had used the alias "Carlos Danger" to continue sending out sexually explicit pictures, including texting them to a fifteen-year-old girl. He pleaded guilty to sending obscene material to a minor. Released from prison in 2019, he is required to register as a sex offender for the rest of his life.

- Senator Ted Kennedy (D-MA). Skip it. This would take too long.

I knew all of these people, and I liked and respected many of them. They came from different backgrounds, regions, experiences, faiths, and temperaments. Each GOP representative joining this unpleasant roll call had something in common: as Republican candidates, they promised their base that if elected they would uphold traditional family values. No matter how sincere the pledge was when made, it crumpled after they went off to serve in one of the most temptation-filled and family-unfriendly swamp in the jungle.

Marilyn Quayle's ominous warning was well-founded.

• • •

Like almost everyone else on the GOP side of the aisle, my voting record upheld traditional family values. It wasn't just a sop to my GOP base. As an evangelical Christian, I believe that God's biblical standards are unerring, so I had no problem voting for measures reflecting those values. However, I never made traditional family values a central theme of my campaigns for a simple reason: I don't live up to them, and I know it. In private I curse like the longshoreman grandfather who raised me (cut me off on the freeway if you want a sample). I'm not averse to laughing at or repeating ribald jokes that I think are funny, and a beautiful woman passing by stands a better than even chance of drawing my gaze (subtly, I hope). The fact that my name isn't on that list of wrecked congressional families is no thanks to me. In almost four decades together, Christine and I faced many major strains along the way, but the ones that put the greatest stress on our marriage, and the ones that almost led to a breakup more than once, came from the incredible pressure brought on by my public life and political ambitions. Like those other failed marriages mentioned above, we hit bleak periods of bitterness, distancing, or bored restlessness that left me quite ready to flip the infidelity switch if a discreet and promising opportunity had presented. Put me in the wrong place at the wrong time and in the wrong frame of mind, and I know from prior close calls my own ready capability of pushing the marriage self-destruct button.

Whenever a supporter told me that they appreciated having a godly man representing them (meaning me), I always corrected their generous but faulty character assessment: "I'm lots of things, but a godly man isn't one of them. The Bible says that I'm a sinner saved by grace through faith in Jesus." That wasn't an expression of false religious humility. Yes, I'm a Christian, but I am a very imperfect one. A godly man? Here I am in my mid-sixties as I write this, and I still haven't developed sufficient spiritual maturity to repent sincerely for many of the sins I have committed and enjoyed immensely back in the day. Given this, how much "traditional family values" finger-wagging moralizing should constituents endure from a guy who bartended while in college at a Hollywood female mud-wrestling nightclub, and who still remembers the experience with fond nostalgia?

Trust me. I'm still a major work in progress, and I know it.

• • •

When I got to Washington as a thirty-nine-year-old married father of twin four-year-old daughters, I sought advice on how I could make the job more family friendly from colleagues who were also the children of former congressmen. One member's reply struck a nerve. Congressman John Dingell (D-MI) was six years old when his father won election to Congress in 1932. As a boy, he served five years as a House page, and then later he worked for his dad. When the elder Dingell died in 1955, John (then age twenty-nine) replaced him in a special election. He had been a congressman longer than I had been alive. He ended up serving fifty-nine years in the House—the longest tenure in congressional history.

One night I sat with him in the chamber. "John," I said, "you were the son of a congressman, you've been here over forty years as a member yourself, and you have four children. What do I need to know to make this job work out for my family, and especially for my young girls?"

"Jim," he answered, "if you stay here long enough, your daughters will resent you as thoroughly as I resented my father, and as thoroughly as my children resent me."

Ouch.

In November 2000, the voters of my district spared me any long-term Dingell family-styled resentments. Five days after losing my bid for a third term, Christine, Dana, Claire, and I were eating a quiet family dinner in our small Arlington townhouse. As we dined by candlelight and quiet music, Christine asked, "How many nights in a row have we had dinner together as a family?"

"Four," I replied.

"When is the last time we had dinner together as a family four nights in a row?"

I did the calculation in my head, and then I answered her: "1993."

She nodded, took a sip of water, and then she changed the subject. I didn't ask if she regretted that I wasn't returning for the 107th Congress.

• • •

The struggles and temptations surrounding the defense of traditional family values are not the exclusive province of politicians. At times, the immediate family members of congressmen must take a stand, too. Just as we have seen with their elected relations, mixed results can occur.

One night I agreed to debate my Democrat colleague, Congressman Jim Moran (D-VA), on Chris Matthews' MSNBC cable show "Hardball." Half an hour before airtime, my brother Pat called me from his local bar hangout in Pacifica, California (a few miles outside of San Francisco). I mentioned my upcoming TV appearance and he said he would watch.

Jim Moran and I broadcast our segment from the House TV gallery. The studio's technicians applied our makeup, seated our earpieces and lapel microphones, and then directed us to sit on adjoining stools. When we went live, Matthews peppered us with questions, and we debated whatever points were on the agenda that night.

Side by side, Jim and I projected different images. He is a big, stocky, tough, Boston-raised Irishman who played football and boxed in his youth. Jim looks and sounds like someone you'd hire as a security guard in case a fight broke out at the union hiring hall. During our debate, his voice rose, his face grew red, he waved his arms, and I think he even jumped off the stool once or twice while accentuating a point. My debate style tends more toward my courtroom lawyer training: legs crossed, hands folded, and a judicial approach to answering questions. Anyway, Jim and I went at it for about five minutes, the segment ended, we shook hands, and then we went back to work.

When I returned home that night, I called my brother Pat to ask if he had watched. "I saw it," he said with no enthusiasm. "In fact, everyone in the bar saw it. The place was packed and pretty noisy. After I turned on "Hardball," I told everyone to shut up—'My brother's coming on TV in a minute. If anyone makes a sound while he's on, I'll kick your ass.'" At a husky six foot three and a veteran of innumerable barroom brawls, nobody questioned Pat's ability to make good on the promise.

Pat shared his thoughts on my performance: "The bar quieted down when you came on. Now, that big Irish guy you were debating—man, he sure knows how to debate! He sounded like he meant business! You sounded like some pussy lawyer. I was so embarrassed that when the debate was over, I told everyone in the bar that the big Irish guy was my brother and that they mixed up your names on the screen."

When I saw Jim on the House floor the next morning, I shared with him Pat's story. I thought he would find it amusing, but I didn't expect the guffaws that followed. When he caught his breath, he told me why Pat's response had tickled his funny bone: "I called my wife and told her to tune in," he said. "When I got home last night, I asked her if she saw our debate. 'Oh, yeah,' she told me, 'I saw it.' She explained that just minutes before we went on the air, a few girls knocked on the door selling candy bars for their school fundraiser. While talking to them, she mentioned that her husband was coming on TV. She invited the girls to come in and watch. When I asked her how I did, she let me have it: 'You looked like a lunatic waving your arms and shouting,' she said. 'Why can't you be more like that judge sitting next to you? He was distinguished and poised. I was so embarrassed that I told those girls that the judge was my husband, and that they had mixed up the names on the screen.'"

As the Bible reminds us, no man is a prophet in his own land.

• • •

There is a postscript to this Jim Moran-Hardball story.

Although my disappointed brother Pat choked at the plate and disavowed me, another sibling defended her big brother's honor without reservation: my sister, Teri. One day not long afterward, Teri called me collect. "I'm in county jail," she told me.

"County jail? What did you do?"

At the time, Teri was bartending in a Northern California-East Bay dive with a lowbrow clientele. A very attractive brunette looked out of place among the regulars when she entered and perched herself on a bar stool. She ordered a drink, Teri poured it, they began talking, and soon became fast friends. It turned out that they had lived in the same town at the same time, attended the same high school in nearby Livermore, and had mutual friends. While they chatted amiably, footage of me appeared on the wall-mounted television tuned to the evening news. Teri told everyone to quiet down so she could hear what her brother was saying. When my televised segment ended, the brunette looked surprised. "Is that really your brother?" she asked.

"Yeah, that's my big brother, Jim. He's a congressman."

The brunette's eyes lit up. "Jim Rogan's your brother! What a coincidence! I know your brother!"

"Really? Hey, small world! How do you know him?"

When the brunette answered, Teri's face contorted in fury. "What did you just say?" my little sister snarled. The brunette repeated her four-lettered description of her claimed acquaintance with me. Determined to defend this slur upon my virtue, Teri came from around the bar, threw the first punch, the brunette swung back, and a few minutes later deputy sheriffs handcuffed and carted off to county jail the two combatants. Teri called to tell me that she needed bail money.

After hearing her story, I chastised my sister about her temper. "Just because some drunk or hallucinating woman in a bar tossed off an unwarranted remark about me was no reason to get into a brawl," I told her. After my severe lecture, I asked Teri if she knew the name of the girl she had slugged. She did, and she told it to me.

"That's the girl you punched?" I asked.

"Yeah. She had it coming."

"Is she in jail with you now?"

"Uh, huh. They arrested both of us. I saw her in the chow line at breakfast. I told her not to talk trash about my big brother again."

I cleared my throat. "Teri, if you run into her at lunch, may I make a suggestion?"

"Sure. What?"

"Apologize."

As it turned out, the brunette and I once had worked together in a pizza parlor in our late teens. Spring was in the air, we had a few beers, her perfume wafted, and, well, you get the point.

"Oh, great," Teri sputtered. "Now you tell me. I feel stupid. Oh, well, that's what I get for sticking up for you, and sticking up for that thing you guys in Congress are always talking about."

"What thing?"

"You know—*that thing*. That thing you guys keep saying we need to stick up for." After fumbling for the phrase that escaped her grasp momentarily, it came to her: "Sticking up for *traditional family values!*"

After getting off the phone, I sent bail money for two.

It's true that my sister's defense of traditional family values proved impetuous, but what the hell—

It's the thought that counts.

Chapter 9

Us vs. Them

If you think Donald Trump's openly hostile relationship with the press during his White House tenure was unprecedented, then you don't know your history of the presidency and the Fourth Estate. Trump's railings against "fake news" and calling out individual reporters for dishonesty was mild compared to how some of his revered predecessors expressed their journalistic dissatisfactions. Thomas Jefferson, remembered as a great defender of press freedoms, viewed the mainstream media of his day—newspapers—as "putrid" and "polluted vehicles" in which "[n]othing can now be believed which is seen in [them]."

He excoriated reporters for their "malignity, vulgarity and mendacious spirit," and he called them "ordures" (French for "garbage") who "are rapidly depraving the public taste."

Harry Truman eschewed Jefferson's Franco-elegant adjectives when he described reporters as "[L]ying, paid prostitutes of the mind" who were "much worse and much more dangerous than the street walking whore who sells her body.... They are the lowest form of thief and criminal."

When reporters and editors rubbed John Adams, Abraham Lincoln, and Woodrow Wilson the wrong way, those iconic leaders ordered them arrested, jailed, and prosecuted: Adams used the sedition laws; Lincoln and Wilson invoked their wartime powers. While vice president, Jefferson opposed President Adams using the Sedition Act against the press, but he changed his tune once he became president and reporters trained their cannon fire on his administration. According to biographer Joseph Ellis, "In [Jefferson's] second term, in response to serious criticism from the New England newspapers… [Jefferson] instructed the state attorney generals [*sic*] in New England to prosecute the newspaper editors for sedition in the same way he had opposed such behavior when it was done by the federal government."

Despite recurring bouts of presidential tantrums over unfavorable news coverage, for most of our history Americans indulged the general belief in the existence of a fair and balanced press. That patina wore off for conservatives after Senator Barry Goldwater (R-AZ) seized the 1964 Republican presidential nomination from the Old Guard GOP establishment. In that campaign, the press often acted as a Democratic National Committee subsidiary by portraying Goldwater as a warmongering kook seeking to place his itchy finger on America's nuclear trigger. Over the next half century, from Richard Nixon to Ronald Reagan to Donald Trump, conservatives saw mainstream press hostility toward them increase in both overtness and volume. By the time Trump started blistering the media for unfairness at his campaign rallies, he stood on the shoulders of three generations of fed-up Republicans ready to cheer that indictment.

• • •

Perhaps I was the rare conservative Republican who viewed my overall experiences with the press during my political years as generally complaint-free (or complaint de minimis). For the most part, I dealt with seasoned and objective professionals in Sacramento and Washington. That didn't mean I always liked their coverage—I didn't—but if they presented both sides adequately, then I was satisfied. However, like other politicians, I also contended with the other kind of "reporter" on occasion and caught shrapnel from their cheap shots. My early days as a member of the California State Assembly introduced me to how some press-credentialed hacks worked in cahoots with the Democrats to push their joint agenda.

In 1994, after winning a special election to the state legislature, I resigned my judgeship and rushed to Sacramento to take the oath in time for the state's annual budget battle. As I settled into my new duties, the Democrat Speaker's chief of staff Mike Galizio dropped by my office to welcome me. A uniformed state police officer accompanied him. "Judge Rogan," Galizio told me, "I've heard that you are a great history buff. We don't do this very often, but I thought you'd like a special perk—a private tour up to the top of the Capitol dome's cupola. It's been closed to visitors for decades, and the only way to go there is with a police escort." Rescheduling my next appointment, I accepted the invitation and accompanied them down the hallways, across the rotunda, and through several locked doors. After entering the inner dome, we climbed a ninety-foot circular ship's staircase to reach the cupola, which is the dome's highest point.

Scrawled across the cupola walls were maybe hundreds of signatures dating back over a century. Galizio showed me the penciled autographs of the workers who laid the gold-leaf ball atop the dome in 1870. "When they finished setting the ball in place," he said, "they signed their names right here on the wall and dated it." I studied the still-visible signatures as my chummy tour guide continued: "Ever since then, it has been a tradition for legislators and VIPs who visit the cupola to write their names on the walls." He pointed out some of these notable autographs, which included governors from Earl Warren to Pete Wilson, Hollywood icon Clark Gable, and many others. Galizio then pointed to a bare space of wall. "Here you go, Assemblyman Rogan," he said. "Time to add your name to the history of the building." The police officer handed me a black marking pen, and I bowed to tradition.

We took in the panoramic view of Sacramento before heading back down. As we cleared the circular staircase, we passed two people making their way up to the cupola. Since one of them carried a camera, I presumed they were VIP tourists. The duo nodded to Galizio, who returned their silent acknowledgment.

The next day, a reporter called and asked if I had visited the cupola and added my name to the wall. Yes, I said, and I explained the circumstances of the honor for what I assumed was a general interest story. Surprise: the next morning, the Sacramento and Los Angeles papers carried banner headlines blaring, in essence, "Rogan Graffities Capitol Dome: Charges of Hypocrisy Fly Against New Legislator." The story portrayed me as a rogue tagger defacing the historic structure on his first days in office. A photograph illustrating the story showed my signature on the wall, cropped tightly to avoid depicting any surrounding signatures. Buried in the lengthy story was some generic defense along the lines of, "Rogan justified his action by saying that everyone does it when they go up there." Within a day or so my district papers carried editorials denouncing me, along with a huge cartoon depicting me scrawling my name on the Capitol while Democrat Assembly Speaker Willie Brown drew back a big paddle to let me have it in the britches for my vandalism.

Of course, the cupola smear was a Democrat leadership set-up, coordinated with press complicity, to stick it to a rookie conservative opponent.

Although angry over the story's shamefully false characterization, I have made it a general practice throughout my public career to avoid complaining to hostile reporters about unfair treatment. I never wanted to give them the satisfaction of knowing that their sucker punch hurt me, which would only add to their sense of professional satisfaction and personal merriment. Instead of sniveling over this cupola treatment, I called the newspaper and asked for a print of the cartoon. After collecting Willie Brown's autograph on it, I framed and hung it in my office reception area. Next, I went to the gift store and bought several cheap plaster Capitol dome paperweights. I signed my name across each dome and gave them out as souvenirs to the reporters responsible for the stories. I made sure they all knew that after explaining to my supporters the circumstances of their hatchet job, my campaign auctioned off four of these signed plaster domes at my next reelection fundraiser, with each bringing a $1,000 winning bid for my campaign coffers.

As they say, revenge is a dish best served cold.

• • •

The Sacramento graffiti episode wasn't the only time I encountered some unprofessional reporter stooging for the Democrats to invent a story. Another example happened when I served in the House of Representatives.

Each year, by tradition, the president and first lady host a Christmas party for members of Congress. I attended the Clintons' party in 1997, which was my first year in Washington. In 1998, my GOP House Judiciary Committee colleagues and I skipped the party because it fell in the middle of our vote on Clinton's impeachment. Under the circumstances, we didn't want our presence there to create awkwardness for the president and his family. Sending regrets that year seemed like the diplomatic thing to do, but the White House gave a friendly liberal Beltway columnist the RSVP guest list, which he used to blast us in print. His version painted a picture of nasty Republicans unable to put aside for one night their Clinton animus and accept a presidential Christmas invitation. He never contacted me (or the others) to ask the reason behind our absence.

The following Christmas, in December 1999, with a year of distance since I had helped to prosecute Clinton's impeachment, and wanting to avoid another cheap shot, I accepted the invitation. Once Christine and I arrived at the White House, escorts steered us to the beginning of the presidential receiving line. Before joining it, Christine and I discussed skipping the handshake ritual. No Clinton fan, she preferred to bypass it, but I felt that protocol mandated that we do it. I recalled for her how the press obtained the guest list from the previous year and blasted me for not attending, adding, "I can just see the reporters' story tomorrow morning if we skip greeting the Clintons: 'Rogan is so petty that he attended a Christmas party hosted by the president and the first lady, and then he refused to shake their hands.'"

We joined the lengthy receiving line.

After moving through the slow ninety-minute procession that wrapped through the ground floor corridor and into the Map Room, we reached the Diplomatic Reception Room, where President and Mrs. Clinton stood near the White House Christmas tree greeting their congressional guests. Per staff instructions, I handed a card bearing my name to a Marine sentry, whose job it was to announce us. While the First Family chatted with the couple preceding us, another sentry whispered stage directions to me: "Congressman Rogan, after you are announced, you will greet the president first, and then you will greet the first lady. Mrs. Rogan, after greeting the president and first lady, you will stand with your husband alongside them, and the photographer will take a group picture."

When I heard my name announced, I approached the president with an extended hand. His face tightened for a moment before it relaxed into a friendly smile. "Jim, Merry Christmas. Good to see you," he said. For the first time since the impeachment trial, I felt a thaw in the ice created by our historic confrontation a year earlier. As I thanked him for his hospitality, I noticed that he glanced over toward Mrs. Clinton as if to gauge her reaction. She remained distracted in conversation with the couple that had been ahead of us, so she had not yet noticed me. He looked back at me with an eye twinkle as if to signal his expectation that my presence might trigger in her a response that he did not want to miss.

I waited to greet Mrs. Clinton, who still looked away while saying goodbye to the other couple. She turned toward me with an outstretched hand, but she had not yet looked up. She was looking at my hand as she reached for it. "Mrs. Clinton," I said, "my wife and I wish you a very Merry Christmas. You and your family are in our prayers."

"Thank you very—"

If she finished that sentence, I never heard its ending. When she looked up and recognized the man who had impeached her husband, her smile froze, her eyebrows arched, and her jaw clenched so tightly that her head appeared to vibrate. "Wel-l-l-l-l! Yes-s-s-s-s!" she hissed through clamped teeth, and then she muttered something inaudible. She looked furious (understandable, by the way), but President Clinton appeared amused. The photographer asked everyone to look this way, he snapped the group picture, Christine and I thanked the Clintons, and then we made a hasty exit.

Once we cleared their earshot, Christine said to me, "Oh my gosh! Did you see the way she looked at you?"

"Do you think I'm blind?"

"I can't believe how she responded to you. I thought the plumes on her dress might fly away."

"Say Cheese": The Clintons and the Rogans at the White House Christmas party, December 6, 1999. The only person in the photo wearing an unforced smile is the president. (Official White House photograph)

Back at our townhouse later that night, as Christine and I got ready for bed, I wondered aloud whether, at that very moment, Hillary Clinton was griping to Bill about my being there. "Don't be paranoid," Christine said. "Hillary has much bigger things on her mind than you showing up for a party."

Oh, really?

The next morning, as I drank my coffee and skimmed the newspaper, I did a double take when I saw an official White House photograph depicting the Clintons and the Rogans at last night's party. Accompanying the photo was a snarky article from the same dissembling liberal columnist from last year. Now he suggested that I elbowed and clawed my way through the receiving line to have my picture taken with the Clintons. How ironic, he added, that I was raising campaign money from impeachment supporters while sucking up to my enemy for a presidential grip-and-grin. He didn't call me a hypocrite directly. He just let the aroma of his fake spin create the stench.

Putting aside that the columnist (once again) never contacted me to get my side before running his lopsided narrative, what amazed me was the Clinton administration's organized choreography with him to whack me with such efficiency. The official White House photographer snapped the photo around 8:30 p.m., and the newspaper went to press around 10:00 p.m. In the pre-digital photography era, this meant that someone at the White House had to tip off the columnist to give him time to pen his screed, and then Team Clinton had to obtain the film from the photographer, get the film to the lab, process it, sort through hundreds of negatives to find the frame depicting Christine and me, print the photo, and get a hard copy of it over to the paper's office before the deadline to make the morning newspapers. As Joseph Heller wrote in his book Catch-22, "Just because you're paranoid doesn't mean they aren't out after you."

I should have taken my own advice about ignoring such cheap

shots, but this time I gave in to temptation. Knowing that Clinton's White House press secretary helped cook up this conspiracy, I wrote to him and explained why we had attended the party and had gone through the receiving line out of respect. I expressed my disappointment in the way his operation played politics with his boss' Christmas invitation. I never received a White House response to my complaint. Instead, Clinton's press hack gave my letter to their columnist buddy, who answered for them in another printed article aimed at me. He quoted selectively from my letter to the press secretary, and then he mocked me as a whiner.

In 1998, the columnist bashed me for not attending the president's Christmas party. In 1999, he bashed me for attending the president's Christmas party. When leftist flunkies in the mainstream media have it in for Republican conservatives (which is all the time), and unless your name is Donald Trump, you will have a hard time winning arguments with people who buy their ink by the barrel.

• • •

As much as I hate to admit it, a hostile press can create an occasional therapeutic byproduct.

One morning in 1998, I perused my district's leading newspaper, the *Los Angeles Times*, and saw my picture in an article alongside a photo of my Democrat colleague, Jim Traficant of Ohio. Jim and I were very good friends, and he was quite a character. Jim may be the only man ever elected to Congress on his notoriety gained from federal prosecutors indicting him for corruption during his time as a county sheriff. At his jury trial, prosecutors played a tape recording of him accepting $163,000 in bribes from local mobsters, and they introduced into evidence his signed confession to the crime. Although not a lawyer, Jim represented himself and, amazingly, he convinced the jury that the damning evidence actually showed him conducting a "private" sting operation against the mob! As an aside, that hat trick worked only once. Twenty years later, another jury convicted him of accepting different bribes and kickbacks. The House of Representatives expelled him after a judge sentenced him to eight years in prison.

Before the unhappy end of his political career, Jim made a notable contribution to congressional sartorial history. On the House floor, where casual attire drew disapproving frowns from traditionalists, Jim sported bell-bottomed denim ensembles and polyester leisure suits, and he topped them off with retro neckties slightly wider than dental floss. Yet it wasn't his static electricity-generating wardrobe or his daily speech tirades, which always ending with the *Star Trek*-inspired phrase, "Beam me up, Mr. Speaker!" that attracted the most notice. That came from his high-piled hairdo, which reporter Neela Banerjee once described as looking like a small puffy mammal resting atop his head.

The fact that Mrs. Traficant worked as a professional hairstylist added to the comic irony. Some speculated that Jim wore a horrible toupee, but the overwhelming consensus held that this hair sprouted directly from his scalp, because no sane man would purchase such a ridiculous wig.

While reading the *Times* article, my teeth gnashed over reporter Faye Fiore's outrageous claim that Jim Traficant and I had the top-two worst hairstyles in Congress. She wrote that my growth had too much bulk on top, not enough bulk on the sides, and it ranked alongside Traficant's as a likely entry into a future *Is It or Isn't It a Rug?* exhibition at the Smithsonian.

I could tolerate Faye's suggestion that my Will Rogers-ish mop looked like a rug. That wasn't an original observation, by the way. People raised that question far too often to suit me. However, her claim that my hair ranked alongside Traficant's roadkill-inspired plume could not stand. I broke my own rule, called her to complain, and I went down the lengthy list of congressmen wearing everything from cat-hair toupees to horrid comb-overs, each of which far outdistanced anything growing out of my head. Since these abominations should knock me well below the top two slots, I demanded a retraction.

Unmoved, Faye dismissed my arguments: "Those guys are all bald," she said. "They have an excuse. You don't. I'm not retracting anything."

"Okay," I challenged her, "then put your money where your mouth is. If you think my haircut is so bad, then you make an appointment for me to see your stylist, come with me to the appointment, you tell him how to cut my hair, and then let's see if you can improve on it." With the gauntlet flung, I set out to bankrupt the *Los Angeles Times* one haircut at a time.

A week later, I found myself in Yvonique's chair at his downtown D.C. salon. After Faye explained our purpose to him, the tall, slender Parisian with long, straight black hair scowled as he circled me a couple of times while studying my locks. Finally, he spoke: "Who deed zees to your hair?"

"Liria cuts my hair," I told him. "She used to work in the Senate's barbershop and salon."

"Duz she steel cut zee hair for zee senators?"

"No. She retired."

"Zhat eez good. Pear-haps zhere eez zum hope for zee Senate yet, no?"

With that, he picked up his scissors and snipped away.

I hated to admit it, but when Yvonique finished, my hair looked more like a barber's cut than a gardener's weed-whack. After that, I turned my skull over to Yvonique every few weeks until our family moved home to California. Faye's harsh in-print comparison of my hairstyle to Jim Traficant's proved a painful but necessary intervention.

It's been many years since I bid au revoir to Yvonique and to Washington. My hair still grows too thick on top and too thin on the sides. My barber, Victoria, has been cutting my hair since we relocated to the West Coast. She does what she can with it, but my genetics force her to bring her scissors-and-clippers artistry to a very faulty canvas. After wearing a decent cut for a week or so, the rug-look returns.

However, with age comes mellowing. In the old days, when someone asked if I wore one, I growled an angry denial. Now I take a different approach: "Yes," I tell them. "It is a toupee. And, to make it look more authentic, I shaved a bald spot into the back of it."

(Left) The King of Bad Hair, Jim Traficant; (Center) Liria's questionable handiwork; (Right) After Yvonique's and Faye's intervention.

• • •

Reporters and politicians endure an uncomfortable codependency. Reporters gain recognition by unearthing scandalous or unflattering information about politicians, but they also depend on their potential victims for their professional lifeblood: inside information. Since politicians need reporters for free publicity, they can't ignore them, especially if they hope to spin a forthcoming story favorably. This bizarre relationship handcuffs together natural enemies needing each other for mutual survival.

Of course, among those politicians and reporters manacled together on the Free Press Chain Gang, some are less natural enemies than others. Politicians curry favor with reporters by leaking to them information or gossip, while reporters cultivate politicians as their secret sources of blabber-mouthing. This romance can be cozy while the ardor lasts, but jilting a suitor in both love and leaking can create a vengeful nemesis.

In late 1998, as the House Judiciary Committee lurched toward approving impeachment articles against President Clinton, reporter Elizabeth Drew, who began covering the Capitol when I was two years old, invited me to lunch. Whether moderating presidential debates, grilling politicians on Sunday morning talk shows, or making her countless print and television appearances, she remained a renowned senior member of the D.C. press corps.

I had hoped to take advantage of our luncheon to hear stories from her distinguished career, but our mealtime conversation proved one-sided and all business. No sooner had we sat down than she pulled out her notebook and questioned me about various impeachment issues. After answering each of her queries, she closed her notebook and told me the true purpose behind her invitation: she wanted me as her "source," meaning she wanted to cultivate me as her inside leaker among the House impeachment managers. When I told her that I would not betray the confidentiality of my colleagues, she closed her notebook, thanked me for my time, and bid me farewell. We never spoke again.

A week later I went to the same restaurant and saw her dining with another future House manager. I don't know whether she turned him into her leaker, but when her book covering Clinton's impeachment came out, she described my colleague with whom I saw her dining in glowing terms: he was a "sharp" and "bright-eyed" prosecutor who made "a strong case" against Clinton during the Senate trial. Oh, yes—my impeachment prosecution skills also earned her notice: I was an ineffective moax with a pale, elongated, funereal puss.

As I read her unflattering assessment, I recognized that her shot at me wasn't so bad.

At least she didn't say I wore a rug.

```
┌─────────────────────────────────────────────────────────┐
│                                                         │
│  INTER-OFFICE MEMORANDUM                                │
│                                                         │
│  TO:     Current and Future Congressmen                 │
│                                                         │
│  FROM:   James Rogan                                    │
│                                                         │
│  RE:     Reporter Elizabeth Drew                        │
│                                                         │
│      If Ms. Drew ever calls and invites you to lunch,   │
│      tell her you have a headache—Or else be ready to   │
│      leak like a goddamn sieve.                         │
│                                                         │
└─────────────────────────────────────────────────────────┘
```

• • •

I'll conclude this chapter with a final press-related story.

Near the end of Clinton's Senate impeachment trial, House Judiciary Committee Chairman Henry Hyde invited a *Time* magazine photographer inside the House managers' private conference room to photograph one of our final strategy sessions. However, she didn't get the first behind-the-scenes shots of us at work. Her competitor at *Newsweek*, Pulitzer Prize-winning photographer David Kennerly, beat her to that punch. I lobbied hard to get Kennerly the scoop, and it had nothing to do with loyalty to his publication.

A month earlier, on the last day of the Judiciary Committee's debate and vote on impeachment, our committee room was jammed with more people in it than I had ever seen. Everyone who could wangle a pass wanted to attend and see history made. With reporters and photographers almost on top of us (and each other), a middle-aged bearded man wearing a chest full of cameras and press badges standing nearby mentioned to me during a break that he also lived in Southern California. After exchanging pleasantries, he tossed out a request: "Hey, when this is done, how about letting me come back and get some exclusive behind the scenes pictures of you guys working on the impeachment trial?"

"Sorry," I replied, "but we haven't let any photographers or reporters into the back room with us. It's a policy" While nixing his request, I noticed the name emblazoned on the press badges around his neck: David Hume Kennerly, whom I knew had been the former official White House photographer under President Gerald Ford and a Pulitzer Prize winner for his Vietnam War photographs.

Once I saw his nametag, I forced an intentionally awkward conversation upon him: "I have a congressional office in California," I told him. "It's in Pasadena."

"Oh. That's a nice place," he replied.

"I have lots of pictures framed on my office wall. You should come and see them sometime."

"Oh, uh, okay. Sure. Maybe someday."

"Some of them are autographed. In fact, some are inscribed to me personally."

"Yeah, that's really nice. Well, I'd better get back to—."

He tried getting away, but I grew more intense in my chatter and pressed the issue: "Some are even from presidents, like Lyndon Johnson, Richard Nixon, Ronald Reagan, and Gerald Ford."

"I really must get back to work."

"I'm especially fond of the Gerald Ford picture. It says, 'To Jim Rogan, with best wishes, Gerald R. Ford.' He signed it for me when he first became president." By now, poor Kennerly looked as if he could hear *The Twilight Zone* theme playing in the distance, at least until I completed the story for him:

In fact, this picture of President Ford was his first official portrait taken after he became president in 1974. I was only sixteen years old when I got a copy of it. I really wanted Ford to sign it, but I knew that if I mailed it to the White House, some staffer would run it through an autopen machine and send it back. Then I read in the newspaper that Ford had just appointed a young guy as his official White House photographer and that he had granted him unlimited and unprecedented Oval Office access. I wrote to the photographer, sent him the picture, and I asked if he might get it signed for me as a favor. He followed through and sent it back with the autograph. I never forgot that Ford's photographer, David Hume Kennerly, did this for me. So here we are, twenty-five years later. And before this is over, Mr. David Hume Kennerly, I'm going to repay that debt and get you inside to photograph the House managers at work!

Making that promise to Dave Kennerly was easy; delivering on it proved a heavy lift. Judiciary Committee Republicans had a standing rule during impeachment that any one of us could veto another's request to allow outsiders into our meetings. Earlier, a couple of managers requested permission for their local hometown newspaper photographers to come in and take a few pictures, but Congressman Steve Buyer (R-IN) always objected. He felt that our discussions should remain secret, and if we made an exception for one, we'd have to do it for all. Steve even blocked a request from Henry Hyde to allow the chairman's own district newspaper photographer into one of our meetings. Once I made my pledge to Dave, I knew that getting Steve's approval would be a tough sell.

At our next managers' meeting, I made a point to sit alongside Steve. Before the session began, I mentioned casually to him that President Ford's former photographer now worked for *Newsweek*, and that I wanted to get everyone's okay for him to come in and take some pictures of us working. As expected, Steve offered his polite rejection. Without warning, I pivoted in my chair, grabbed Steve by the shoulders, shook him as I leaned forward until our noses almost touched, opened my eyes wide, and behaved as if on the verge of lunacy. "Goddamn it, Steve!" I shouted, "I owe this guy! I've owed him a favor for twenty-five years. You gotta do this for me, Steve! You can't say no! Please, Steve! Please! I'm begging you! Steve—I *need* this favor!"

The element of surprise worked. Looking concerned for my mental health, a stunned Steve replied, "Okay, Jim, if it's that important to you."

Twenty-five years after Dave Kennerly had President Ford sign that picture for me, and thanks to Steve Buyer, I repaid a big favor to a great guy. When I look at that old Ford photo today, I remember the look on Steve Buyer's face when I launched my offensive—a look that suggested he thought someone in a white coat should drop a net on his clearly overstressed colleague from California.

With my pal Dave Kennerly in my congressional office a couple of weeks after the Clinton impeachment trial ended, February 1999. (Author's collection).

• • •

On July 24, 2002, the House voted 420-1 to expel Jim Traficant from Congress. He called me on the telephone a few days before surrendering to federal prison. "Well, Jimmy," he lamented, "those bastards that I went after years ago got the ole' sheriff. The average murderer does seven years in prison. The judge gave me eight. Who the hell did I kill, Jimmy?" He refused all visitors during his incarceration, and he never responded directly to any of my letters. Released in 2009, he died at age 73 on September 27, 2014, four days after the tractor he was driving flipped over and landed on top of him.

Chapter 10

Nobody Pranks the Pope

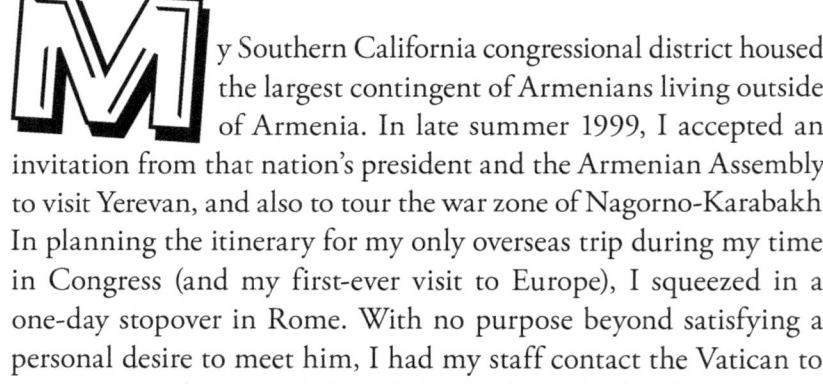y Southern California congressional district housed the largest contingent of Armenians living outside of Armenia. In late summer 1999, I accepted an invitation from that nation's president and the Armenian Assembly to visit Yerevan, and also to tour the war zone of Nagorno-Karabakh. In planning the itinerary for my only overseas trip during my time in Congress (and my first-ever visit to Europe), I squeezed in a one-day stopover in Rome. With no purpose beyond satisfying a personal desire to meet him, I had my staff contact the Vatican to request an audience with Pope John Paul II, who by then was one of the world's most respected figures.

Over two decades into his papacy, the once-athletic pontiff who skied and climbed mountains had become increasingly feeble and showed the infirmities of old age. None of that dampened my enthusiasm to meet the man who, along with President Ronald Reagan and British Prime Minister Margaret Thatcher, had helped catapult Soviet totalitarianism into oblivion. I was thrilled when the Vatican notified my office that His Holiness would see me during my visit, but my excitement proved short lived.

A few days before my scheduled Rome departure, a high-placed Clinton loyalist at the U.S. State Department pressured the Vatican to scuttle my audience as payback for my earlier role as a prosecutor in the president's impeachment trial. With profound apologies, a papal representative explained that it would create a diplomatic protocol breach to sanction a public meeting with an American citizen when the U.S. ambassador registered an objection. Upon learning of this petty sabotage, I told my scheduler, "I'll take this to a much higher authority." I picked up the phone and called my old friend, Los Angeles political consultant Joe Cerrell.

The former head of the California Democratic Party, Joe had been a campaign aide and advisor for fifty years to presidents and presidential candidates such as Adlai Stevenson, John F. Kennedy, Lyndon Johnson, Hubert Humphrey, Bill Clinton, and every other major party leader of his generation. At the time, Joe served as president of NIAF (the National Italian American Foundation). "Joe," I told him, "Your fellow paisan needs a favor." [1] I explained to him the situation.

"Let me get back to you this afternoon," he said, and then the phone went dead.

A couple of hours later, Joe called back. "Your meeting is back on," he said. "I'm going to meet you in Rome to make sure it happens." Joe had called the Vatican and received clearance for him and an unnamed guest to attend the pope's weekly public audience, and then (in his capacity as NIAF president), he arranged an informal private meeting for me with the pope following the public ceremony. "The State Department did you a favor," Joe told me. "Had they not screwed you over, you would have met the pope briefly with dozens of others at the end of his public audience. Since they pulled the rug out from under you, now you're getting a private unscheduled

---

1   How, I hear you asking, is a guy with the Irish last name of Rogan a paisan to an Italian guy named Cerrell? Answer: Rogan was my stepfather's surname. My biological father's last name was Barone (the Anglicized version of Baroni). My paternal ancestors all hailed from Italy.

meeting with him, which is not subject to the same diplomatic protocol." To avoid State Department sabotage or a diplomatic rupture, Joe ensured that the Vatican kept his special guest's name off of any official schedule on roster. Clever people, those Italians.

The lesson: having Democrat friends in high places comes in handy. Well done, Joe.

• • •

Exercising my writer's prerogative, I share a side story before returning to my pope saga.

The night before my Vatican visit, and despite the State Department blackballing my formal papal meeting, I checked into my Rome hotel and found a message from the U.S. ambassador to the Holy See inviting me to be her guest at a special dinner she was hosting that night at the American embassy. Why would Bill Clinton's hand-picked ambassador buck her own team and invite her patron's arch nemesis to her formal embassy soiree? To answer that question, I must take you back a quarter century.

By October 1972, polls showed that the campaign of Democratic presidential nominee George McGovern appeared headed for an overwhelming defeat at the hands of President Richard Nixon in the general election four weeks away. Anticipating the White House loss, Democratic Party leaders turned their attention to protecting their congressional majorities by scheduling a few high-dollar fundraising dinners around the country. They held one in San Francisco on October 5, 1972. I was fifteen years old and a confirmed political junkie, so along with my twelve-year-old brother, Pat, we took the bus downtown and slipped into the hotel's ballroom when a security guard had left the entrance door unattended temporarily.

I had hoped to meet one of the dinner headliners that night: U.S. House of Representatives Majority Leader Hale Boggs (D-LA). First elected to Congress in 1941, Boggs had served on the so-called Warren Commission that investigated President Kennedy's assassination and had reported the government's official version of the tragedy. With House Speaker Carl Albert's pending retirement, Boggs was his heir apparent. Who better to ask questions about my future congressional aspirations than the next Speaker of the House? That proved easier said than done. Throughout the evening, each time I tried approaching Boggs, the crowd surrounding Mr. Leader appeared impenetrable.

When the dinner program ended that evening, and as the room emptied, I saw Boggs in a corner of the room huddled with Congressman Phillip Burton (D-CA) and his brother, California State Assemblyman (later Congressman) John Burton. Pat and I hung back and waited for their animated conversation to end, so I could meet the future Speaker.

While we lingered, a diminutive woman tapped me on the shoulder and asked if I was waiting to meet Mr. Boggs. I told her yes, but I didn't want to interrupt his discussion with the legislators. Determined to introduce me to the majority leader, she took my arm and started leading me toward the object of my interest. I balked, pulled back, and said that I really didn't want to intrude.

"Oh, he won't mind," she said with a smile as she continued tugging.

"No, really lady," I insisted. "That's okay. I'll just wait."

"Trust me. He won't mind. I'm Lindy Boggs, Hale's wife." With that, Mrs. Boggs broke up her husband's powwow and introduced us. Then she took my camera and directed our group to pose together for a photograph. When she told her husband of my interest in politics and government, he urged me to stick with it. "Maybe I'll see you back in Washington someday," he said.

Eleven days later, Majority Leader Boggs went to Alaska to campaign for Congressman Nick Begich's reelection. In Anchorage, they took off in a small twin-engine Cessna bound for Juneau. The plane disappeared somewhere in the Alaskan wilderness. Despite the lengthiest search in U.S. history, authorities to this day never have located the plane or the victims' bodies. On January 3, 1973, the House passed a resolution declaring Boggs' seat vacant due to his presumed death. His widow Lindy ran successfully in the special election to fill the seat, and she took office a few months after our San Francisco encounter.

I wrote the new congresswoman a condolence letter and enclosed a copy of the photograph she had taken that night at the Fairmont (one of the last pictures ever taken of her husband). In her gracious reply letter, she recalled our conversation regarding my goal of one day serving in Congress. She noted that in ten years I would be twenty-five, which is the constitutional age for congressional eligibility. "I'll wait for you," she wrote.

In the rebellious early 1970s, teenage boys like me often wore their hair long. I suspect that the depiction of me in this photograph ended that fad single-handedly. From left: me, Assemblyman (later Congressman) John Burton, House Majority Leader Hale Boggs, Pat Rogan, Congressman Phil Burton, San Francisco, October 5, 1972. Twenty-five years later, when John Burton and I served together in the California State Assembly, he had a blow-up made of this photo, and then he displayed it prominently in the legislative chamber to tease me. (Photograph by Lindy Boggs but disseminated heavily by John Burton.) (Author's collection)

Fast-forward twenty-five years later: After I won a seat in Congress, I tracked down former Congresswoman Boggs' address (she had retired after serving there for almost two decades) and sent her a copy of the photo and her letter to me from long ago. On my congressional letterhead, I ended my message with this postscript: "I am so disappointed—you didn't wait for me!" Soon thereafter, she visited me in Washington for a lovely reunion lunch. The next day, President Clinton nominated her as the United States ambassador to the Holy See.

When I arrived in Rome in 1999, Ambassador Lindy didn't care if the White House and State Department liked it or not. She invited me to her embassy banquet and treated me as an honored guest. During the round of toasts, I feted her as "The most distinguished photographer I have ever employed."

As I said earlier, having Democrat friends in high places comes in handy.

Reunited in 1997 with my 1972 photographer: The very dear former Congresswoman Lindy Boggs and me in my congressional office. (Author's collection)

• • •

With that detour completed, let us now return to my Vatican visit.

The night before my private meeting with His Holiness, I reflected on Poland's Karol Wojtyła, the man who now presided over the Catholic Church. Unlike his long line of dour-faced predecessors, John Paul II had been nicknamed, the Smiling Pope. Everything I had read about him indicated that he was a friendly man with a wonderful sense of humor. As I thought more about it, I suspected that nobody dared tickle his funny bone the moment the College of Cardinals sent up the white smoke signaling his selection, and perhaps long before that. "He's probably surrounded every day by an army of stiffs who view their encounters with him as a religious experience rather than a friendly visit," I told myself. "I'll bet nobody has played a joke on him in many decades. I wonder if he misses the days when people treated him as just a regular guy. I wonder... I wonder...."

Trust me: I understood that executing a practical joke on the pontiff was fraught with potential diplomatic ramifications and social disaster. Still, as the concept churned over in my mind, the temptation grew stronger until the challenge became irresistible:

I decided to prank the pope.

• • •

On the morning of my meeting with him, and before I rendezvoused with Joe Cerrell, I purchased two sets of high-end rosary beads at the Vatican Museum gift shop. Then, in Saint Peter's Square, I bought a dozen or more cheap varieties from a pushcart vendor.

After connecting with Joe, I told him what I contemplated doing—if I didn't lose my nerve at the last minute. He shook his head. "I'm glad I'm not going in with you for the off-the-record audience," he said. "I don't think I want to be within lightning strike distance if you go through with it."

Joe and I followed the crowd of people lining up outside the Basilica for the pope's traditional Wednesday morning audience.

Each person clutched an admission ticket printed in various colors that determined where one sat during the service. Joe's and my purple admission tickets bore the words Prima Fila (First Row). An escort led us into Aula Paolo VI (Pope Paul VI) Auditorium, a modern building constructed within Vatican City and adjacent to the Basilica. The lack of security around and inside the building surprised me, especially since a would-be assassin had shot and wounded the pope over twenty years earlier. People carried into the service backpacks, camera bags, and purses without submitting these items to hand inspection or metal detectors. "This sure ain't Washington," Joe replied when I commented on it.

The auditorium filled quickly. By the official start time of 9:30 a.m., no vacant seats remained, and overflow visitors filled a second-floor level. The crowd did not await the start of the service in reverent silence. Visiting choirs broke out in spontaneous gospel songs from their seats in the pews, people clapped in unison, pilgrims waved their national flags, and they applauded when those from other countries hoisted their own flags. The scene reminded me of a stadium filled with fans anxious for the start of a sporting event. After a half hour delay, the restless crowd whistled and clapped in sync as if signaling readiness for their team to take the field. When a Swiss Army honor guard took its position on the stage and stood at attention, the audience cheered with heightened anticipation.

Finally, at 10:15, the door opened at stage right and Pope John Paul II walked through it.

An ear-splitting ovation greeted him. People waved arms, flags, and banners. Thousands of flashbulbs illuminated the stage, and cries of Viva Il Papa! roared throughout the hall.

The pope leaned on a simple wooden cane as he shuffled across the stage. He stopped every few feet to wave, but I suspected that he did so to rest. Navigating the distance to center stage appeared to take great physical effort. Reaching it, he eased into a high-backed gold fabric chair. A bishop and monsignor flanked him; to his left stood the six priests who would read greetings in their native languages. Behind him rested the massive (and controversial) sixty-six-foot by twenty-three-foot bronze sculpture of Jesus rising from a nuclear bomb crater blasted out of the Garden of Gethsemane.

The pope's eyes appeared tired as he squinted at the crowd. He raised his arm several times to acknowledge the continuing ovation. When he did, his hands shook—an early indicator of the onset of Parkinson's disease that the Vatican later acknowledged.

The service began when the priests lined up at a microphone. After bowing to him, each read in his native tongue (English, French, German, Italian, Spanish, and Portuguese) a greeting and a blessing to all attending. At the conclusion of each, the pope read a formal reply in the same language. In his English translation, he urged the church to repent and, as Christians approached the Jubilee Year 2000, he called on believers to show greater faithfulness to the Gospel. As he listened to each greeting, the pope tried to stabilize the involuntary muscular shaking in his hands by clasping them in front of his chest or by gripping the chair arms.

The lengthy ceremony appeared a physical ordeal for him, but he endured it without complaint or hurry, although I caught him glancing a few times at his wristwatch.

Pope John Paul II presides over his weekly audience, Vatican City, September 1, 1999. (Photograph by the author)

When the public audience ended at 11:20, thousands of people held up rosary beads, religious medals, and other artifacts for his blessing. A guard approached and spoke to Joe and me in Italian. I understood only his accompanying body language: "Follow me." Carrying in my hand the two sets of expensive rosary beads that I had bought in the museum gift shop that morning, Joe and I stepped from the pew and trailed the guard up to the stage.

John Paul II remained seated while blessing the priests who had read to him the various greetings. Each knelt and kissed the pope's ring before stepping away. When my turn came to meet him, the pope offered me a warm greeting as he grasped my hand in both of his. After a brief introduction, he blessed the rosaries I carried, and then he offered a blessing for my family and me. Joe followed me in the papal receiving line, and then we returned to our pew until the ceremony concluded and the pope retired.

Joe had a plane to catch, so we said goodbye. When he left for the airport, he carried with him my debt of forever gratitude.

With my old pal Joe Cerrell—he fled Rome to avoid conspiratorial liability for my contemplated papal prank. (Author's collection)

My escort led me out of the auditorium, down several corridors, and into an ornate room where I found John Paul II seated. He beckoned me to enter. Once again, he took my hand as I thanked him for the audience. When I asked how he was holding up, he closed his eyes and shook his head as if in sorrow. "Physically," he sighed, "not well." Then a smile lit his careworn face. "But," he added as he pointed his index finger upward, "spiritually, well!"

While we talked, I started losing my nerve about playing a joke on him. Here I stood with one of the century's most beloved and respected voices of moral and spiritual authority, and the clock was ticking. Should I, or shouldn't I? Once started, I knew there was no turning back. Oh, well, you only live once.

I pulled the grenade pin.

Reaching into my pocket, I removed a few sets of rosary beads—the cheap variety purchased from the vendor. "Your Holiness," I began, "after your public audience you blessed a couple of rosaries for my daughters. As you can imagine, when the news of our meeting got out among members of my Irish-Catholic family members, some nieces and nephews asked me to have their beads blessed, too. I didn't want to hold up the line during your public audience, but I was wondering if you would bless the rosaries I'm carrying for my young nieces and nephews?"

"Of course, my son," he replied, and then he blessed the ones in my hand.

"Well, Your Holiness, to be honest, I only held these out to nail down the commitment from you." With that, I started pulling cheaper-variety rosary beads out of every pocket sewn into my clothing—trousers (front and back pockets), suit jacket (outer flap pockets, outer and inner breast pockets), and shirt. Then I reached up my sleeve and pulled out a set that I had secreted inside my forearm cuff (much the way a magician produces a hidden scarf). I even bent down and pulled out a couple of rosaries from inside the calf bands of my socks. I draped each set of beads over my arm, and when I ran out of arm room I said, "Oh, I hope you don't mind," and then I draped the last couple across his lap. When I finished, I fought back a grin as I looked at him and awaited his reaction.

Pope John Paul II studied me for a moment, and then he nodded. "Congressman Rogan," he said, "they told me that you were a lawyer before you were a congressman. I can see that you were a very good lawyer." With that, he started blessing each set of rosaries.

"Oh, Your Holiness," I interrupted, "please don't! That isn't necessary. I only did it as a gag. I thought that you probably haven't had anyone joke with you since you became pope and that you might get a rare chuckle from someone doing it."

"Ah, but I made a promise. And promises must be kept." Ignoring my entreaties to quit, he blessed each set individually. When he finished, and as I collected the relics amid expressions of profound gratitude, he asked, "Congressman Rogan, where did you acquire this cornucopia of rosary beads?"

"Where else? I said with a shrug and a wink. "I bought out the pushcart vendor in Saint Peter's Square!"

"I'm sure your purchases blessed him, just as your visit has blessed me." He put his hand on my forehead, blessed my family and me again, and then he grasped my hand once more as we said goodbye.

Here I am with Pope John Paul II at the Vatican, September 1, 1999. Just as the photographer snapped this shot, a monsignor photobombed our picture. Thanks to the miracle of Photoshop™ and my pal Jeff Ferguson's proficiency with it—voila! He sent the monsignor back to his diocese. (Author's collection)

• • •

My escort led me to the office of the Secretariat of the Vatican, Monsignor Giovanni D'Ercole, for my next unofficial meeting. During our amiable chat, he shared with me his Vatican responsibilities: "I act as the pope's personal secretary. In your country you might refer to me as his 'body man.' I'm there for him when he gets up in the morning and when he goes to bed at night. It is not generally spoken of, but I also write his speeches. I wrote the remarks he delivered today."

"Monsignor," I replied, "if I could coax you to move to California and be my speech writer, I'd go up five points in the public opinion polls."

We had a delightful visit that went over our allotted time. We hit it off so well that I made a suggestion: "When you put the pope to bed tonight, and if you aren't doing anything, I'm addressing the Italy-American Chamber of Commerce over at the Piazza Tempio di Diana. Come by if you can. When I'm done, we can go find a place and have some gelato."

"That would be wonderful if it works out. We'll see how late His Holiness stays up tonight."

The monsignor arranged for me a private tour of the Vatican, which included visits to the Sistine Chapel and the pope's private chapel. It was overwhelming to walk through rooms so rich in history, tradition, and faith.

• • •

Later that evening, as I neared the finish of my chamber of commerce speech at the banquet hall, Monsignor D'Ercole arrived in a small motorcade. I introduced him as he entered the room, and the audience responded with an enthusiastic ovation. Many patrons reached for his hand and kissed his ring.

After the event, he and I walked to an outdoor restaurant near the piazza. As we enjoyed cappuccinos and gelatos, he told me, "When I was with the Holy Father tonight during his evening meal, I told him that I was coming to see you. His face brightened when I mentioned your name, and then he told me about the rosary beads."

I buried my face in my hands. "Oh, no," I groaned. "I only did it as a joke. I figured nobody ever plays jokes on a man once he becomes pope. I thought he might—"

"Don't be embarrassed!" he interrupted. "He thought it was very funny. However, he wanted me to tell you something. He said he noticed that in your loving Christian heart, and thinking only of others, you never requested anything for yourself." The monsignor reached into his pocket, retrieved a white jeweler's case bearing the pope's seal imprinted on the lid, and then he handed it to me. The box contained a beautiful silver and mother of pearl set of rosary beads. Attached to them was a small silver charm bearing the pope's signet. "His Holiness asked me to give these to you," he said, "and he wanted me to tell you two things about them. First, he wanted you to know that these are his personal rosary beads that he has used in his own private devotions and prayers. In fact, he used them this evening in chapel, and then he blessed them for you."

"I don't know what to say. This is the most precious—"

The monsignor raised his hand as if to request silence. He had not yet finished his explanation: "There was one more thing His Holiness asked me to tell you. He said that you would understand." A broad smile crept across the monsignor's face:

"He wanted you to know that unlike the ones that you shoved in front of him this morning, these *did not* come from the Saint Peter's pushcart vendor!"

Here's proof that a gutsy prank can turn into a lifetime blessing: the personal rosary beads of His Holiness Pope John Paul II (now Saint Johannes Paulus), September 1, 1999. (Author's collection)

• • •

After almost twenty-seven years in the papacy, John Paul II died at age eighty-four on April 2, 2005. Nine years later, Pope Francis presided over the canonization ceremony that proclaimed sainthood on John Paul II.

Monsignor Giovanni D'Ercole headed the General Affairs Office for the Vatican's Secretariat of State until Pope Benedict XVI made him vicar general of the archdiocese of L'Aquila in 2009. In 2014, Pope Francis appointed him bishop of Ascoli Piceno, where he ministered until his retirement in 2020.

Former Congresswoman and Ambassador Lindy Boggs died at age ninety-seven of natural causes on July 27, 2013.

Joe Cerrell remained as one of America's most respected political consultants until his death from pneumonia at age seventy-five on December 3, 2010.

Chapter 11

More Swag

When I was ten years old, my growing interest in American history collided with the epic 1968 presidential campaign. This convergence inspired in me the political bug. Miss Firpo's fifth grade class spent weeks studying the campaign's shifting developments. Living in California brought added excitement to the race as all eyes turned to our state's June 4 presidential primary, which many commentators thought might prove decisive in the Democratic nomination contest. Vice President Hubert H. Humphrey, a late entry into his party's sweepstakes to succeed President Lyndon B. Johnson, wasn't on the ballot, so California was make-or-break for HHH's two main challengers, Senators Robert F. Kennedy (D-NY) and Eugene McCarthy (D-MN). Miss Firpo urged us to visit the local Kennedy and McCarthy campaign headquarters and bring back posters and stickers to decorate our classroom.

I rooted for McCarthy because the cute girl in class (and upon whom I had a secret crush) supported him. On the morning of the primary vote, and as a joke, a classmate in the rival camp pinned to my jacket a blue Kennedy campaign button. I yanked off the offending badge and hid it in my pocket before my heartthrob saw it and thought me a traitor. Late that evening, Kennedy eked out a narrow victory over McCarthy. Disappointed at the result, I went to bed around midnight after McCarthy had conceded and as Kennedy joined his jubilant supporters in a Los Angeles hotel ballroom. I didn't learn until the next morning that moments after the victorious candidate exited the stage, Sirhan Sirhan had shot and mortally wounded him.

In class that morning, and while Kennedy's life ebbed away, I reached into my jacket pocket and pricked my thumb on the campaign button that I had stashed there the day before. Once destined for my junk drawer, now I viewed it as a historic relic. I took it home and nested it inside a small cardboard box lined with cotton. I didn't know it at the time, but I had just started a lifelong passion. For me, collecting political and historic memorabilia brought to life those biographies and stories from America's past that I enjoyed reading.

During the next few years, I spent countless hours in the Daly City public library poring through the Who's Who in America reference books and looking up the addresses of old retired political leaders. I wrote to them requesting autographs, seeking advice on how to get into politics, and (on occasion) asking if they had any unwanted memorabilia to send to a young collector. It is amazing how many once-famous but by then long-forgotten people were happy to correspond about their glory days with an enthusiastic boy. Along the way, many of my pen pals sent me wonderful items for my growing collection:

- Evelyn Lincoln, the longtime personal secretary to President John F. Kennedy, gave me his Esterbrook dip-style fountain pen (captioned on the barrel "The President—The White House"), its matching Esterbrook inkwell that JFK had kept on a desk in his White House study, and one of his gold PT 109 tie clasps personally worn by him.[1]

- The wife of General James Doolittle, the legendary aviator who earned the Congressional Medal of Honor in World War II after leading a daring bombing raid over Japan, sent me an embroidered patch from his old 1943 Eighth Army Air Force Command flight jacket that she found in an attic trunk.

- Former First Ladies Mamie Eisenhower and Bess Truman both sent me old campaign buttons that came from their husbands' remaining personal stashes.

- When I was in the sixth grade, California Governor Ronald Reagan sent me an inscribed copy of his early and pre-politics memoir, "Where's the Rest of Me?" A few years later, when I met him during a reception in Walnut Creek, California, he signed and then gave me his handwritten speech notes from that event. The charming story of how this chance acquisition made a profound impact on my later life is recounted in one of my earlier books.[2]

- As New Mexico governor, Edwin W. Mecham appointed himself to a U.S. Senate vacancy in 1962, where he served when President Lyndon Johnson signed the 1964 Civil Rights Act.

---

1 "Perhaps the most popular campaign item [from John F. Kennedy's 1960 presidential campaign] was the tie-clasp replicating the form of PT 109, the boat captained by JFK during the Second World War. In an effort to quell public concerns about what some called candidate Kennedy's 'inexperience,' the Kennedy campaign sought to publicize his heroic service in the Navy." John F. Kennedy Presidential Library and Museum, https://www.jfklibrary.org/media/8601 (accessed May 16, 2021).

2 James Rogan, *And Then I Met.... Stories of Growing Up, Meeting Famous People, and Annoying the Hell Out of Them* (Washington, DC: WND Books, 2014), 49–54.

Mecham owned one of the pens LBJ had used to authorize the landmark legislation (an interesting expression of presidential largesse in that Mecham had voted against final passage). The pen remained in Mecham's desk drawer for a quarter century until I wrote and asked him if he had any unwanted political memorabilia that might fit in my collection. He sent me the pen. In 2000, I loaned the pen to the Smithsonian Institution's National Museum of American History where it remains on public display.

Saved from the junk drawer! One of the pens used by President Lyndon B. Johnson to sign the 1964 Civil Rights Act, July 2, 1964. (Author's collection)

- A surviving member of President Truman's cabinet sent to me a cigarette case given him by the president and emblazoned with the words, "I Swiped This from Harry S Truman."

- Former Treasury Secretary Donald T. Regan gave me the framed shadow box display from his personal office containing the pen President Ronald Reagan used to sign Regan's commission as White House Chief of Staff.

Long before I made it to Congress, my collection brimmed with many such treasures. But the opportunity to score booty exploded once I arrived in Washington. Legendary comedian Bob Hope gave me a silver money clip emblazoned with his famous ski-nose profile. Three-time heavyweight champion Muhammad Ali signed for me a pair of his boxing gloves. The architect of the U.S. Capitol gave me one of the original bricks from the building's Monumental Staircase (in service from 1851 until removed by engineers during repairs almost 150 years later), along with the large flag flown over the Capitol dome on the day of America's bicentennial, July 4, 1976. Apollo 11 astronaut Neil Armstrong gave me medallions cast from medal taken from NASA's Saturn V launch tower that shot Armstrong and his crew to the Moon. Former President Gerald Ford gave me his heavy Air Force One pewter ashtray. Former Nevada Governor and U.S. Senator Paul Laxalt, the man who nominated Ronald Reagan for the presidency three times, gave me his personalized delegate's badge from the 1968 Republican National Convention in Miami. House Judiciary Committee Chairman Henry Hyde gave me the battle-scarred gavel that he used during our committee's debate and vote on President Clinton's articles of impeachment. After Clinton's impeachment trial ended, Senate Majority Leader Trent Lott and Minority Leader Tom Daschle, on behalf of the U.S. Senate, gifted to each of the House managers and the president's attorneys our leather chairs and desk nameplates used in the Senate chamber during the trial. (We used two sets of nameplates during the trial; the Senate transferred the second set to the Smithsonian

Institution's collection.)[3] As I noted in a previous chapter, House Speaker Newt Gingrich signed and presented to me the gavel that he and I both had used to preside over the House of Representa-

---

3   Each of the House managers and the president's attorneys received a framed display from the Senate. A large shadow box frame encased our nameplate, a group photograph taken during the trial, and original tickets to the first and last day of the trial.

After my defeat in 2000, President George W. Bush nominated me to be his U.S. Under Secretary of Commerce. Following my Senate confirmation, I paid a courtesy call on the new chairman of the House Judiciary Committee, Jim Sensenbrenner (R-WI). Jim and I had been colleagues in the House and, more importantly, we had been in the foxhole together as House managers in the impeachment trial. When I dropped in to say hello to Jim and to congratulate him on his accession to the chairmanship, I assumed that I was visiting an old friend.

"Mr. Secretary," he greeted me with undue formality, and so I played along with the gag. I bowed slightly and replied, "Mr. Chairman, nice to see you." Without smiling, he directed my chief of staff, Wayne Paugh, and me to take seats in front of his desk. He sat behind his desk flanked by his note-taking aides.

As the conversation began, it became quite clear that this was not an informal get-together between pals. He treated me as if he didn't know me, and he spent our meeting lecturing these two Bush Administration flunkies on his expectation of cooperation when it came to his committee's priorities. The more he stiffed me with his officious attitude, the more I felt an inward burn.

When our meeting drew to a close, I glanced around his private office and noticed that he had only a few framed items hanging inside his cavernous digs. On opposing walls were two large formal paintings of himself in different poses from when he served as chairman of both the House Science and Judiciary Committees (1997 and 2001 respectively). When I commented on them, he told me that he had commissioned the committee's official artist to paint copies of his formal portraits for his personal office. The other framed item on Sensenbrenner's wall was hanging behind his desk: it was his impeachment trial shadow box presented to him by the Senate and identical to the one given to me and the others.

As Wayne and I stood to leave, I pointed to the shadow box and asked Sensenbrenner, "What's that?" (Of course, since I had one, I knew the answer.)

"Oh, this is one of my prized possessions," he told me. "At the end of the Clinton impeachment trial, the United States Senate presented this to me in recognition of my service as a House manager."

I couldn't believe it. Did he think that he was the only guy in town who got one of these? I walked over and pretended to study the contents more closely. "Wow, this is an amazing gift," I said. Then I pointed to the photograph displayed in the shadow box that depicted all thirteen of us House managers seated together in the Senate. "Mr. Chairman, do you ever look at this display hanging here on your wall?"

Sensenbrenner straightened up: "Of course," he replied. "That's why I hung it right here behind my desk. I look at it every day."

I smiled: "Well, Mr. Chairman, let me make a suggestion. The next time you look at it—" I stepped closer and whispered the end of my sentence into his ear so that his two staffers couldn't overhear my comment: "The next time you look at it, Jim, don't forget who's in the fucking picture with you." With that, Wayne and I left.

A week or so later, I ran into Sensenbrenner at a Capitol Hill function. "Hi, Jim!" he greeted me with a friendly smile and handshake. "How's my old colleague doing over in the Commerce Department? Let me know if you need anything."

tives during the debate and vote on America's first balanced federal budget since the Vietnam War.

Despite that impressive haul, two of my favorite freebies—favorites because of the stories behind the gifts—came from a pope and a president. The story of Pope John Paul II giving me his personal rosary beads is recounted in the previous chapter. Read on to learn how President Bill Clinton augmented my wardrobe in an unexpected way.

• • •

A few days after the Senate voted to acquit Clinton in his impeachment trial, nationally syndicated political columnist Morton Kondracke wrote, "Coming from a majority Democrat district carried by President Clinton, Congressman Jim Rogan will be Target One of the Clinton-Hollywood vengeance machine."[4] Speaker Newt Gingrich echoed the sentiment when he noted that Clinton and the Democratic National Committee named me as their number-one target for retribution in the 2000 congressional election cycle.[5]

The passage of time did nothing to cause Clinton and Company to adopt a "Let bygones be bygones" attitude. A year after the trial had ended, Congressman Chris Cox (R-CA) visited with his onetime Harvard classmate Susan Estrich, who was a close Clinton friend. A dozen years earlier, she had served as the national campaign manager for 1988 Democratic presidential nominee Michael Dukakis. Estrich told Cox (who told me) that she had spent several days with Clinton during the impeachment trial. One day she and Clinton were in the Oval Office watching the proceedings and that Clinton "was full of profane threats. [Clinton] kept saying, 'Fuck them! Fuck them! They're all fucking me, so I'm really gonna fuck them.'" When it came to me, she described Clinton as "a very angry

---

4   Morton Kondracke, *Roll Call*, February 15, 1999

5   James Rogan, *Catching Our Flag*, xii.

and bitter man bent on personal revenge."[6]

I never faulted Clinton for this lingering displeasure, which was understandable under the circumstances. That is why, as my obnoxiously expensive reelection donnybrook appeared on the horizon—a race that became the most expensive House campaign in American history—an unexpected phone call to my congressional office left me bewildered.

And very suspicious.

• • •

"Congressman Rogan!" exclaimed the cheerful voice on the other end of the line. The woman calling was from the White House congressional liaison office. She told me that President Clinton was flying to Los Angeles the next day on Air Force One, and he wanted me to join him on the trip.

"I beg your pardon?"

She repeated the invitation. I suggested that she must be calling the wrong congressman. No, she insisted, there was no error: "The president knows that Los Angeles is in your congressional district, and he thought that this might be a good bipartisan signal for you to send to your voters back home. You will be the president's guest on the flight, and when he deplanes in front of your local press, you'll deplane with him. He has a few hours scheduled on the ground, and then he will return to Washington that evening. You are also invited to fly back on the return trip if you choose not to remain in California."

"This must be a mistake. I helped lead his impeachment. In fact, since then, he's frozen me out from every White House perk, right down to cutting off my monthly complement of White House tour passes for constituents. You guys even stopped sending me those standard Happy Birthday form letters sent to every other

---

6   Ibid., 413.

congressman. I'm telling you—you've called the wrong guy."

She laughed. "No, we have the right man. The president wants you to join him. May I tell him that you accept?"

I told her that I was honored by the invitation, but that I would have to check with my scheduler and get back to her. She gave me her callback number.

I tried making sense of this confusing situation. My first thought was that Clinton wanted his pilot to fly over the Grand Canyon, and then have his staff toss me out of Air Force One's bomb hatch, thereby getting even and saving his party's coffers the millions of dollars we expected them to spend against me.

After mentally running through alternative explanations for this unexpected development, it dawned on me that the invitation might be connected to tomorrow's scheduled congressional votes. I asked my legislative director if we had anything important coming up in which we were battling Clinton, and our margin was tight. After checking the calendar, he told me that there was a defense weapons system vote tomorrow that the Republican leadership supported and that Clinton opposed, but he had heard that we had enough votes to pass it. I decided to check with the best vote counter in the history of Congress, Republican Majority Whip Tom DeLay (R-TX), nicknamed the Hammer because of his knack for bringing off-the-reservation GOP colleagues into line when leadership needed them. Tom had an uncanny ability to predict an accurate tally.

It was no secret that Tom despised Clinton and that such feelings were mutual. In an earlier House Republican Conference meeting, Tom had called Clinton a sexual predator, and he never backed down from the slur when the press got wind of it.[7] During impeachment, he had tagged Clinton as an immoral disgrace to both America and to the presidency.[8] *Mother Jones* senior reporter

---

7   Ibid., 52.

8   Ibid., 109.

Stephanie Mencimer wrote, "As president, Bill Clinton didn't have many political enemies more dogged than Tom DeLay."[9]

I walked over to Tom's office, told him about my suspect invitation, and I asked if we had any tight votes tomorrow. He told me that the only important vote scheduled was to approve the weapons system. He pulled a card from his pocket and studied it. "As of right now," he told me, "we have a firm six vote margin. I'd say that we don't need you here. If you want to go with Clinton tomorrow, go. But be careful. Don't trust him."

Still wary of this bizarre twist, I ran the situation by Speaker Dennis Hastert (R-IL) and Majority Leader Dick Armey (R-TX). Both agreed with Tom: "Go if you want, but watch your back. This smells fishy," was the unanimous sentiment.

I returned to my office and called the White House liaison officer to confirm my acceptance. "This is wonderful news!" she exclaimed. "The president will be pleased to hear it." She gave me directions regarding what time to arrive tomorrow morning at Andrews Air Force Base. We would be wheels up for Los Angeles International Airport as soon as the president and I were aboard.

An hour or so later, a White House courier arrived at my office and delivered a large box. Inside was a heavy wool and leather flight jacket with an embroidered presidential seal and *Air Force One* emblazoned on one side, and *James E. Rogan—Member of Congress* embroidered on the other. It made for a stunning presentation. A few minutes later, my new liaison friend called to confirm that I had received it. "The president wanted you to have this," she told me. "Be sure to wear it when you come aboard tomorrow. You and he will be the only people on the plane with these jackets. It's a special gift and a special honor that he wanted you to enjoy."

---

9   Stephanie Mencimer, *Mother Jones*, "There's a Big Problem with One of Hillary Clinton's Favorite Campaign Stories," August 29, 2016, https://www.motherjones.com/politics/2016/08/tom-delay-hillary-clinton-foster-care/ (accessed January 15, 2022).

• • •

The next morning, with my new jacket folded on the car seat next to me, I left at dawn for the nineteen-mile drive from my Arlington townhouse to Andrews Air Force Base. As I neared the destination, my pager beeped. Tom DeLay had messaged to call him immediately. Spotting a pay telephone booth outside a convenience store (this was in an era when cellular telephones were not ubiquitous), I pulled over, dropped a couple of quarters into the coin box, and dialed Tom's number.

"Where are you?" he asked in a tone suggesting that this was no casual inquiry.

"I'm a few blocks from Andrews."

"Get back here. We need you. That son-of-a-bitch Clinton had a better whip count than we had. He knew before we knew that several of our members wouldn't be here for today's vote. I don't know how he knew it, but that doesn't matter. You're the swing vote on this weapons system. That's why he invited you to go with him to LA. He wanted to get you out of town for today's vote. Whatever you do, don't go to Andrews. They might drag you onto the plane. Turn around and get back to the Hill—now!"

I promised Tom that I'd return as soon as I made another call. After hanging up, I dialed the White House congressional liaison office and got my new friend on the phone. I told her something had come up and, most regrettably, I would be unable to fly with the president.

"Please hold the line," she said in a voice that no longer exhibited cheerfulness. After hearing a couple of clicks, another person came on the line. I couldn't hear his name over the static, but I did hear him tell me that my call had been patched through to him on Air Force One. "Congressman," he asked, "is there a problem? We're waiting for you."

"Well, yes," I replied. "I'm sorry to disappoint you, but something has come up. I won't be able to fly with you today. Please pass along my regrets to the president."

"I'm sorry—what?"

"I said I won't be able to make it. Please extend my apologies to the president and my thanks for the invitation."

For the next few minutes, I was treated to a running litany of angry denunciations. After hectoring me, he enumerated each known violation of civilized behavior that I now offended. It covered everything from the massive protocol breach of blowing off a presidential invitation to the need for a true gentleman to keep his promises. "I understand all of that," I responded when he finished, "and I'm awfully sorry. Something's come up. I can't make it."

"Are you telling me," the furious aide now screeched into the phone, "that you want me to walk into the private cabin of the president of the United States right now and tell him that Congressman Rogan is refusing to fly with him? Are you telling me that you want me to do that? The president of the United States is on board Air Force One right now. He's waiting for you. Do you understand that? *The president is waiting for you.* Are you seriously suggesting that I go and tell the president of the United States that you are refusing to join him?"

I cleared my throat. "Well, when you put it to me that way, basically, yes," I replied. "But when you do, please tell him one more thing."

"WHAT?"

"Please thank him for the nice jacket. It'll be something to remember him by."

When Air Force One taxied down the runway that morning, it probably didn't need jet fuel in its tanks for takeoff. The intensity of vulgarities that the aide blasted into my ear before he slammed down the telephone would have been sufficient to levitate that aircraft to its cruising altitude.

This is a very subpar photograph of my beautiful Air Force One jacket—replete with shadows and reflections off of the glass. To take a better photo, I'd have to disassemble the frame. This image will have to do. (Author's collection)

• • •

What does one do with a flashy Air Force One flight jacket? The coat proved so bulky that it took up almost half of the closet space in our small townhouse. I wore it once to a convenience store to pick up some orange juice. The stares and questions it elicited relegated the jacket back to the closet to collect dust for the next half-dozen years.

In 2006, after returning to the state court trial bench, my wife Christine surprised me with a gift. She had my Air Force One flight jacket mounted and framed. "I was tired of this huge beast that you don't wear taking up so much closet space," she told me. "It came down to two choices: frame it to hang in your chambers or donate it to Goodwill. Here you go. If you bring it home and put it back in the closet, I'll switch to Plan B."

For the next quarter century, my framed Air Force One jacket hung in a prominent spot on my office wall. Thanks to Christine's thoughtfulness, it makes for a great conversation piece. It also lets me keep my promise to that angry presidential aide aboard Air Force One who shrieked at me decades ago:

Each time I look at that jacket, I think of Bill Clinton.

Chapter 12

So You Think We Read the Bills?

Laws, like sausages, cease to inspire respect in proportion as we know how they are made.

—JOHN GODFREY SAXE, 1869

First, we have to pass the bill so that you can find out what is in it.

—HOUSE SPEAKER NANCY PELOSI, 2010

At the risk of unintentional exaggeration, my guess is that even the most diligent members of Congress will possess a deep understanding of maybe 2 percent of the measures upon which they will cast votes. As to the other 98 percent, they rely on instinct, persuasion, staff-generated analyses, luck, or a combination thereof.

Before I came to Washington, I should have known, based upon my experience as a state legislator, that deliberation wasn't exactly what one should expect when voting in a large lawmaking body. After winning a special election, I joined the California State Assembly eighteen months into its two-year session. On the day I arrived in May 1994, the Democrat speaker called the session to order, he administered the oath to me, the escort committee led me to my seat, and then we turned to business. Atop my assigned desk sat a thick three-ring binder filled with summaries of the fifty or so bills scheduled for a vote that day. Fifty bills—in one sitting! Every Republican desk had a binder prepared by our caucus staff; the Democrats had one prepared by their team. With each bill summary came: (1) the recommendation of our party leadership as to how we should vote, and (2) a list of the major proponents and opponents of the measure, particularly those with political action committees that might donate money to (or against) a lawmaker's future campaign.

I learned that our GOP caucus staff usually did not prepare these analyses weeks or even days in advance. Often, they prepared them the night before the vote, and sometimes hours or minutes before sessions began. Bills came up for a vote at the discretion of the Democrat speaker, and giving the minority Republican staff sufficient time to prepare a timely analysis was not among his priorities. Republican bill summary binders never arrived for our advance review: they landed on our desks while we assembled in the chamber to begin voting. We debated and voted on bills faster than an Evelyn Wood[1] disciple could read the summary. Suffice to say that my first day as a state legislator left me appalled over how little time we had to familiarize ourselves with bills or ponder their

---

1   In the 1960s, Evelyn Wood (1909–1995) popularized the "speed reading" craze through her business, *Evelyn Wood Reading Dynamics*. She claimed that she could teach people to read up to three thousand words a minute while preserving and even improving their comprehension. See, e.g., https://en.wikipedia.org/wiki/Evelyn_Wood_(teacher).

merits before pushing the aye or nay button.

In frustration, I shared my complaint with my seatmate. She said that the rushed protocol didn't bother her particularly. Instead, her angst came when reviewing the list of those in support and opposition to the bills. "On some of these," she told me, "I have supporters and donors on both sides. I don't know what to do. No matter which way I vote, I'll make someone mad at me. The bill we're debating right now is a perfect example." She pointed to the bill's "support/oppose" list and showed me the groups in both camps that had spread financial largesse to her campaign.

"Putting that aside, do you support the bill?" I asked.

"Yes. It's a good measure."

"Then vote for it."

"But if I do, I'll make donors on the other side angry."

Oh, Lord.

Having resigned my state court judgeship only hours earlier, I couldn't comprehend such indecisiveness. In the courtroom, judges make dozens of rulings every day, and each one produces a winner and a loser. With me, decision-making came with the turf in these jobs; with my colleague, it was creating a self-induced ulcer.

As the weeks went by, I learned that this first day's voting experience was the status quo and not an aberration. In the last hours of that 1994 session before sine die adjournment,[2] we voted on over 300 bills in one day, and with the summaries jammed into three large binders—none of which I saw in advance. The debate and vote on those individual bills often took a minute or less, which was faster than I could turn the page and locate the next one's analysis. Later, I asked the Assembly clerk how many bills our eighty legislators had introduced that session. He told me that the number exceeded three thousand.

---

2   Sine die adjournment: the final adjournment before a new legislative body is sworn in after the election of its new members.

Wanting to unmask this obnoxious process, I lugged those bulging bill summary binders home as visual aids, and I displayed them to constituents at my local town hall meetings and to the press at my editorial board interviews while lambasting the process. Every now and then a reporter followed up with an article about how legislators vote on bills with little or no understanding as to content, but no public pressure for change came from my efforts to expose the practice.

The reality: unless a member served on a committee where a particular bill came through for a hearing and received proper vetting, when the measure came to the floor for a vote, there stood a very strong chance that he voted based on some overworked junior staffer's summary and recommendation. As the saying goes, that ain't no way to run an airline.

In January 1996, twenty-one months after my Sacramento debut, we Republicans captured our first Assembly majority in thirty years. As the new majority leader, I authored a resolution limiting the number of bills a single member could introduce per session. It passed, but the reform didn't last. I left for Congress at the end of that year, the Democrats reclaimed (and have held ever since) their majority, and once they regained power, they vaporized my bill limitation rule.

Nothing has changed since I first joined the State Assembly thirty years ago. According to *Capitol Weekly*, during the 2019–2020 legislative session, California's eighty-member Assembly introduced a whopping 3,374 bills. That does not include the additional 1,474 bills introduced in the State Senate. When the Senate passed its own bills, those additional measures went to the Assembly for more debates and votes, thereby adding to the Assembly's already substantial stack of legislation.[3]

---

3   Chris Micheli, Capitol Weekly, *By the Numbers: The 2019–2020 Legislative Session*, October 1, 2020 (accessed January 23, 2022), https://capitolweekly.net/by-the-numbers-the-2019-2020-legislative-session.

And so, as the sun sinks slowly into the west, we bid farewell to those ill-informed Golden State lawmakers who now merrily run their one-party state by jamming down the throats of almost 40 million constituents their witch's brew of oppressive taxes, freedom-crushing regulations, and inexhaustible unfunded mandates—and they still vote to adopt most these abominations in overall ignorance.

No wonder so many Californians keep moving to Texas.

• • •

Given my Sacramento experience, you might be surprised to learn that I found the State Assembly's voting procedures preferable, even superior, to what I encountered in Congress. In California, when the Assembly met in session, under its rules no committee hearings interrupted the proceedings. Similarly, on committee days, no floor sessions distracted from the hearings. When we entered the Assembly chamber to debate and vote on bills, the sergeant-at-arms locked the doors behind us. That is not a metaphor—he locked the door! We could not leave the chamber without a pass signed by the speaker. Because the sergeant sometimes confined us for so long and so late that we had to send out for food, members came to know each other. I had a personal relationship with almost all of my colleagues on both sides of the aisle. Bipartisan friendships blossomed.

Unlike Sacramento, working in Congress was like working in a large multinational corporation. When I arrived in Washington for freshman orientation, a former Assembly colleague who had already served one term in Congress lamented the impersonal nature of the House of Representatives. She told me that other than the members whose offices adjoined hers, and the few members who sat next to her in committee hearings, she really didn't know any of her colleagues.

This social isolation was not due to her limited tenure. As I mentioned earlier, John Dingell spent almost sixty years as a House member. One night he sat alongside me during a lengthy floor session. As we chatted, he motioned with his thumb to a Republican congressman walking by us. "Who's that?" he asked me. I told him the member's name and the state that he represented.

"Has he been here very long?"

"A while."

"How long?"

"Over twenty years, John."

He shrugged. "Hmm," he said. "I've never met the guy." As he stood to go, the tall, lumbering House dean looked back at me and said, "Big place, ain't it."

The Dean of the House of Representatives, John Dingell (D-MI), who served from 1955 to 2015 and set the record for an unprecedented fifty-nine years of consecutive congressional service. (Author's collection)

• • •

Voting in Congress wasn't the stirring and patriotic exercise that I had anticipated. As a youth, I had romanticized that weighing in on grave issues of war and peace for constituents would be a thoughtful enterprise. In fact, the task carried about as much romance and thoughtfulness as using a credit card in the supermarket checkout line.

In Congress' pre-technology days, the clerk called the names of each legislator to record their votes. As the House grew from its original 54 to its current 435 members, roll calls became a tedious and time-consuming process. In 1973, the House installed electronic voting machines. Members now carry a microchipped card. Except when a matter requires a verbal roll call, votes are cast by inserting the card into one of the forty-seven boxes stationed around the chamber. As an aside, the symbolism of this process resembling a debit card raiding an ATM machine is not lost on me. Anyway, the member then presses either the green "Yes" or the red "No" button.[4] By removing the card, the vote is recorded, and a green or red light illuminates next to the member's name on the tally board.

• • •

On the positive side, when I served there, the U.S. House of Representatives had far fewer bills introduced per member per session than their Sacramento counterparts—an average of 11.5 bills per member in the 105th Congress (1997–1999), and 13.4 in the 106th (1999–2001). By comparison, in the California State Assembly, the average ran to almost forty bills per member. The bad news was that, with 435 House members in Washington, it added up to 5,014 House bills introduced in the 105th Congress, and 5,815 in the 106th. Add to those totals the bills passed by the Senate and sent to the House for consideration, and that brings the totals up an extra 586 bills (105th), and another 819 bills (106th).[5] If you think

---

4   There is a third button on the voting station box that allows a member to vote "Present."

5   https://www.brookings.edu/wp-content/uploads/2016/06/Vital-Statistics-Chapter-6-Legislative-Productivity-in-Congress-and-Workload_UPDATE.pdf (accessed January 27, 2022).

this is outrageous, consider that during President Lyndon Johnson's elected term (1965–1969), his fellow Democrats controlled both the Senate and House—and those two bodies introduced a whopping 50,263 bills during this brief four-year period.[6]

• • •

Unlike our lockdown situation in the State Assembly chamber, debate on a bill in the House of Representatives usually occurs in a near-empty room. Other than the handful of members addressing the merits or demerits of the legislation under consideration, the rest of the congressmen are spread out in committee or subcommittee hearings, working in their offices, making fundraising calls at the Republican or Democratic National Committee offices, or attending functions elsewhere in or around Capitol Hill.

A loud discharge of bells throughout the Capitol and the House office buildings is the signal for members to drop everything and rush to the chamber for a vote. At the clanging, members have fifteen minutes (or less, depending on the measure) to record their votes. The variety of bell signals and their meanings are so numerous and confusing that one almost needs a Rosetta stone to interpret them. Clerks issue to new congressmen laminated cards for translating the earsplitting blare. After four years in the House, I still couldn't tell what most of those signals meant without using my magic decoder ring.

---

6 https://www.brookings.edu/wp-content/uploads/2016/06/Vital-Statistics-Chapter-6-Legislative-Productivity-in-Congress-and-Workload_UPDATE.pdf (accessed January 30, 2022).

House Legislative Bell Signals

1 long ring and a pause, followed by 3 rings	Signals the start or continuation of a notice quorum call. This call is terminated if and when 100 Members appear.
1 long ring	Termination of a notice quorum call.
2 rings	Electronically recorded vote.
2 rings and a pause, followed by 2 rings	Manual roll call vote. The bells will ring again when the Clerk reaches the R's.
2 rings and a pause, followed by 5 rings	First vote under suspension of the rules or on clustered votes. There will be 2 more rings after five minutes. The first vote will take 15 minutes, with successive votes at intervals no shorter than five minutes.
3 rings	Quorum call (possibly converted from a notice quorum call). The bells will ring again in five minutes. Members have 15 minutes to be recorded.
3 rings and a pause, followed by 3 rings	Manual quorum call. The bells will ring again when the Clerk reaches the R's.
3 rings and a pause, followed by 5 rings	Quorum call in the Committee of the Whole. This may be followed by a five-minute recorded vote.
4 rings	adjournment of the House.
5 rings	Five-minute electronically recorded vote.
6 rings	Recess of the House.
12 rings at two second intervals	Civil defense warning.

*lights on the clocks (where they exist) will correspond with rings.

This pocket reference card, prepared by the House Committee on Administration, is carried by members to decode the bell signals.

Most members rushing to the House chamber for a vote have no idea of the awaiting policy issue motivating their sprint. That is why the chamber's leadership tables become centers of vital information. About a third of the way back from the Speaker's dais are tables for the majority and minority leaders. By tradition, the Republicans sit on the right side and the Democrats on the left (hence the political labels of "right wing" and "left wing"). At each vote, committee staffers familiar with the bill under consideration are stationed at these designated party tables to dispense information and to answer questions from the mass of members racing into the chamber.

Chamber of the U.S. House of Representatives. Circled at left are the Democrat leadership tables; those at right belong to the Republicans. (U.S. Government photograph)

Most congressmen might not know much (or anything) about why the bells beckoned, but they all want to maintain a high percentage of answering the roll, lest opponents back home attack them for lazily missing votes. For campaign propaganda purposes, a congressman is better off voting 100 percent of the time in ignorance, rather than voting 50 percent of the time after study and meditation.

• • •

Although far from perfect, siding with one's party is usually a safe way to create the public illusion that members gave considered thought to their voting. However, I learned that blind voting based on partisanship alone is not foolproof. One afternoon, I raced to the chamber for a vote on some unknown matter. With only two minutes left on the clock, and as I fumbled for my voting card, I summoned a Republican staffer and asked, "Hey, what's this?"

"This is a George Miller amendment to a Republican labor bill," he explained.

A no-brainer, I concluded. George Miller, a hardcore leftist Democrat from Northern California, always had one of the most liberal voting records of any congressman. If George offered an amendment to one of our labor bills, that fact alone told me it had to be an awful, and probably socialist, idea. I inserted my cart into the voting station and punched the red "nay" button. As I was leaving, I glanced back and noticed something peculiar. Over four hundred green lights illuminated the tally board. Only three red lights were posted, and one of them was mine. I rushed back to the staffer and asked for more details.

"Mr. Miller's amendment," he explained, "would ban the importation into the United States of any clothing manufactured overseas by child slave labor."

Oh, shit.

The Speaker pro tempore, Ray LaHood (R-IL), had picked up the gavel and was about to bang it, which would close the roll and enter the votes as recorded.[7] "Don't bang the gavel, Ray!" I shouted from the back of the chamber. I rushed forward to fill out the necessary card to change my vote from nay to aye. Ray awaited my vote change, and then he again prepared to close the roll. "Hang on for a second," I called up to him. I wanted to see if any of our Republican members had also cast an accidental "no," just as I had. The two red lights remaining on the board were Republican colleagues Ernest Istook and Steve Largent, both from Oklahoma. "Ray, keep it open," I urged. "I need to find Istook and Largent so that they can change. Their votes are a mistake."

"Okay," he replied, "but hurry up. We need to move on."

I scanned the chamber, and, as luck would have it, I spotted Ernie and Steve seated together. I rushed over to them: "Hey, guys, thank God I found you before Ray closes the roll! You need to change your vote! This isn't just a normal George Miller commie amendment. This one bans child slave labor imports. You two guys are the only no votes in the House."

Ernie and Steve looked at each other, and then they looked back at me. Ernie said, "We know what it does. Thanks, Jim."

---

7   My best recollection is that Mr. LaHood was in the chair at the time this occurred.

Oh.

From the rear of the chamber, I hand-signaled for Ray to close the roll. He banged the gavel, and the measure passed with only two no votes, both of which were registered by the gentlemen from Oklahoma.

The father of modern economics, Adam Smith, wrote in his 1776 classic book *The Wealth of Nations:* "In every country it always is and must be the interest of the… people to buy whatever they want of those who sell it the cheapest." In two Oklahoma congressional districts, it appears that they took that free market advice far more seriously than did my Los Angeles constituents. In any event, if you're looking for dirt-cheap bargain clothing, you might want to do your shopping at the Muskogee Dollar Tree.

• • •

Although the thousands of bills introduced in each Congress makes it impossible for even the most conscientious member to read, reflect on, and understand them, Congressman Sonny Bono[8] knew how to beat the system and avoid my frustrations with the system.

Of all my House colleagues, Sonny became my favorite. Our friendship started shortly after I arrived in D.C. when a tour group of disadvantaged students scheduled both of us to address them. Sonny arrived late to the event and stood in the back of the room listening as I discussed my early life far from Washington's powerful center of gravity. I spoke of being the illegitimate son of a bartender and cocktail waitress and of growing up in San Francisco's hard-scrabble Mission District and never knowing my father while my mother (a convicted felon) raised her four children on welfare and food stamps. Later, I bartended at (among other places) a Hollywood stripper bar while scrapping through law school on my way to becoming a prosecutor, judge, state legislator, and congressman.

---

8   For background on Sonny Bono, see chapter 7.

Sonny liked what he had heard. "You're a no-bullshit guy who doesn't put on airs," he told me as we walked back to our office building. "Some of these other guys around here really have their heads up their asses." We became friends.

During votes, Sonny often joined me in the House chamber and talked about everything from his Hollywood years, his three ex-wives, his current family, the private sex lives of almost every colleague in sight (I couldn't believe how much he knew), and the old days of Sonny and Cher. He felt humbled by the privilege of serving in Congress. I felt the same way, but he harped on it too much during one particularly long day. The session began at 10:00 a.m. By 2:00 a.m. the next morning, an unending string of procedural votes had kept us trapped on the House floor for sixteen hours and with no end in sight. While Sonny and I sat in the back of the chamber together, he jabbered endlessly about what a thrill it was to be a congressman. "Damn, Jimmy," he exclaimed, "look at this place! Here we are members of the United States House of Representatives!"

"Yep. Here we are."

His voice grew more emphatic: "Abraham Lincoln once served here!"

"Yeah. Lincoln."

"And Webster!"

"Uh, huh, Webster."

"And the presidents! Kennedy, Johnson, Nixon, Ford! All of them!"

"All of 'em."

Growing irked that I wasn't in the proper reverential spirit, he smacked me with his rolled-up papers, and then he grew serious. "Look at you," he said. "You're a guy who used to bartend on the Sunset Strip. Here I am—a guy who used to drive a meat truck on the Sunset Strip. Don't you ever look around this chamber and wonder how in the hell we ever got here?"

"Sonny," I told him, "I know how I got here. I went to law school. But I look around this chamber every day and wonder how the hell you ever got here!" We laughed so hard that the Speaker rebuked us with a gavel bang.

Although he sometimes lacked political polish, nobody could diffuse a hostile situation like Sonny. Some months into my first year in Congress, Newt Gingrich's speakership almost collapsed when a rump group of disgruntled conservatives organized a coup to try and depose him. As news stories leaked of the secret rebellion, Newt summoned his 228 GOP members to a private confrontational meeting in the Capitol basement. Angry charges of treachery and lying flew among the rebels, Newt's leadership team, and outraged members. I watched helplessly as the wheels appeared to be falling off the historic Republican Revolution.

Late into the tense evening Sonny rose to speak. A few chuckles broke out. Whenever Sonny talked at our Conference meetings, everyone expected it to end up being funny (intentionally or otherwise). As usual, he couldn't resist slipping into a nostalgic look at his Tinseltown years while trying to tie in a lesson for us: "I remember being on top of the entertainment world," he began. "I had a hit show, a great wife, and a beautiful little girl. I had everything. Then, in a single day, it was gone." He told of the simultaneous demise of both his marriage and his Hollywood career. Oblivious to the eye-rolling glances of some colleagues, he continued: "I ended up being one of those celebrities spending all of his time trying to regain his fame. I knew I had hit rock bottom when I became a regular on a TV show that was the elephant graveyard for washed-up celebrities: *Fantasy Island.*"[9]

The titters grew as Sonny told of sitting alone in his trailer on

---

9   *Fantasy Island:* a weekly television drama show that aired on ABC from 1977 to 1984 and starred Ricardo Montalbán and Hervé Villechaize. See https://en.wikipedia.org/wiki/ Fantasy_Island (accessed January 30, 2022).

the *Fantasy Island* set. Feeling sorry for himself, he got drunk while waiting to shoot the next scene: "The script called for me to walk up to Herve Villechaize [the three foot eleven show costar who played Tattoo, the island host's diminutive assistant], and say, 'Isn't it a lovely day, Tattoo?' When the cameras started rolling, I walked up to him and said, 'Isn't it a lovely day, Harpoon?' Instead of calling him Tattoo, I called him Harpoon. I don't know where the hell Harpoon came from. The director called 'Cut!' Herve started yelling and calling me a stupid asshole. I just stood there looking at Herve and thinking to myself, 'I've lost my money, my family, and my fame. I've lost it all. I've written ten gold records, and all I have to show for it is having to stand here and get screamed at by a goddamn midget.' "

The room broke into howls. It didn't matter if the story had relevance to our political warfare. Sonny had returned calm to the fractured conference. "Let's retire for the evening to reflect on the lesson shared by the gentleman from California," Newt proclaimed. "Meeting adjourned." The next morning, the Republicans started working together again.

Later that night over dinner, Sonny shared with me this insightful observation: "Washington is just like Hollywood. In both towns you run a big risk of falling hard if you ever start believing your own bullshit or your own press agent. People need to keep a sense of perspective here." Sonny maintained this sense of perspective when voting on bills with no knowledge as to their content. One day I was in my office when the bells clanged for a vote, so I started making my way to the Capitol. In the Cannon Building rotunda, I ran into Sonny. We walked together across the plaza, up the Capitol steps, and entered the House chamber with just a couple of minutes to spare. Sonny and I made our way to the Republican leadership table manned by a pimply-faced young GOP staffer working for the committee handling the measure. I picked up from the table two copies of the bill's summary and handed one to Sonny for his review. He tossed it back on the table without looking at it.

"Hey, kid," Sonny called to the staffer manning our Republican table.

"Yes, Mr. Bono?"

"What is this?" The young man started to give Sonny a complicated macroeconomic analysis of some hyper-technical subject before the House. Sonny's face went blank as the staffer prattled on in wonkish detail. After thirty seconds, Sonny waved off any more explanations. "Listen, kid," he interjected, "I didn't ask *what's in the bill*. I'm asking: Am I *for* it or *against* it?"

The uneasy staffer cleared his throat. "Well, Mr. Bono," he replied, "I believe that our committee chairman and the Republican leadership are seeking a *yes* vote on the measure."

"Thanks," Sonny said. He slid his electronic voting card into the nearby station box, pressed the green button, and then he stepped aside for me to do the same. With our duties completed, we made our way toward the exit. Halting halfway down the aisle, Sonny turned and went back to the leadership table. Pointing his finger at the young staffer whose detailed information had exceeded his interest level, Sonny told him, "Hey, kid, do me a favor:

"The next time I ask you a simple fucking question, give me a simple fucking answer."

With my beloved buddy Sonny Bono in 1997, just a few months before his untimely death. (Author's collection)

• • •

What explains the avalanche of bills introduced in Congress? When citizens tolerate or encourage the federal government's continued reach far beyond the limited and enumerated constitutional powers crafted by our Founders, the predictable result is a giveaway free-for-all. For statists, the most expedient means of consolidating their rule is to seize trillions of dollars from the wallets of taxpayers who worked for the money, and then redistribute those funds to purchase loyalty from organized and politically connected interest groups that grasp tirelessly for every piece of this unearned pie. How do collectivists gain power, and how do they maintain it once gained? By our ignorance. By our indifference. By our leave.

As Thomas Jefferson warned two centuries ago, "The government you elect is the government you deserve."

• • •

After serving fifty-nine years in Congress, John Dingell retired in 2015. He died of cancer at age ninety-two on February 7, 2019.

On January 5, 1998, Sonny Bono died in a skiing accident at age sixty-two. A few months later, his widow, Mary, won a special election to fill his seat. She became my seatmate on the House Judiciary Committee, and, like her late husband, a cherished friend.

Chapter 13

Nunc Pro Tunc

If you want a friend in Washington, buy a dog.

—HARRY S TRUMAN

To people of my generation, the following snippet is reminiscent of those old 1960s TV mouthwash commercials: *Are you unpopular? Are friendships fleeting? Do people ignore you in a crowd? Is your dating life empty? Does everyone forget your name? Is there dead silence when you tell a joke? If so, cheer up. A simple remedy for these and other social maladies has existed for over two centuries:*

Win a seat in Congress.

The Latin phrase *nunc pro tunc* means "now for then." As a judge, when I granted a *nunc pro tunc* motion, it meant that whatever I just did, the lawyers and I pretend, and the official record reflects, that I did it earlier than I just did it. Winning elective office is one of life's few ventures where, once you gain club membership, you acquire *nunc pro tunc* friendships.

I experienced this phenomenon the morning after my first election to Congress. Letters from political action committees (PACs) and latecomer donors cascaded into my office with campaign donation checks attached. Some came from people who wouldn't return the repeated phone calls that I had placed over the preceding year. "Our PAC account is pretty much depleted, but because we know that you're in a really tough race, we dug down deep to send this check to you. No sacrifice is too big to get a quality leader like you in Washington. Sure hope this helps!" was a common theme. Funny that the dates on these letters and checks predated the election, but the postmarks showed that the senders mailed them hours after the Associated Press called the race for me. A few of these straggling letters came from donors savvy enough to know that a tell-tale postmark would give them away. Dated the morning after the election, this category of writer exclaimed elation over my victory: "Enclosed is *another* check to help with any end-of-campaign debts. Combined with the *earlier* check that we sent you, please know how proud we are to have been a *continuing* supporter of your path to victory." *Another* and *earlier* check? *Continuing* supporter? When my treasurer called to tell them that no prior check ever arrived, these writers expressed shock: "What? Our earlier check didn't make it? Must have been lost in the mail. So sorry! We'll stop payment on the old one and mail a replacement today."

• • •

It isn't just the putative supporters and donors that nunc pro tunc their love for the incoming freshman. The newly elected members' telephone lines burn up with calls of congratulations from incumbents. Most of these are sincere and appreciated messages of welcome. A few come from congressmen who (like the aforementioned PACs) never returned the underdog candidate's urgent calls for help, but now append to their congratulations the advisement that the caller is seeking a House GOP leadership position, and that they hope to have the new member's support. "By the way," goes the postscript, "I sure hope that the PAC check you received from *X* lobbying group helped, which you got only because I called and personally pleaded with them to support your uphill race." One would-be House leader, a Midwestern Republican, adopted the business model of those salesmen who shill a free Lake Las Vegas weekend to anyone attending their ninety-minute timeshare pitch. He cornered me in D.C. and said that he would donate $1,500 to the campaign coffers of every GOP freshman who came to a private meeting and listened to his pitch for a leadership position. I replied that I would attend as a courtesy, but that he didn't need, nor did I expect him, to pay tribute for my presence. Instead of appreciating my willingness to hear him gratis, he snapped at me, "Well, if you don't want the money, I'll give it to someone who does."

After that exchange, had she been in the running, I would have endorsed Leena the Hyena over this guy. In the end, he didn't win his leadership race. Maybe he ran out of beer money. Or maybe Leena ran stronger in the border states.

• • •

I don't know about other newly elected members of my freshman class of 1996, but when I ran, I needed all of the help I could get. I owed my victory to thousands of hardworking volunteers and donors. One senior congressman (I'll call him Joe—not his real name) gave me the opportunity to fill his gratitude cup to overflow. Joe and I were both members of the California Republican delegation, but the geographical similarity ended there. He enjoyed a very safe Republican seat, and I had a Democrat-majority district that hemorrhaged Republican registrations daily. I liked Joe, but from the day I won my first House election, whenever something positive in Washington came my way, he called me and took credit for it. At first, I believed his claims and I expressed repeated expressions of sincere gratitude. It didn't take long to recognize that for him to have secured all the things for which he took a continuous bow, he would have needed to dedicate his entire term solely to advancing my welfare.

To explain the depths of Joe's credit-hogging, I must share some background. In 1994 (two years before I came to Washington), Republicans won their first House majority in forty years. With this new Republican Revolution headed by Speaker Newt Gingrich, my predecessor, Carlos Moorhead (R-CA), was in line to chair either the Commerce or Judiciary Committee because of his twenty-two years of seniority. Newt and his leadership team viewed Carlos as too weak, too nice, and too accommodating to the Democrats, so they denied him the gavel and gave those chairmanships to less-senior members. Team player Carlos, keeping silent about his hurt and humiliation, chose retirement at the next election. Years later, Newt told me that after I had won the election to succeed Carlos, my predecessor had visited him. "When you bypassed me for two chairmanships," Carlos told the Speaker, "I made no public complaint, and I went along with it like a good soldier. Now I'm calling in the favor. I want Jim Rogan to replace me on the Commerce Committee. He's in a very tough district, and it will get tougher each year he's here. He needs to be on a powerful committee to help raise money for his reelection. I'm vacating a California seat, so it needs to go to a Californian anyway. Give Rogan my slot on Commerce and I will call the debt paid."

Like it or not, reelection in a district where the opposing party has a significant voter registration advantage depends on raising a massive campaign war chest, a job always made easier for congressmen on key "juice" committees. The House Commerce Committee is not only the House's oldest congressional committee, but it is also the juiciest. A lobbyist once told me that during John

Dingell's reign as Commerce chairman, Dingell enjoyed demonstrating his committee's vast and powerful reach by pointing to the framed map hanging on the wall behind his desk. "What's that?" Dingell would ask his visitor.

"A map of the world," came the standard reply.

"Wrong," the chairman corrected. "It's the jurisdiction of my committee."

During my orientation week, the House Steering Committee met and approved committee assignments for the new freshmen. A senior member of the GOP leadership team (and also a Steering Committee member), Congressman Bill Paxon (R-NY), called and gave me the good news: the committee had just approved me for Carlos' Commerce slot. When I asked Bill if there was anyone in particular whom I should thank, he responded without hesitation: Speaker Gingrich. "We were kicking around your name [for Commerce] among the Steering Committee members," Bill told me. "Gingrich interrupted us. He said, 'Rogan will be one of the most talented guys in our Conference. We need him on Commerce.' Boom! That was it. You went through without a hitch. Truthfully, I was surprised. Newt usually doesn't intervene on these committee assignments. He did for you."

Within minutes of Bill Paxon's call, Joe (my self-proclaimed benefactor) called to congratulate me on my selection. "It was a tough battle," he told me, "but I was able to pull you across the finish line after calling in quite a few chits."

"Oh. Uh, thanks—again."

Joe's ongoing claims of beneficence metastasized over the next four years. If a positive editorial or news story about me ran in my local papers, Joe told me that he had called the reporter or the editor and demanded that they write the sympathetic piece. If a favorable editorial cartoon of me appeared on the opinion page, Joe said that he had called the artist and told him what to sketch. Each time we published our campaign contribution reports, Joe pointed out the many thousand-dollar checks that he had steered my way, and he usually appended that claim with another: "I told them to withhold the contribution to my race and to give it to you instead." He even claimed that the large crowds attending my campaign rallies showed up because he had turned loose his political operation in my district. For my two terms in Congress, Joe's credit-taking mania became a standing joke between my office staff and me.

The morning after State Senator Schiff defeated me in my bid for a third term in 2000, my former chief of staff, Greg Mitchell, called me to commiserate. He felt very badly about my loss, and at one point he became emotional. Wanting to cheer him up, I told him, "Greg, look on the bright side:

"I finally did something in Congress for which Joe won't take credit."

• • •

These "you owe me" friendships are not directed solely to incoming freshmen. In June 1999, I attended a Republican members-only meeting with Texas Governor George W. Bush at the Library of Congress. Bush, at the time an unannounced presidential candidate, was gearing up to battle Senator John McCain (R-AZ) for the 2000 Republican nomination.

At this meeting I ran into three-term Congressman Charlie Bass (R-NH). Because New Hampshire's first-in-the-nation primary draws inflated attention, and because New Hampshire's elected officials often hold back their much-coveted early endorsements, I told Charlie that I was surprised to see him back a contender so soon in the process. Charlie said that about a year earlier he had started getting phone calls and notes from McCain, who began inviting Charlie to dinners and sporting events. McCain sent flowers and boxes of chocolates to Charlie's wife on anniversaries and birthdays. This went on for over a year. "Finally," Charlie said, "McCain called recently and said, 'Charlie, I've decided to run for president, and

I'm counting on your support.' I told him, 'Gee, John, I'm sorry, but I'm for Bush.'" Charlie laughed as he quoted from memory McCain's explosion of name-calling four-letter expletives that ended only when McCain slammed down the phone in Charlie's ear.

• • •

When it comes to the Washington "What have you done for me lately?" mindset, a perfect example from my congressional tenure came from my contact with a historical figure from my youth, the onetime chairman of the House Judiciary Committee, former Congressman Peter Rodino (D-NJ).

A decorated World War II veteran and lawyer, Rodino began his forty-year House career in 1948. He served there for a quarter century in anonymity until 1973, when seniority elevated him to chairman of the House Judiciary Committee. Within weeks, President Richard Nixon's administration began unraveling under the weight of the Watergate scandal. Ultimately, Rodino's Judiciary Committee adopted articles of impeachment against Nixon in July 1974. Nixon resigned two weeks later, and Rodino's calm approach during Watergate made him a national media hero. He remained committee chairman until retiring from Congress in 1989.

I came to know Rodino when I visited him in Newark in 1998 (where, at age ninety, he still taught a law school class) to seek his advice as the House moved toward impeaching President Clinton. Taking back to Washington his recommendations derived from this three-hour meeting, our House GOP leadership adopted these "Rodino Rules" from the Nixon impeachment as our model for fairness.

At the end of my 1998 visit with Rodino, he invited me to stay over and come to his home for dinner. Late-night scheduled votes precluded my accepting, but I promised to take a raincheck during my next visit to his area. The opportunity to return to Newark did not present itself until seven years later when I accepted a speaking invitation there. I debated whether to call Rodino. By then he was almost ninety-six, and we had fallen out of contact after I left Congress. Would he remember me? If he did, would he be angry that I ended up playing a key role in impeaching a president of his own party that he did not believe deserved that sanction?

Despite these reservations, I kept my promise and called. He remembered me and, to my relief, he was glad to hear from me. I told him of my upcoming Newark trip and suggested completing our elusive dinner plans. He apologized and said that now was not a good time for a visit because he was home recovering from major surgery, and he wasn't receiving visitors. However, as our call progressed, he sounded more chipper. "Maybe you could pick up dinner and bring it over," he suggested. Still later, near the end of our call, he was naming Italian restaurants where we could go during my visit. The more he talked about my upcoming visit, the more his desire to get out of bed increased.

The only melancholy note during our chat came when we talked about his recuperation. "I served in Congress for forty years," he told me sadly. "I chaired the Judiciary Committee for fifteen of those years. Now I'm recovering from major surgery and nobody from Washington calls me to see how I'm doing. In fact, the one guy who does call is a congressman with whom I never served and is in the wrong party to boot. I guess it shows that when you're gone from Congress, people forget you quickly." His voice cracked with emotion.

I tried cheering up the ailing legislator: "Mr. Chairman, you left Congress more than fifteen years ago. Yet, when the House of Representatives faced the grave duty of considering another presidential impeachment, a Republican-controlled Judiciary Committee adopted your precedents. You set a standard for fairness that outlasted your service. In fact, [House Judiciary Committee Chairman] Henry Hyde and [Speaker] Newt Gingrich kept saying publicly that we Republicans were relying on the Rodino Rules. If you don't mind my saying so, that's a hell of a legacy for a kid who grew up in a Jersey tenement."

• • •

Sometimes a simple act of kindness between natural political opponents can develop unlikely and genuine congressional friendships.

When I served in Washington, among the veteran congressmen, they just didn't come much grumpier than John Conyers (D-MI). Republicans disliked the cranky senior Democrat on the House Judiciary Committee, and the feelings appeared mutual. First elected to the House in 1964, John had over three decades of seniority by the time I arrived, when the only thing standing between the Michigan liberal and the chairman's gavel was a switch of six GOP House seats to the Democrat column. John had coveted the chairmanship for many years, so it wasn't surprising that he brushed off new Republican members as irritants and wanted little or nothing to do with us.

None of that mattered to me. As a teenager, I sat spellbound watching Chairman Peter Rodino's 1973–1974 televised Judiciary Committee impeachment hearings against President Nixon. Now, twenty-four years later, John remained the last Watergate member still serving on our committee. As a history buff, I longed to talk to him and hear his first-hand accounts of that historic period, but whenever I tried, he offered only a discontented grunt before walking away.

I formulated a plan to crack through his unresponsiveness. Having collected old political memorabilia since the age of ten, I knew from experience that most politicians never saved their own campaign items, only to regret it years later when their grandchildren want it. Determined to find an icebreaker, I rummaged through my collection for a relationship building opportunity.

The next time I saw John sitting alone on the House floor, I went over and sat alongside him. Before he could run me off, I asked him if he remembered doing a campaign rally with Senator Edward Kennedy (D-MA) in Michigan almost thirty years earlier. John gave me a quizzical look as if wondering how I knew about that obscure event of long ago. Coincidentally, he told me that he had thought about that rally just the other day: "This was back when everyone believed Ted Kennedy would be the next president," he said. "It was the biggest rally I ever held in my district." I asked if he remembered seeing yellow campaign badges circulating at that rally bearing the legend "The People's Choice in 1972: Edward Kennedy for President—John Conyers for Vice President."

His eyebrows raised and his voice showed excitement: "I remember those badges!" he said. "In fact, I wanted my staff to save one of them for me, but they never did."

I reached into my pocket. "I saved one for you, John," I told him. Pressing the coveted badge into his hand, I winked and left.

My childhood hobby, once again, helped forge a friendship.

John's newfound kindness toward me caused some concerns at my maiden appearance as a member of the House Judiciary Committee. On March 3, 1998, Lindsey Graham (R-SC), another new committee member, and I attended our first hearing, which was also the first scheduled hearing after the Monica Lewinsky scandal threatened to end Bill Clinton's presidency via impeachment. The national and international press crowded the hearing room for the expected fireworks and partisan confrontations.

As the senior Republican, Chairman Henry Hyde drew the duty of introducing Lindsey and me as the new members. After Henry finished and then called up the first bill, John Conyers interrupted unexpectedly: "Mr. Chairman, will you yield?"

Everyone looked around nervously. "Here it comes," remarked a GOP congressman seated behind me. Republicans hunkered down for a high voltage Conyers tirade. Instead, jaws dropped as he made a lovely speech welcoming me to the committee and expressing his belief that I would prove myself a valuable member. As he extolled my virtues, Republican colleagues began eyeing me suspiciously. Even Henry Hyde stared at me while looking baffled. I shrugged my shoulders.

When Conyers finished paying tribute to me, he turned an icy gaze toward the other new member, Lindsey Graham, who now smiled in anticipation of Conyers hailing his arrival. "Mr. Chairman," Conyers growled, "I yield back the balance of my time."

• • •

Sadly, former House Judiciary Committee Chairman Peter Rodino and I didn't keep our planned dinner engagement in Newark. A few days after our telephone conversation, he died of congestive heart failure at age ninety-six on May 7, 2005.

When Democrats regained control of the House in 2006, John Conyers became chairman of the House Judiciary Committee, which he held until Republicans took back the majority in 2010. Retiring in 2017 after serving fifty-two years in Congress, he died in his sleep of natural causes at age ninety on October 27, 2019.

Chapter 14

Vignettes

While working in Congress, I looked for opportunities to ask my senior colleagues and others I met to share stories of some of the historic people and experiences that they encountered during their time in government. Below are some vignettes from those conversations.

• • •

Congressman George Brown (D-CA) could have given John Conyers[1] a run for his money in the cranky category. Born in 1920 and a World War II veteran, Brown won election to the city council and state legislature before coming to Congress in 1963. In 1970 he vacated his safe seat to run for California's Democratic U.S. Senate nomination. After losing a bitter primary fight to fellow California Congressman John Tunney (the son of former heavyweight boxing champion Gene Tunney), Brown left Congress, but he returned two years later and remained for the next quarter century.

---

1   See chapter 13.

Brown was yet another grouchy old Democrat bull who had lost his powerful committee chairmanship with the 1994 Republican House takeover. When I served with him, he usually sat alone in the chamber during votes and, like John Conyers, had no interest in getting to know his younger Republican colleagues. I tried a couple of times to chat with him, but his standoffish demeanor let me know that my conversational interest remained one sided.

Just as my political memorabilia collection had helped me break the Conyers Freeze, I tried the same approach with Brown. One day I plopped into the empty seat next to him in the House chamber. "Hey, George," I told him, "I remember when you ran against John Tunney for the Senate in 1970."

He looked surprised. "How the hell do you remember that?" he asked. "You're too young."

"I was in junior high," I replied. "As a school project, I walked precincts for Tunney."

After he grumbled an expletive-laden reply, I asked if he had ever saved any of his campaign memorabilia from that race. "No," he snapped, "and I wish that I had. My grandkids want some of my old items. I never thought to save any of it back in those days." I handed him a large envelope loaded with buttons, pamphlets, and stickers that I had picked up during a boyhood visit to his 1970 San Francisco campaign office. Brown's eyes widened when he saw the assortment, and he appeared genuinely touched.

With this happy opening, and after some friendly small talk, I asked Brown to share his impressions of two political giants who had always fascinated me, and with whom he had served in Washington: President Lyndon B. Johnson and LBJ's arch-nemesis, Senator Robert F. Kennedy (D-NY).

"Oh, I knew Lyndon and Bobby well," he told me. "Ask me whatever you want. I'm happy to tell you all about those two guys."

"Thanks, George. That's great. Let's start with LBJ. What kind of guy was he?"

George reflected on my question, and then he said, "Lyndon Johnson was one of the meanest son of a bitches that I ever knew."

I waited for a further explanation. None followed. "That's it?" I asked. "He was just a mean son of a bitch? Nothing else?"

He nodded. "Yeah, that about covers it."

Regrouping, I tried again: "That was very informative, George. Let's move on. How well did you know Bobby Kennedy?"

"Oh, I knew Bobby very well. In fact, in my office foyer there's a large photo of Bobby and me taken shortly before his assassination. We were pretty good friends."

"What kind of guy was he?"

Once again, George paused in thought before replying: "Bobby was one of the meanest son of a bitches that I ever knew."

"George, I'm seeing a pattern here. Can't you tell me anything else about both of them?"

"Well, there was one big difference that I remember."

"What?"

"Between the two of them, Lyndon was the meaner son of a bitch." George stood to leave. "This was great, Jim. I enjoyed our conversation. Thanks again for the campaign items. Let me know if I can tell you about anybody else."

• • •

A veteran of Senator Barry Goldwater's 1964 presidential campaign, Congressman Phil Crane (R-IL) won a special election for an Illinois seat in 1969. Over the next thirty-five years he regularly ranked as one of the House's most conservative members. He formed and chaired the Republican Study Group, a faction of right-wing GOP congressmen acting as watchdogs over their more center-left Conference leadership. In 1976, he chaired Ronald Reagan's Illinois campaign for the Republican presidential nomination against incumbent Gerald Ford. Later, after gaining national exposure from his leading role in battling President Jimmy Carter's attempt to give back to Panama the canal built by the United States, and believing that Reagan wouldn't run again, Crane entered the 1980 Republican presidential nomination contest. Reagan later jumped in and romped to victory, first against his primary challengers, and then against Carter in the general election. After Reagan crushed Crane in the Illinois congressman's home state primary, Crane ended his presidential campaign, endorsed Reagan, and ran successfully later that year for reelection to the House.

By the time I came to Washington, Crane was well past his prime. Moreover, he appeared to be a loner. During our weekly GOP House Conference meetings, and when he dined at the Capitol restaurant, he always sat by himself. His hands trembled, and I heard repeated rumors of a drinking problem.

One afternoon I entered the House Members Dining Room. Seeing Crane seated alone, I walked over to his small table against the back wall, introduced myself, and asked to join him. I pretended not to notice the awkward hesitation before he invited me, reluctantly, to do so.

Over bowls of chili, I asked about his challenge to Reagan for the presidency in 1980. "Well," he told me, "I didn't run much of a campaign. I was as conservative as Reagan. In fact, we agreed on just about everything. The main difference was that I was forty-nine and Ronnie was sixty-nine. I only got in the race because I didn't think Reagan would run that year. He was too old. If he ran, he'd be older becoming president than Eisenhower was when leaving the presidency. After Reagan got in the race, it was too late for me to fold my tent, so I kept going. I told everyone that if elected I'd be just like Reagan, only I'd be a younger version." Crane laughed as he finished that thought: "As it turned out, everyone preferred the older version to the younger one!"

Regarding Richard Nixon, another Republican president with whom Crane served in Washington, he told me that he had won a special election to the House in 1969 after Nixon opened the seat by appointing his predecessor to an administration position. "I liked Nixon," he said, "but he was never one of us. He was never a conservative. After the Watergate scandal broke, our House Republican leader, [future President] Jerry Ford kept telling us not to worry. 'Nixon has assured me that there are no smoking guns,' Jerry kept repeating. Finally, after a year or so of Nixon never addressing Watergate with any of us personally, we demanded that Jerry set up a Republican Conference meeting with Nixon so that we could discuss the scandal and strategize with him on how to handle it in the press. Eventually, after Ford kept pressing the issue, Nixon invited all Republican congressmen to the White House. We assembled in the East Room. When Nixon arrived, he was animated, relaxed, and confident as he walked around the room and spoke without using any notes. In fact, I never saw him so relaxed. The damn thing is that after talking for over an hour, he never mentioned Watergate! He talked about Russia, Medicare, draft dodgers—everything but the thing we all cared about. Finally, one of our members raised his hand and asked him about Watergate."

With this, Phil transformed his face, voice, and mannerisms as he slipped into a dead-on impression of Nixon. The smile faded; his eyes narrowed, his shoulders hunched, and his arms began wrapping and rolling around each other in a feigned nervous movement. Finally, Phil (still imitating Nixon) extended his right arm forward with his index finger pointing at the imaginary questioner. Wagging his finger up and down as his folded arms raised upward to help conceal his face, Phil mimicked Nixon's voice: " 'That's a *very* good question,' Nixon said, and then he ended the meeting summarily and left the East Room."

"When I saw that performance," Phil added, "with Nixon shrinking physically before my eyes and trying to hide his head behind his arms, I leaned over to the guy sitting next to me and told him, 'I don't care what Jerry Ford keeps telling us. I think we're in a hell of a lot of trouble.' "

· · ·

Historians remain consistent in ranking Sam Rayburn (D-TX) as among the most powerful and influential men ever to serve in Congress. Born in 1882, Rayburn, a former schoolteacher, won election to the House in 1912. For the next half century, and in a congressional career spanning two world wars and eight presidencies (Woodrow Wilson to John F. Kennedy), Rayburn still holds the record for the longest speakership tenure in American history.

By the time I had arrived in Congress, only two of the 435 House members remained who had served with Rayburn (Sidney Yates of Illinois and John Dingell of Michigan). Although I never had much of a chance to get to know Yates, I did get to know Dingell, and during our occasional private luncheons in the House Members Dining Room, he shared with me a few recollections of having served under Texas' iron-fisted, beloved, and feared "Mr. Sam."

"Rayburn was Speaker back when my dad served in Congress,[2] and he was Speaker when I was elected in 1955," John told me. "There's a statue of him in the Rayburn Building, and if you look at it standing on that pedestal, he looks like a shrimp. He was a little guy. His physical stature was tiny, but to me he seemed like a giant. On a personal level, he was pretty aloof. He was very proper and insisted on proper decorum when he ran the House. He also insisted on proper dress for members. He didn't like sport coats, although he grudgingly gave in to that as time went on. He had these blazing eyes that would stare right through you when you made him mad. I know. I got that stare often. He would hit you with that stare when you voted against the [Democratic] party line. Back in those days, there was no electronic voting, so we voted by roll call. Whenever I voted against the party, he'd give me a stare from the dais that would melt my collar button."

---

2   John Dingell Sr. (1894–1955) represented Michigan's fifteenth congressional district from 1933 until his death in 1955, when his son, John Dingell Jr., succeeded him in a special election.

I will return to my John Dingell vignettes momentarily, but let me divert to a Rayburn story as told to me by another longtime congressional member: Daniel K. Inouye (D-HI), who won the Congressional Medal of Honor for valor during World War II. When Hawaii became a state in 1959, Inouye became its first congressman. Three years later, he moved up to the U.S. Senate, where he served for almost fifty years. I had interviewed him for a school project in 1973; a quarter century later, we served together in Congress. While we chatted in the Senate chamber one afternoon, he teased me about inheriting presidential impeachment responsibilities during my freshman term. Then he shared with me this story of his own introduction to Congress and Speaker Sam Rayburn:

> After winning a special election in 1959, I arrived in Washington and joined a Congress already in session. This was only fourteen years after World War II ended, and there was still plenty of anti-Japanese bigotry around. My election made me the first American of Japanese ancestry ever to serve there, and quite a few congressmen snubbed me when I showed up.
>
> The Speaker of the House back then was Sam Rayburn, a gruff, no-nonsense Texan who by then had served in Congress for almost fifty years. Rayburn called me forward into the well of the House and told me to raise my right hand to take the oath of office. Of course, I couldn't do that because I had lost my right arm in combat. When I raised my left hand instead, I heard congressmen and visitors in the gallery weeping. In that moment, I think the bigotry began fading.
>
> Anyway, after I took the oath, I wanted to meet Rayburn, but he left the chamber after swearing me in. Over the next few weeks, I kept looking for a chance to introduce myself to him, but the opportunity never came. Then, about a month or so later, I was standing in the lobby of the Longworth Building talking to someone on the payphone. I saw Rayburn walking down the

hallway alone and in my direction. Here was my chance. I got off the phone, approached him, and said, "Mr. Speaker, I'm sorry to interrupt, but I wanted to introduce myself. I'm Dan Inouye, the new congressman from Hawaii."

Rayburn was a very dour-looking and serious man. He looked me in the eye and said, "You don't need to introduce yourself to me, Dan. I know who you are."

"You do?

"Of course, I know you," Rayburn said. "How the hell many one-armed Japs do you think we have in Congress?" Then he continued on his way.

A few senators had gathered around and joined me in listening to Danny's story. When he reached the climax of his Rayburn yarn, everyone erupted in laughter and, to his credit, Dan Inouye laughed the loudest.

• • •

Now, back to John Dingell. Because his own House career ran parallel to an astounding twelve presidential administrations (Dwight D. Eisenhower to Donald Trump), I asked about his impressions of some of the chief executives that he had known over the years:

JOHN F. KENNEDY: "I knew Kennedy when he was a senator, and then also as president. I wasn't very close to him. Kennedy viewed himself as an aristocrat. He really didn't want to hang out with congressmen once he went to the Senate."

LYNDON B. JOHNSON: "Johnson was very earthy, but probably also one of the most insecure men that I have ever met."

RICHARD NIXON: "My marriage to my first wife was a disaster. She was a clinical paranoid schizophrenic. I came to know the signs and symptoms well. I honestly believe that Nixon suffered from the same condition. Nixon reminded me of how Lord Cromwell described Winston Churchill: 'A great bad man.' "

GERALD FORD: "Jerry Ford is a dear friend. We served together in the House for almost twenty years in the Michigan delegation. Ford's longtime goal was to one day serve as chairman of the Appropriations Committee. Toward the end of his time in the House, he dreamed of becoming Speaker. Of course, he never achieved either goal, but he went on to become vice president and president."

GEORGE H. W. BUSH: "Bush is also a very close friend. We served together in the House for six years. He used to be my paddle ball partner when we played together in the members' gym."

During one of our visits, John asked me what I liked best about serving in Congress. I told him that I had presided over the House for a couple of hours the previous evening. When I returned home late that night, I turned on the TV and watched a historical retrospective on World War II that included the 1941 newsreel footage of President Franklin Roosevelt asking Congress to declare war on Japan. Behind the president during that historic speech sat Speaker Rayburn in the same high-backed leather chair that I had just vacated an hour earlier, and on the very spot where I had presided. That surreal connection reminded me of the incredible privilege I now enjoyed serving in the body.

"Well," he told me, "the next time you watch that old film, look about fifteen feet to the president's right. You'll see a young House page standing against the wall. That's me. I was there that day working as a page appointed by my father." John might have ended up as the last surviving witness to that monumental day in American history, and I asked him to tell me about it:

It was a very scary day," he reflected. "We all thought that the Japanese had invaded the West Coast as well as having bombed Hawaii and other areas. Roosevelt was stern and firm when he spoke. Later, my dad introduced me to him. He was like a god to me when I met him. I can't describe what I felt when I shook his hand.

He said that when the House debated the war resolution, pacifist Congresswoman Jeannette Rankin (R-MT) was the only no vote in either house of Congress: "She was the first woman ever elected to the House. In her first term [1917–1919], she voted against entering World War I, and that unpopular vote led to her defeat at the next election. Over twenty years later, she returned to the House in 1941 in time to vote on our entry into World War II. Once again, she voted no. Once again, she didn't come back in the next election. Montana voters defeated her, and she never again held elective office."

"She only served four years in the House," John added, "but now her statue is in the Capitol Building. Not bad for a short-timer!"

• • •

When I served on the House Judiciary Committee, a perennial proposal came before us to break up the vast Ninth Circuit Federal Court of Appeals. A group of their circuit's judges visited me to lobby against the bill. At the end of our meeting, I stood and thanked the judges for coming to see me. As the last one in the group, Judge James Browning, shook my hand, I whispered to him, "I know that you're the guy in *The Picture*. I'd love to hear the story."

The short, elderly man told his colleagues, "Go ahead without me. I'll catch up with the rest of you." He and I returned to my office and sat on the couch. "Most people don't make that connection any longer" he told me.

"Why do you think I took the meeting today?" I joked. "When I saw your name on the list of judges requesting an appointment, I told my staff that I'd handle this one myself." With that, I asked him to tell me the story of how he came to hold the Bible upon which John F. Kennedy placed his hand while reciting the presidential oath of office at his inauguration on January 20, 1961:

> Chief Justice Earl Warren had appointed me as clerk of the United States Supreme Court in 1958. Back in the old days, it was the tradition for the Supreme Court clerk to hold the Bible when the chief justice swore in the new president. We had no rehearsal for the ceremony. Chief Justice Warren and I just showed up at the Capitol and, at the appointed time, I held Kennedy's 1850 Fitzgerald family Bible, and the chief swore in Kennedy. Maybe we should have rehearsed it first, because halfway through the oath Kennedy absent-mindedly let his hand slip off the Bible. That kicked up a later stir over whether that invalidated the oath. The Constitution does not require the use of a Bible in reciting the oath, but it gave the press something to write about.

Supreme Court Clerk James Browning holds the Bible while Chief Justice Earl Warren swears in President-elect John F. Kennedy, January 20, 1961. Note that JFK's left hand and arm are at his side because his hand had slipped off of the Bible during his oath recitation. (U.S. Government photograph).

Browning recalled that a heavy snowfall had hit Washington the night before Kennedy's inauguration. Because the morning of the event proved so bitterly cold, workers had installed a small portable heater on the presidential platform. "Just as the invocation began, an electrical issue with the heater started a small fire under the lectern. Smoke began billowing around the praying man! It looked like a staged spectacle."[3]

Browning became the last Supreme Court clerk doing Bible honors on Inauguration Day. Four years later, President Lyndon Johnson's wife held it during his oath, and that established a new tradition that continues to this day. I asked Browning what caused the change. "I'm not sure," he replied with a smile. "But I suspect that someone figured out that the person holding the Bible has the best camera position!"

• • •

Because my Los Angeles-based state legislative and congressional districts had so many Hollywood studios and entertainment-related industries sited in it, and because I served on the Judiciary Committee's Intellectual Property subcommittee (copyrights and trademarks are the lifeblood of that community), I worked closely with many studio heads and other industry leaders during my service in both Sacramento and Washington. My favorite was a Hollywood legend that is likely unknown to the average reader: A. C. Lyles.

Born in 1918, A. C. rose from a lowly office clerk to become a movie producer in an unprecedented seventy-six-year career at Paramount Studios (1937–2013). A. C. always dressed as though he had

---

3   "Once the festivities were underway, the podium—the same one from which Kennedy would go on to deliver his iconic address—caught fire during Cardinal Richard Cushing's invocation. As Cushing spoke and as the then president-elect looked on, smoke began to billow out of the podium. But as video from the event illustrates, officers were on their knees working to fix the problem and appeared to have it under control as the cardinal walked away." Ree Hines, "JFK's Inauguration was 60 Years Ago Today: A Look Back at the Day's History-Making Moments," *Yahoo! News*, January 20, 2021, https://news.yahoo.com/jfk-inauguration-60-years-ago-201914341.html?fr=sycsrp_catchall (accessed March 12, 2022).

just walked out of a gentleman's gazette: "When I started working at the studio," A. C. told me, "Adoph Zukor, one of Paramount's founders, told me that if I wanted to be a success in moving pictures, I needed to 'Dress British and think Yiddish.'" An engaging man, A. C. counted among his lifelong friends everyone in Hollywood from James Cagney to Ronald Reagan. My favorite A. C. story is the one he shared with me about his first day on the Paramount lot in 1937, where he hired on as an office boy:

> One of the reasons that Mr. Zukor hired me was because I had a bicycle, and he figured that he could use me as a delivery boy. On my very first morning, he called me into his office and handed me a large envelope with some documents in it. He told me to bring it to W. C. Fields at his home. At the time, Fields was the studio's top film comedian and one of the biggest stars in Hollywood.
>
> I rode my bike over to Mr. Fields' house in Toluca Lake. A butler answered the door, and then he led me out to the rear yard. There, in a canoe out on the lake, I saw Fields as he cursed and swung a paddle like a madman at a quacking duck, who kept flapping its wings and splashing water all over Fields. No matter how hard Fields tried, he couldn't hit the duck.
>
> Frustrated with his failure, Fields paddled back to shore and walked over to me. "Mr. Fields," I told him, "my name is A. C. Lyles from Paramount Studios. They asked me to deliver this envelope to you." He took the envelope and tossed it onto a nearby table, and then he put his face close to mine. The smell of gin on his breath was overpowering.
>
> "Listen, kid," he told me. "Here's what I want you to do. I want you to get into that canoe, row out on the lake, and then take this paddle and beat that duck to death."
>
> I was aghast. "But Mr. Fields," I pleaded, "I don't want to kill a harmless duck. Please don't ask me to do that."

Fields' gaze grew more intense as he replied: "Any young man who won't climb into a canoe, row out on a lake, and use a paddle to kill a vicious duck is no goddamn good and is bound to fail in life." With that, Fields turned and walked into his house.

Crestfallen, I returned to the studio. The encounter left me depressed all day. Finally, when I got off work that night, I had decided to redeem myself with the great star. I rode my bicycle back to his house, knocked on the door, and told the butler that I needed to see Mr. Fields again. The butler led me into the study and announced me to Fields, who now appeared far more clear-eyed than he had been that morning.

"Mr. Fields," I said, "remember me? I'm A. C. Lyles from Paramount Studios. I'm ready to get into your canoe, go out on your lake, and use your paddle to beat to death the duck that's swimming out there." Fields gave me a blank look.

"You want to do what?" he asked me.

"I said that I want to get into your canoe, go out onto your lake, and use your paddle to beat to death the duck that's swimming out there."

"Listen, kid," Fields told me. "Any young man who would come to my house, get into my canoe, go out onto my lake, and then take a paddle and beat to death a poor defenseless duck is no goddamn good and is bound to fail in life." Fields got up and walked out of the room."

"And that," A. C. concluded, "was my introduction to what became a lifelong career at Paramount Studios!"

• • •

Early in his 1992 presidential campaign, a sex scandal nearly upended Arkansas Governor Bill Clinton's White House trajectory. Cabaret singer Gennifer Flowers claimed, on the eve of the crucial New Hampshire primary, that she and Clinton had maintained a "torrid twelve-year love affair." After voters had accepted his repeated denials and sent him to Washington, she produced recorded conversations to corroborate her claim. Clinton then admitted to it.

One night I returned home late from the Capitol and turned on the TV. The History Channel was airing a documentary of Clinton's 1992 race. The broadcast included a snippet from then Governor Clinton's press conference denying the Flowers accusation. I noticed that Louisiana Governor Edwin Edwards and Congressman Billy Tauzin (D-LA) had flanked Clinton during this infamous fib.

Edwin Edwards was perhaps one of the most flamboyant politicians and biggest rascals since the days of his predecessor Huey Long. A four-term populist governor with an unrepentant reputation for high stakes gambling and womanizing, he boasted that the only way any Republican could beat him for reelection was to catch him "in bed with a dead girl or a live boy." He survived one indictment in 1985, but his luck ran out in 2000 when a jury convicted him on seventeen counts of racketeering, mail and wire fraud, conspiracy, and money laundering. Released from federal prison at age eighty-three, after serving an eight-year sentence, he married his third wife (fifty years his junior) and ran unsuccessfully for Congress.

I never knew Governor Edwards, but by the time I had watched that vintage news clip, Congressman Billy Tauzin and I were colleagues and friends. A former House Democrat, Billy had switched parties in 1995 and joined our Republican ranks.

The morning after I had watched the old Clinton-Gennifer Flowers retrospective, I ran into Billy in the House chamber. When I mentioned what I had seen, he laughed and told me the backstory behind that infamous morning:

It was a couple of weeks before the critical New Hampshire primary of 1992. Gennifer Flowers had told reporters that she and Clinton had enjoyed a "torrid twelve-year affair." Edwin [Governor Edwards] and I were up in Clinton's hotel suite in

Louisiana when the story hit, and all hell broke loose. Clinton was already running behind in New Hampshire, so he knew that this story could end his presidential campaign just as a similar sex scandal had destroyed Gary Hart's four years earlier.[4] Clinton had scheduled a press conference to address Gennifer's charges, and he and his aides were almost shouting at each other over how to handle the damage control. I got caught up in the drama and made suggestions, but Edwin sat silently and calmly in a chair smoking a cigar and taking in the whole scene.

When the time came to leave for the press conference, I climbed into the back seat of the limo with Clinton and Edwin, who still hadn't said anything. Clinton remained frantic over what to say when we arrived, and he kept yelling at his staff that he needed help to get this under control.

Finally, just before we got to the press conference location, Clinton asked Edwin for his advice. Edwin took the cigar out of his mouth. "Bill," he said, "there's a very simple way to deny these charges and make everyone believe your denial." Now at a near-panic level, Clinton begged Edwin to tell him what to say.

Edwin smiled. "Bill," he replied, "just go into that press conference, look those reporters in the eye, and say this: 'Ladies and Gentlemen, I submit to you that there is such a thing as a torrid affair. And I also submit to you that there is such a thing as a twelve-year love affair. But I defy anyone to prove there has *ever* been such a thing as a torrid twelve-year love affair!'

Clinton stared at Edwards, and then he shook his head in exasperation. "That's not gonna help me, Edwin," he said, and then we all exited the car. We went into the press conference where Clinton gave a lame denial, which of course nobody believed. Later, he was forced to admit that he had lied.

---

4   The frontrunner for the 1988 Democrat presidential nomination, U.S. Senator Gary Hart (D-CO), dropped out of the campaign after reporters uncovered episodes of marital infidelity. See generally, https://www.history.com/news/gary-hart-scandal-front-runner (accessed March 20, 2022).

In the end, Clinton lost that New Hampshire primary, but he was able to bounce back from the loss and the scandal. But to this day, I remain convinced that if Clinton had taken Edwin's advice, he would not only have won the presidency in 1992, but he would have won the New Hampshire primary, too!

• • •

Congressman George Brown died of complications following heart surgery at age seventy-nine on July 15, 1999.

Congressman Phil Crane died of lung cancer at age eighty-four on November 8, 2014.

Judge James Browning served on the Ninth Circuit Court of Appeals for over fifty years. He died at age ninety-three on May 6, 2012.

After working at Paramount Studios for almost eighty years, A. C. Lyles died at age ninety-five on September 27, 2013.

Chapter 15

Cold Shoulder

y fascination with the American presidency began as a nine-year-old boy in 1966 when I stumbled upon a small booklet, *American Presidents Album*, that my mother picked up from our local grocery store during its weekly promotional giveaway. Knowing nothing about the presidents beyond Washington's cherry tree and Lincoln's top hat, the photos and brief profiles in the brochure teased my interest. I read and reread it, and then I checked out a book on presidents at my school's library. When I finished it, I went back for another book, and then another. After reading all the books on presidents at the library, I found another library. This early interest fueled my love of American history, government, and politics, which in turn led to my eventual career in law and public service.

During my boyhood, I often cut school and took the bus into downtown San Francisco whenever a national political figure came to town. I snuck into their events to take pictures, collect an autograph, and get advice on entering politics. As a youth in the 1970s, I met Congressman Gerald Ford, Georgia Governor Jimmy Carter,

California Governor Ronald Reagan, United Nations Ambassador George H. W. Bush, and Arkansas Attorney General Bill Clinton. When meeting these future chief executives back then, I never dreamed that I would become acquainted with each of them in later years.[1] In the following chapters, I'll share some behind-the-scenes presidential glimpses from my perch as an elected official. We begin with America's thirty-eighth president, Gerald R. Ford.

• • •

Born in 1913, the Eagle Scout and college football star earned the University of Michigan's most valuable player award before entering the Navy during World War II. He returned home to Grand Rapids and practiced law until winning a congressional seat in 1948. Elected minority leader in 1964, he served as the top House Republican until President Richard Nixon tapped him for the vice presidency following Vice President Spiro Agnew's 1973 resignation. Ford succeeded to the presidency upon Nixon's resignation on August 9, 1974. Running for a full term in 1976, Ford bested former California Governor Ronald Reagan for the Republican presidential nomination, but he lost the election to Jimmy Carter in a close race. He retired to the Palm Springs area (Rancho Mirage) where, over the next three decades, he penned his memoirs, oversaw the construction of his presidential library, played in charity golf tournaments, maintained a busy speaking and travel schedule, and joined corporate boards.

---

[1]   The stories of my boyhood encounters with these future (and some former) presidents of the United States are memorialized in two of my previous books: *Rough Edges: My Unlikely Road from Welfare to Washington* and *And Then I Met: Stories of Growing Up, Meeting Famous People, and Annoying the Hell Out of Them.*

Congress of the United States
Office of the Minority Leader
House of Representatives
Washington, D.C. 20515

September 11, 1970

Mr. Jim Rogan
25 Poncetta Drive
Apartment 110
Daly City, California 94015

Dear Jim,

I have your recent letter and am glad to know that you are interested
in politics.

You will find enclosed one of my photographs which I have autographed
for you. I am sorry that I cannot send you my autograph on an admission
card to the United States Senate since I am not a United States Senator.
The members of the House of Representatives are not permitted to sign
the passes for admittance to the Senate.

Because of your interest in our government and its leaders, I thought
you would like to see the enclosed booklet entitled, "How Our Laws Are
Made."

Kindest personal regards.

Sincerely,

Gerald R. Ford, M.C.

GRF:h

Encl.

"Because of your interest in our government and its leaders...." At age twelve, I wrote to Michigan
Congressman Gerald Ford and told him of my attraction to history and government. He replied on
September 11, 1970, with this letter, and he sent me a booklet on how Congress works. (Author's
collection)

• • •

I had not quite completed my first year in the House of Representatives when fellow California freshman Congressman Walter Capps
(D-CA) died of a massive heart attack in October 1997. The governor called a special election to fill his Santa Barbara coastal seat.
Republican Brooks Firestone, a close friend with whom I had served

in the California State Assembly, joined the field of contenders for the vacancy. In late November, Brooks called and asked me to emcee a district campaign event for him featuring former President Ford as the guest speaker. The Ford and Firestone families were longtime friends: Brooks' father Leonard had served as Ford's U.S. Ambassador to Belgium. When he left the White House in 1977, Ford built his retirement home next to the elder Firestone's house on the thirteenth fairway of the Thunderbird Golf Course.

• • •

A few days later, and as the only passenger, I boarded a small Beechcraft twin engine jet in Van Nuys and departed for Palm Springs to pick up Ford and escort him to the Santa Barbara area to campaign for Brooks. When I landed at a private terminal in the desert early that morning Nancy DeLuna, a friend of both the Fords and the Firestones who had organized the day's events, met and briefed me on the schedule while we awaited Ford's arrival. Lovely, bright, and charming, she proved a very pleasant addition to our small traveling party.

During Nancy's briefing, a lone Secret Service agent performed a cursory check of the jet. After conducting his inspection, he asked me to join him inside the four-seat cabin. Pointing to my briefcase and small camera resting on the left rear aisle seat that I had occupied on the inbound flight, he requested that I switch over to the right aisle seat. "President Ford always prefers the left aisle seat," he told me. No problem. I picked up my things and moved them to the opposite chair.

I rejoined Nancy on the tarmac just as a dark sedan carrying Ford and a few agents pulled alongside the plane. Ford exited carrying a battered leather briefcase and walked toward us. At eighty-four, he looked erect, husky, and solid. The only telltale sign of advancing age came from his stiff gait caused by multiple knee surgeries to repair old football injuries.

As a boy in San Francisco a quarter century earlier, I had stood outside Ford's hotel with a large crowd of onlookers hoping to catch a glimpse of the incumbent president as he arrived for a speech. Now he and I would spend the day together, with much of it on a private jet. I felt thrilled by the honor as I offered my hand and greeted him: "Mr. President, I'm Jim Rogan, the new Republican congressman from Los Angeles County. It's an honor to join you today and to help Brooks. He and I served together in the State Assembly. We're close friends."

Ford looked beyond me as he gave my hand a single pump before dropping it. "Hi," he replied in a monotone voice suggesting boredom, and then he turned from me and walked away. His indifference caught me off guard, and it contrasted sharply with his sudden joviality when approaching our traveling companion. "Oh, hello, Nancy!" he said cheerily as he kissed and then engaged her in simpatico small talk: "How is X doing these days? Have you seen A and B lately? Are you going to their party in Indio this weekend?" I felt like an unwelcome country cousin crashing a private family reunion. Ford and Nancy continued chatting while boarding the plane; I shuffled up the stairs behind them.

When Ford reached the two forward facing side-by-side aisle seats in the small cabin, his eyes fixed on my belongings on the seat where the Secret Service agent had asked me to relocate them. Without making an inquiry as to ownership or whether anyone minded, Ford scooped up my stuff in his arms, flung it across the aisle into my original seat, and then he dropped himself into the chair that the agent had asked me to occupy. I started to tell Ford that he had parked himself in the wrong one per his agent's direction, but I caught myself when I remembered the story of President Lyndon Johnson deplaning from Air Force One. LBJ made his way toward the two helicopters that waited to whisk him back to the White House. Johnson's Secret Service-designated helicopter was positioned on the right, with the decoy helicopter alongside it. Johnson marched to the wrong helicopter to board it. A frantic young Marine tried to intercept him: "Excuse me, Mr. President," he said, "but the other helicopter is *your* helicopter." Johnson never blinked as he continued on his way. "Son," he replied, "they're *all* my helicopters."

In the spirit of recognizing that *all* the seats on the plane were Ford's seats, I picked up my briefcase and camera and settled into the chair across the aisle from him. In the narrow cabin, only eighteen or so inches separated us. Nancy sat in a seat facing Ford, while the two Secret Service agents traveling with us sat forward on a small couch next to the cockpit.

During takeoff, Ford motioned with his finger toward the camera in my lap. "I don't know whose camera that is," he groused, "but I don't want any pictures taken in here."

No pictures? How often does a green congressman spend a day flying around in a private plane with an ex-president? In a voice betraying my disappointment, I replied, "It's mine. I'll put it under my seat."

"Well, be sure and keep it there," he snapped. "I don't want a bunch of pictures taken in here." I slid the offending instrument under my chair.

This promised to be a very long day.

• • •

Things didn't improve between us once airborne. Ford ignored me and spoke exclusively with Nancy. He even snubbed me on sports talk—a traditionally male conversational topic—by sharing with Nancy his views on college football, his favorite coaches, and the ongoing NFL season. Here I didn't mind Ford's cold shoulder. Since my knowledge of (and adult interest in) sports is near-nonexistent, dealing me out of this chatter proved merciful. As they talked, I nodded my head up and down as if I understood and agreed with whatever the hell they were gabbling about.

When he reminisced with Nancy about his own days of playing college football ("Back when we wore leather shoes, leather helmets, and used a round football!"), I saw an opening to inject myself into the exchange. I asked him if it was true, as press accounts reported, that a young Iowa sportscaster named Ronald Reagan had once broadcast a Michigan football game in which Ford had played.

"I've heard that one before," Ford sniffed. "I don't know if it's true." Then he scowled as if confronting an unpleasant odor in the cabin. "It makes for a good story," he added.

During the flight, I tried on other occasions to join the discussion, but no matter what I asked or said, I drew curt replies. By the time we neared our destination, my feelings of awe and excitement over spending a day with him had morphed into irritation. For the remainder of the flight, I sat in silence and nursed my grievances: the airport brush-off, tossing my belongings like a petulant child, griping about my camera, ignoring me throughout the flight, and, worst of all, subjecting me to a god-awful spew of sports trivia.

Dr. Rogan had diagnosed the patient as suffering from *ex-president-itis*. Indulging the symptoms had exacerbated them, so I decided to bide my time to poke a needle in this inflated balloon if the opportunity presented.

• • •

Our plane landed at Santa Maria Airport at 11:00 a.m. and taxied next to the rear entrance of the Hilton hotel, where Brooks and Kate Firestone awaited our arrival. Ford ran a comb through his hair before he disembarked and greeted the Firestones on the tarmac. Brooks escorted us into the hotel and up to Room 418, where Ford and I joined a dozen of Brooks' major donors seated around a large conference table for a private briefing. Ford thanked everyone for coming to support Brooks, who then updated Ford and his donors on his campaign's progress. Brooks then asked me to share my insights.

I didn't know anything about sports, but as the California State Assembly's recent Republican majority leader, I made it my business to know the political lay of the land in every district of my GOP members. In off-the-cuff remarks, I discussed Brooks' political strengths and vulnerabilities against each of his declared Republican and Democrat opponents. As I broke down the demographics of the district and laid out my thoughts on Brooks' potential path to victory, I noticed Ford leaning toward me and listening with apparent concentration. When I finished, Ford questioned me about the national congressional scene. Each answer brought from him nods of agreement. At one point he made a comment about the current GOP House leadership with which I disagreed. Rather than ignore our differences, and looking to get even for his earlier high-hatted treatment of me, I differed with him openly and (I grimace now at the memory) dismissively. To my surprise, rather than showing annoyance or offense over my challenge to his political calculation, when I finished my point, he said that on reflection he agreed with me. As this hotel room discussion continued, his earlier coolness had dissipated. Now he spoke to me with respect, and even with a hint of warmth.

Progress, I thought.

Over the next few hours, Ford and I attended a private cocktail reception with Brooks' major donors; we did a photo-op line with individual key supporters, and then we both spoke at a general luncheon for three hundred party faithful. During my introduction of Ford, and still bent on settling my airplane score, I joked about his famed clumsiness and his penchant for hitting spectators on the fairways with errant golf balls. Once again, instead of taking umbrage at my poking the bear, he laughed heartily and appeared to enjoy the mild roasting. When he spoke, he built on my jokes by telling of golfing with comedian Bob Hope recently. Ford recalled that as Hope teed up his shot, a woman in the gallery yelled out, "Hey Bob, what's your ideal foursome?" Hope replied, "Jerry Ford, a priest, and a paramedic!"

Following the luncheon, I escorted Ford outside to his sedan. He had planned a two-hour excursion to visit his son Steve's San Luis Obispo ranch. We synchronized our watches and agreed to meet back at the airplane at 4:30 p.m. for a 4:35 takeoff. With a California Highway Patrol escort car as the lead vehicle and a Secret Service chase car behind, Ford's small caravan departed.

With a couple of hours to kill, Nancy and I drove with Kate Firestone to her family's ranch and winery in Los Olivos. Our visit proved so delightful that we lost track of time. When I checked my watch, it was 4:00 p.m., which left us only thirty minutes to drive twenty-seven miles back to the airport and rendezvous with Ford. We jumped into Kate's car, and she sped toward Santa Maria.

At 4:20, with ten minutes and a few miles remaining, Nancy's cell phone rang. She listened for a moment, and then her face lost all color. "Yes, Mr. President," she said. "We're almost there." When she ended the call, she turned to Kate and told her in a somber voice, "The president is at the airplane and waiting for us. He's ready to leave *now*. The president doesn't like to be kept waiting. *This is not good.*"

I told the ladies to relax. We'd still get there before our scheduled departure time. Besides, Ford had arrived early, so he shouldn't have expected us to anticipate his last-minute change to a schedule that he had dictated. My reasoning did nothing to soothe their concerns. Kate slammed down the accelerator pedal and sped to the freeway exit. In her anxiety, she couldn't locate the entrance to the air strip. Growing desperate, she screeched her car to a stop outside the main Hilton entrance. The three of us raced through the lobby and out the back door to the airfield, which we reached at 4:32—two minutes behind our scheduled return time, but still three minutes ahead of departure.

We encountered a very disconcerted Gerald Ford pacing alongside the plane on the windy tarmac. The strong gusts had blown the hair straight out on the sides of his otherwise bald head, making him look like a crazed circus clown. I suppressed any show of amusement at this offbeat sight while Nancy and Kate offered profuse apologies that did nothing to satisfy him. "I've been waiting for ten minutes!" he barked. "No excuses! Let's get this damned plane in the air." Nothing that the ladies said assuaged Ford's prickly impatience, which made another mild jab irresistible to me. With a smile I cracked, "Next time you synchronize watches with someone, maybe you should wind yours first. We're three minutes early. Since we're ahead of schedule, why don't we go in the terminal and pick up some magazines and Hershey bars?"

Ignoring me, Ford shouted over the noise of the nearby jets, "All right, everyone, get aboard! Let's go!" Nancy and I waved goodbye to poor Kate, who stood on the tarmac looking stricken, and then we followed *el Jefe* up the stairs into the plane.

Once inside, Ford yelled at the pilots, "All right, you guys, let's go! Get this plane in the air—now!" With growing agitation, he slumped into his seat while complaining about the cabin temperature. "Damn it, turn on the heaters, somebody!" he shouted over the engine turbines. Then he started squirming in his chair while looking down as if in search of something lost. He fumbled with his hands at his sides before blaring in frustration, "Where's my goddamn seat belt?"

Once again, the *ex-president-itis* bug had bitten our patient.

By now I had come to like Jerry Ford, notwithstanding my earlier feelings from our morning flight and his current tantrum over our two-minute late arrival. In the twenty-five years since he entered the White House, I guess that he had grown accustomed to having things go his way and to having people indulge his whims. Based on my daylong experiences with him, I sensed that he respected people who pushed back a bit. That's why, when he shouted a second time and in a louder and angrier tone, "Where's my goddamn seat belt?" I leaned across the aisle and told him, "Excuse me, Mr. President, but I believe that your ass is sitting on your goddamn seat belt."

Ford (with his hair still sticking out in an amusing coif) turned and scowled at me. Nancy looked down at her shoes, no doubt fearing that any eye contact with me might implicate her as an aider and abettor. Then, in a welcome reaction to my less-than-deferential reply, he laughed. "Well, so it is!" he exclaimed as he fished out his belt and buckled it.

We were back on track.

• • •

Ford relaxed once we took off. On this final leg of the trip, he talked—with me!—throughout the return flight. My thrill at having full rein to question a former president about his career ran at full throttle.

Ford expressed deep disappointment in the recent failure of Congress to pass "fast track" trade legislation, which President Clinton had identified as his highest economic priority. The bill lost by a narrow margin, with GOP congressmen supporting it overwhelmingly. Under union pressure, House Democrats had joined with recalcitrant Republicans to kill it. Ford told me that, at Clinton's request, he had lobbied wobbly Republicans personally for their support, and then he added, "I'm sure that Clinton did the same thing with House Democrats."

"I don't know what Clinton's been telling you," I said, "but I helped whip that bill [act as a GOP leadership vote counter]. At least a dozen junior Democrats who ended up as no votes told me that Clinton had never bothered contacting them. They said that if Clinton had let them know that the bill was important to him, they might have voted differently."

Ford's jaw clenched. "I worked *very hard* for that thing," he said. "I was under the impression Clinton was doing the same thing. This is inexcusable."

• • •

During the return flight to Palm Springs, Ford shared with Nancy and me a potpourri of insights about his life in politics:

HIS FIRST CONGRESSIONAL CAMPAIGN IN 1948 — "Nobody gave me much of a chance. I was a young attorney and World War II veteran. With a push from our Michigan senator, Arthur Vandenburg, I challenged an isolationist Republican incumbent in the primary. Since I had served in the war and he had not, we set up a military Quonset hut as our campaign headquarters. It was a reminder to the voters that I had served and that he hadn't, despite the fact that many members of Congress had enlisted and gone to war. Ultimately, I won the race by a two-to-one margin."

PRESIDENT HARRY S TRUMAN — "I liked Truman, and he liked me. We had a good relationship because I supported him in his foreign policy objectives. He was president when I first went to the House in 1948. Years later, when Truman was dead and I was president, Betty and I were at the 1976 Republican National Convention. The night I beat Ronald Reagan for the presidential nomination, Mrs. Truman wrote Betty a handwritten note. It said, 'Congratulations— Our boy won!' Betty cherishes the note to this day."

SPEAKERS OF THE HOUSE — "Sam Rayburn was a great Speaker. He understood power and how to get things done. He was a little fellow with a bald head, but he had an immense presence when he walked into a room. I got along fine with him, as well as his successors John McCormack and Carl Albert. Carl's big problem was that he drank too much, and so did his wife. I'm surprised that they're both still alive. Tip O'Neill and I were very close friends. He was about as partisan as they came, but we had a wonderfully close relationship. Newt Gingrich's current problem is something I discussed with him recently. I told him that he had to remember that he is Speaker of the *House*, and not just Speaker of the Republican Conference."

Referring to a rump faction's attempt to topple Gingrich from the speakership a few months earlier, Ford distinguished that failed effort from his own overthrow of House GOP Leader Charles Halleck following the 1964 elections in which Democrats swept the presidency and both houses of Congress. "These guys made two mistakes when they ran their failed coup against Gingrich," he said. "First, they tried it in mid-session. Second, they couldn't agree upon a single leader. When I deposed Charlie Halleck after the Goldwater debacle of 1964, I did it just before we had our organizational meeting after the election results. Everyone there had just survived a disastrous year for Republicans and dissatisfaction ran high. Change was ripe, and I benefitted from that sentiment. Further, there was only one insurgent candidate to pick from—me. In Gingrich's case, the rebels couldn't decide who should replace him, so it all fell apart." He laughed as he told me, "In 1964, we lost 47 GOP House seats. We were down to 140 Republican members. When they counted the secret ballots cast for Halleck and me, there were 141 turned in! Nobody ever fessed up as to who had voted twice. I won by 73-67, but after I won, all 140 Republican members later told me that they had voted for me!"

PRESIDENT RICHARD NIXON – "I had known Dick Nixon for many years. We served in the House together for a couple of years and I knew him back then. I had campaigned for him in 1960 when he ran against Jack Kennedy, and I was mentioned briefly as his possible running mate that year. It was a brief mention! Some of my Michigan supporters made a small push for me to be selected as his vice presidential running mate. Instead, he chose [former Senator] Henry Cabot Lodge, who was a pathetic candidate. Lodge didn't want to campaign, took naps, and only wanted to do one speech a day.

"Nixon became president when I was House Republican leader. We generally had a good personal relationship. However, we often had problems. Not personal, but problems working with his senior staff. He was cloistered by people like [chief of staff] H. R. Haldeman, [domestic advisor] John Ehrlichman, and [White House counsel] Chuck Colson. They would call me on the telephone and order me around, saying, 'The President wants you to do this or do that.' Sometimes I would pick up the phone, call Nixon, and complain about his directives. Nixon would tell me he didn't know what I was talking about. These guys were really evil."

ON SUCCEEDING SPIRO AGNEW AS NIXON'S VICE PRESIDENT IN 1973—
"Richard Nixon did not want me to be his vice president. He really wanted his treasury secretary, former Texas Governor John Connally. Connally was a long-time Democrat who later became a Republican, but his shift to Nixon in the 1972 campaign angered the Democrats who controlled Congress. Further, Connally had been investigated over some legal and ethical lapses, so Connally could never be confirmed, and Nixon knew it. Nixon's next choices were New York Governor Nelson Rockefeller and California Governor Ronald Reagan. However, the moderates would never vote to confirm Reagan because he was too conservative, and the conservatives would never support Rockefeller, whom they viewed as too liberal. Finally, the Democrat leadership—House Speaker Carl Albert and Senate Majority Leader Mike Mansfield—went to see Nixon. They told him the only person they could guarantee would be confirmed by the Democrat-controlled Congress was Jerry Ford. Nixon needed a candidate who would be confirmed swiftly, and that is what turned the tide toward me.

"After Congress confirmed me as vice president, they had the swearing-in ceremony for me in the House chamber. It was a very emotional moment for me. I had served there for twenty-six years. Now I was saying goodbye to so many of my oldest and dearest friends. I was given a thunderous ovation from my colleagues on both sides of the aisle. I'll never forget that day.

"When Agnew resigned the vice presidency in 1973, he moved to Palm Springs. A few years later I retired from the presidency and moved to nearby Rancho Mirage. During the twenty years that I lived near Agnew, I rarely saw him—maybe four times in twenty years. He had many lucrative business deals all around the world, but he was a political recluse. He went to nothing and kept a very low profile. I got my updates on him from Mrs. Ford, who would run into his wife, Judy, at the shopping mall now and then."

BECOMING PRESIDENT ON AUGUST 9, 1974 — "Well," he sighed, "it had been a very rough seventy-two hours [leading up to Nixon's resignation]. Once it became clear that Nixon's support in Congress was gone, I kept a very low profile and kept my distance from the issue. I didn't want to appear to be like a vulture. Nixon announced his resignation on August 8. The next day he made his farewell speech. We escorted him from the White House to a waiting helicopter, and then we returned for my own swearing-in ceremony.

"When I had my hand on the Bible and I recited the oath to become president, truthfully, I wasn't thinking much about the historical moment. It had been a long, hard day. I just wanted to get through it and appear strong and in control of the situation."

ON SURVIVING TWO ASSASSINATION ATTEMPTS WHILE PRESIDENT— Ford grew somber as he reminisced about the two attempts on his life during his presidency, both of which occurred in California and within two weeks of each other in September 1975. "It was a scary thing to go through," he said. "The first one happened in Sacramento. I had just left the hotel and was making my way across the street and through the park to the Capitol. As I was shaking hands with spectators along the police line, I could see a young woman dressed in red following along the back of the crowds. A few moments later, I was looking at the people in the line where I was shaking hands. I saw the young woman in red. As I looked down to take her hand, I distinctly saw a large handgun pointed right at me. It scared the hell out of me. Before I could react, a Secret

Service agent grabbed the gun. He wedged his thumb down where the hammer would strike the firing pin. He may have kept her from firing it. The agents hustled me into the Capitol, where I met with Governor Jerry Brown before I addressed the legislature. Nobody in the Capitol knew that I had been the victim of an attempted assassination just a few minutes before.

"A couple of weeks later, I was coming out of the St. Francis Hotel in San Francisco. As I was waving to the crowd gathered across the street from my car, I heard a gunshot. This time, the lady with the gun actually pulled the trigger and got off a shot at me. A Marine in the crowd standing next to her had deflected her arm and the bullet hit the side of the hotel. The Secret Service rushed me into the car and drove directly to the airport, where they hustled me aboard Air Force One.

"When we were on the plane, I sat in my compartment with [White House photographer] Dave Kennerly and [White House Chief of Staff] Don Rumsfeld having a drink when Betty arrived. She hadn't heard about the shooting. 'So,' she asked innocently, 'how did they treat you in San Francisco today?' We all broke out laughing, especially when we saw the puzzled look on her face. It really broke the tension. I told her that I almost gave up my support for the Equal Rights Amendment because of that question!"

FORMER PRESIDENT RONALD REAGAN—"I visited with Reagan in his Los Angeles office recently. I remained for about twenty minutes. Because of his Alzheimer's disease, he didn't recognize me when I arrived, and he didn't know who I was. We sat, I told him stories from our political days, and I talked about people we had known. By the time I was ready to go, Reagan knew that we had been friends, but he didn't comprehend or remember my position or his own. One of his staffers told me that Reagan still goes out and plays golf regularly, but he doesn't talk with the people he plays with. He just goes out and plays. It's good for him at this stage, I guess."

THEN-INCUMBENT PRESIDENT BILL CLINTON—"The trick for congressional Republicans in dealing with Clinton is to keep him from reverting to his old liberal ways. Clinton moves to the right when he thinks he needs to do so. But his true gut instincts are that of a big-government liberal."

ON THE FIELD OF POSSIBLE 2000 REPUBLICAN PRESIDENTIAL CANDIDATES—"I have no current favorite, but I think a fresh face is needed and probably will surface. George Bush Jr. [Texas governor] and John McCain [U.S. senator] are both fine men, and both would make excellent candidates. [Publisher] Steve Forbes is a one issue candidate—the flat tax reform. That didn't get him very far when he ran in 1996. [Former Vice President] Dan Quayle is a good guy, and he got a bum rap by the press when he ran for vice president in 1988, but I don't know that he can ever overcome that handicap. Jack Kemp [former congressman and 1996 Republican vice presidential nominee] is a great friend of mine. When I was House minority leader, I campaigned for him in New York when he ran for Congress in his first campaign. But Jack is another 'one-note' candidate. When he debated [Vice President Al] Gore last year, it didn't matter what was the question. He turned it into a tax question, and he gave a tax answer. He didn't do very well against Gore." When I asked him about Elizabeth Dole (wife of 1996 Republican presidential nominee Bob Dole) and her rumored interest in running, Ford shook his head. "I don't think the country is ready for that," he said.

• • •

As we compared impressions of our day campaigning for Brooks Firestone, I asked if he did many events for Republican candidates these days. "I've done a few," he said. "The Firestones are old friends. I did one for Sonny Bono[2] out in the desert and Steve Horn[3] in

---

2   Sonny Bono (1935–1998) served as Ford's congressman in the Palm Springs area.

3   Steve Horn (1931–2011), a liberal Republican and former university president, served in the House from 1993 to 2003.

Long Beach. That's about it. I feel that after all these years, I've done my duty electing Republicans. I've paid my dues. I don't like doing them anymore." Ford took a sip of coffee from a Styrofoam cup, and then he surprised me with an unexpected and dazzling potential: "Brooks tells me that your reelect next year will be pretty brutal. Give me a call in the spring. Maybe I can come out your way and do something for you."

If I had any complaint with Gerald Ford at the beginning of the day, all was forgiven.

• • •

Mild turbulence told me that we had begun our descent into Palm Springs. Remembering his earlier irritation over seeing my camera that morning and his arbitrary demand of "no photos," I hoped that he had softened enough for me to spring my request to get a picture with him aboard the plane. Since the day neared its end, it was now or never. I approached my appeal in a roundabout way: "Mr. President, I read that one of your biggest political heroes was President Eisenhower. I'm curious: when you were a young congressman—as I am now—did you ever get the chance to meet him when he visited your state?"

"Oh, my, yes!" he exclaimed as his face brightened over the pleasant recollection. "Ike's train came through my hometown of Grand Rapids when he ran for president, and I was running for reelection to Congress. I got to go aboard and meet him!" As Ford recalled Ike's trip to his district, he shared how excited he had been to spend private time with Ike aboard the train and how much it had meant to him.

"Did you ever get any pictures of you with Eisenhower that day?"

"Oh, yes, lots of them! I still have them. They're among my prized possessions."

With the big game now lined up in my sights, I pulled the trigger: "Well, aren't you glad that Ike didn't tell you 'No pictures' and make you shove your camera under your seat when you boarded his train?"

Instead of connecting the dots, Ford looked puzzled at my question. "Uh, no, Ike never told me 'No cameras' or 'No pictures,'" he replied. "Actually, I got quite a few pictures with him that day."

With my shot missing the mark, I bit the bullet: "Mr. President, right now I'd sure like to get a picture with you and me on the plane. I'd treasure it just as much as the ones you have with Ike."

"Well, all right," he said. "But just one or two. I don't want a bunch of pictures taken."

I remain glad that Ford stretched out his largesse to *two* photographs. Nancy took them both, and because of a sudden turbulence bump, the first one ended up blurry. It took some doing, but thanks to Nancy DeLuna's steady hand, my flight with Jerry Ford is memorialized on film.

Here I am with President Gerald Ford aboard the plane, December 1, 1997. His protruding hair from the windy tarmac still hadn't settled down, and mine doesn't look much better. (Photo by Nancy DeLuna)

We landed in Palm Springs a few minutes later. I carried Ford's briefcase for him as he negotiated his way through the cramped cabin and down the stairs. We shook hands as he thanked me for joining him and for helping Brooks. As Nancy and I walked him to his waiting car, I looked back and saw the disappointed faces of the two pilots who had told me earlier that they had hoped to get a picture with him. With Ford prepared to depart, that chance appeared lost. Pressing my luck, and at the risk of annoying him, I told him about the pilots' request and that it would mean a lot to them. "If you do it," I said in a hushed voice, "I promise I'll only take one picture, and then I'll shove the camera back under my seat! Come on—do it for old Ike."

"Well, okay," he said. "For old Ike. But just one or two. I don't want a bunch of pictures taken."

"Trust me, sir. By now, I know the rules."

• • •

During my two terms in Congress, I saw Ford a few times in Washington. He always greeted me as an old friend. In mid-1999 I cohosted a private meeting for him and former First Lady Betty Ford at the Capitol with some younger Republican congressmen. He spent an hour regaling us with stories of his early days in the House in what sounded like a more innocent, and a more fun, time to be in politics.

Enjoying a joke with Jerry and Betty Ford, the U.S. Capitol, June 3, 1998. (Author's collection)

• • •

For every ten political figures that offered or promised to do a fund-raising event for me, a small percentage actually came through. The rest of these big talkers were just that. Unlike those "summer soldiers and sunshine patriots" who shrank from their pledge of help when I needed it, Jerry Ford came through in spades. Over the next three years, he attended three events for me, and he would have attended a fourth had we not canceled it because I was stuck in Washington for House votes. In October 1998, a month before I won a tough reelection, he headlined a fundraiser for me at the Richard Nixon Library in Orange County (just outside my district). After standing on painful knee replacements while doing a hundred-person "grip and grin" photo line with my high-dollar donors, he spoke on my behalf for almost half an hour to a large gathering of my supporters in the library foyer. He told them that at his advanced age he rarely appeared at political events, but that he drove out from the desert to do one for me because he felt it important to return me to Congress. Five days later, he made the long round-trip drive again and spoke for me at a Pasadena Republican fundraiser in my congressional district.

Here I am introducing former President Ford to several hundred of my supporters at the Nixon Library, October 16, 1998. We handed out these serial-numbered (and whopping) nine-inch commemorative campaign buttons to everyone attending. (Author's collection)

In mid-1999 my campaign scheduled a Palm Springs fundraiser to raise money for my 2000 reelection effort. A couple of weeks before the event, Ford called me on the phone and asked if he could drop by and speak at it. His incredible generosity moved me deeply. Unfortunately, the House ended up missing its targeted adjournment date. Late budget votes kept me in Washington, and so my campaign canceled the fundraiser. When we rescheduled it in January 2000, I didn't call and invite Ford. At age eighty-seven, I had heard that his health was starting to fail, and I didn't want to add a burden to his schedule. He surprised me and showed up anyway.

After greeting me outside the hotel ballroom, he pulled me aside for a private word: "Jim," he whispered in a noticeably weaker voice, "I hope you'll forgive me. I fully intended to say a few words at your event tonight. Would you mind if I begged off on a speech? I'm feeling pretty beat. I'm not up to making a big deal out of my being here." I told him how grateful I was for his presence, but I insisted that he head home and get some rest. That is what he did—after he made a point of walking unannounced into the ballroom, surprising everyone there, and thanking them for coming out to support his good friend Jim Rogan. He remained behind for some time signing autographs and posing for pictures with many of my donors before departing.

Nancy DeLuna, my friend from our earlier Santa Barbara soiree for Brooks Firestone, had accompanied Ford to my Palm Springs event that evening. "Thanks for not pressing him into service tonight," she told me as Ford mingled with the crowd. "He really wanted to do this for you, but in the last year I've noticed he's slipping. Tonight, when he entered the hotel, he grew disoriented and almost walked into a potted plant. I'm worried about him. I guess it's just age catching up."

God bless Nancy. She was there looking out for him.

• • •

In August 2000, on the second night of the Republican National Convention in Philadelphia, I sat with the California delegation when Jerry and Betty Ford arrived in the hall. A huge cheer greeted them, and later the convention paid tribute to the thirty-eighth president for his lifetime of public service. That night, after he returned to his hotel, he suffered a stroke. It proved the first in a string of health-related scares. Still, he remained active for several more years even after battling pneumonia, another stroke, and the increasing infirmities of old age. A competitor to the end, when he died at age ninety-three on December 26, 2006, he had set the record as the then-longest surviving former president. At Ford's funeral, Jimmy Carter spoke for America when he recalled the man that he had defeated for the White House. In an elegant eulogy, Carter recalled the tribute he had paid to Ford in the opening line of his own 1977 inaugural address:

"For myself, and for our nation, I want to thank my predecessor for all he did to heal our land."

From the man who had sent me a booklet when I was a twelve-year-old boy on how Congress works: "To my very good friend Jim Rogan, with appreciation for a great job in the House." (Author's collection)

Chapter 16

The Secret to a Long Life

When little-known Georgia Governor Jimmy Carter announced his longshot bid for the White House, few took his 1976 campaign seriously, including his own mother. When he told her that he was running for president, she asked him, "President of *what*?" As a community college student that year, I registered Democrat to vote in my first election. I had opposed Carter's preconvention bid, but after he secured the nomination, I cast my ballot for him in the general election. As president, he enjoyed some successes, but I found his overall performance weak and ineffective. When he sought reelection in 1980, although still a registered Democrat, I voted for Ronald Reagan.

I met Carter a number of times beginning with his first White House bid and into his post-presidential years. To be candid, I wasn't very fond of him on a personal level. I found him prickly, somewhat moody, and, on occasion, borderline rude. In my 2014 book, *And Then I Met*, I reported some of these earlier encounters with him (including two visits to his hometown of Plains, Georgia in 1988 and 1990). These recollections were not particularly warm toward the man for whom I had once voted. I did soften toward him temporarily when he wrote me a brief note complimenting the job that I did during President Clinton's impeachment trial, but even that cordiality failed to offset my overall coolness toward him.

In 2014, Bobby Linzey, a former Georgia Democratic Party official and longtime pal of both Carter's and mine, called me not long after I had sent him a copy of my book that included those Carter stories. After sharing his divergent opinion of the former chief executive, he delivered an unexpected invitation: "Jimmy's ninetieth birthday is in October, which coincides with the Plains [Georgia] Peanut Festival. We're planning a birthday dinner for him. We want you to come to Plains and be the guest speaker."

I thought Bobby was joking. "You did read the chapters I wrote on him?"

"Yes, I read them. But that's okay. We view some things differently about him, but I know you'll be sensitive and will do a good job."

"Have you run this by Jimmy? I don't want to show up and have my presence ruin his birthday."

"He's fine with it, and he'd like to welcome you back to Plains."

"I sure hope you know what you're doing. In fact, I hope we both know what we're doing." When I hung up, I booked a flight to Georgia for late September.

With Rosalynn and Jimmy Carter on my first visit to Plains, 1988. (Author's collection)

• • •

Born James Earl Carter Jr. on October 1, 1924, in Plains, a small Georgia farming town, the United States Naval Academy graduate served as an officer on a nuclear submarine under Admiral Hyman Rickover. At the death of his father in 1953, Carter left the Navy and returned to Plains to run the family peanut farm and business. Elected to the Georgia legislature in 1962, he ran unsuccessfully for governor in 1966, but he won four years later. After capturing the 1976 Democratic presidential nomination, he defeated Gerald Ford in the general election. Over the next four years, he presided over an administration bogged down in major crises at home and abroad, including high inflation, high unemployment, and low economic growth; soaring gasoline prices and long lines at the pump; the Soviet invasion of Afghanistan; an Iranian revolution that left fifty-two American diplomats held hostage by Islamic terrorists for over a year; and other problems for which voters blamed him. After his 1980 defeat, he and his wife Rosalynn returned home to Plains. Over the next four decades he wrote thirty books, established his presidential library, founded the Carter Center, traveled the world to promote democracy and human rights, strapped on a tool belt and built homes for countless needy families, and taught a weekly Sunday school class at his local church. In recognition of his "decades of untiring effort to find peaceful solutions to international conflicts, to advance democracy and human rights, and to promote economic and social development," the Norwegian committee awarded him the 2002 Nobel Peace Prize. As Carter's ninetieth birthday approached, the former first couple's still hectic schedules now were crowded with campaign appearances around the state for their grandson, State Senator Jason Carter, Georgia's Democratic gubernatorial nominee.

• • •

As mentioned earlier, I first visited Plains in 1988, which was seven years after the Carters left Washington. When I returned twenty-four years later for Carter's ninety birthday party, little about the town had changed. With a population of about seven hundred living within less than a square mile, things like movie theaters, fast-food establishments, and department stores didn't exist there. The nearest ones were ten miles away in Americus. Main Street still had eight contiguous brick-and-wood buildings dating from the early twentieth century, each of which bore historical significance in Carter's early life. These structures once housed the Carter family's peanut office, farm business, and Jimmy's early legislative and campaign offices. In 1988, most of these buildings stood vacant, with only Hugh Carter's worm farm and his antique store (where Hugh personally hawked mementos of his famous first cousin to visiting tourists) in operation. With business in decline, Hugh closed his two shops in the mid-1990s. By 2014, souvenir merchants had taken over the buildings.

After checking into the Americus Quality Inn (also the location for the birthday banquet), I drove to Plains for the start of the Peanut Festival. During Carter's administration, up to ten thousand people visited Plains each day. In his post-presidential years, the town remained a tourist destination, but the once mighty flood of visitors trekking there in the old days had receded substantially. For this year's fiesta weekend, several hundred came to enjoy the carnival-like celebration. Fast food vendors (including some selling Gator-on-a-Stick—unimaginable snack fare to a native Californian), a jump house, pony rides, lemonade stands, a live band, and craft vendors lined the flag-bedecked streets.

I wandered over to the train depot and joined the small crowd watching as former President Carter passed out dozens of small trophies to the winners in each category of that morning's one mile and 5K foot races. Ignoring the slight drizzle, he smiled and posed for photos with every recipient; their ages ranged from grade school to elderly. Other than a slight stoop in his posture, and his hair and eyebrows now snow-white, he hadn't changed much since the 1980s. He dressed casually in black sneakers, blue jeans, dress shirt with sleeves rolled up, and a tooled leather belt with a large brass horseshoe buckle emblazoned with "JC". A handful of Secret Service agents, also dressed casually but wearing dark glasses and earpieces, kept their distance while studying the onlookers.

When the awards ceremony ended, Carter and his security detail departed in a van, but twenty minutes later he reappeared on Main Street with Mrs. Carter for the start of the parade. Appearing on the balcony of the Plains Inn and Antique Mall Store (formerly Hugh Carter's antique shop), the Carters acknowledged the applause and shouts of birthday wishes from the assembled crowd. Speaking into a microphone, he kicked off what he called "the biggest small-town parade in America" by sharing his secret for a long life: "Eat lots of peanuts!" Mrs. Carter, wearing a sweatshirt promoting her grand-son's gubernatorial candidacy, also welcomed everyone to Plains, and then she signaled for the parade's start. A Planter's "Mr. Peanut" drum major waving a baton and leading a high school marching band led the procession, followed by a tractor carrying the town's Shriners, a motorized peanut bus, beauty pageant winners, and various local elected officials and political candidates.

When the parade ended, I skipped the remaining festivities and returned to my motel room to draft my banquet speech for that evening. Approaching this task left me nervous. I faced the challenge of preparing a favorable talk about a man whom I had just spanked in my newly published book. Also, since the organizers billed my presentation as a "roast," this included the added stress of making my speech entertaining. Finally, and not the least of my concerns, the thirty-ninth president of the United States and former First Lady would judge it while sitting a few feet away from me.

No pressure here.

When I sat down at the small desk in my motel room with pen in hand, I decided that success depended on making Jimmy Carter look good and making myself the butt of any jokes. Through this prism I began constructing my presentation.

• • •

The intervening hours flew. That evening I went to the banquet room fifteen minutes before the designated 6:00 p.m. start time. Some of the attendees already there asked me to autograph their dinner programs or copies of my books. I was still signing when Jimmy and Rosalynn Carter arrived. The crowd cheered as the couple waved and then took their seats at the head table, where I joined them. After we exchanged brief greetings, the emcee asked the three of us to lead the procession to the dinner service. Rather than tuxedoed waiters bringing us the food, and in keeping with Carter's preference, this banquet proved both humble and democratic in nature. All guest—including the former presidential couple—walked to the motel's coffee shop where we collected dishes, served ourselves from buffet-style carts, and then we carried our filled plates back to the banquet room.

• • •

Settling back with him at the head table, Carter and I talked at length during supper. In an unexpected surprise given my prior experience with him, I found myself warming up to the nonagenarian.

Here I am with former President Jimmy Carter as we await the introductions at his ninetieth birthday party, September 27, 2014. (Author's collection)

He asked about my experience during President Bill Clinton's impeachment and trial. I told him that House Judiciary Committee Chairman Henry Hyde divided the main case between Arkansas Congressman Asa Hutchinson and me. I handled Clinton's perjury and Hutchinson covered the obstruction of justice charge. I mentioned that when I left Congress, my onetime impeachment nemesis who later became my friend, Clinton's White House Counsel Lanny Davis, had tried to recruit me to his law firm. Back then Lanny told me that he had attended a farewell party at the mansion during Clinton's last few nights in the White House. When they were alone, Lanny broke the news to his former boss of his recruitment effort. Instead of recoiling at the idea, Lanny said that Clinton grew wistful as he recalled that their team had defeated me for reelection in a very bloody House race. Despite this two-year onslaught against me, Clinton said that every time he encountered me during it, he found me very respectful and polite. Clinton told Lanny that he had concluded that I voted as I did because, as a former prosecutor and trial court judge, I felt that the evidence compelled me to do so. He said that there was no political advantage for me in impeaching him. Just the opposite—it had cost me my political career. After sharing this insight with Carter, I leaned in closer to him and lowered my voice so that Mrs. Carter wouldn't overhear the coda to the story: "Lanny also told me that Clinton said, 'Yeah, Rogan did what he did because *he* thought it was the right thing to do—not like those other two fuckers from Arkansas, Asa Hutchinson and Jay Dickey! Fuck those guys!'"[1] His born-again Christianity notwithstanding, Carter (an old Navy man) erupted in laughter upon hearing Clin-

---

1   President Clinton, a former Arkansas governor, expressed his simmering ire over two homegrown representatives, Arkansas Republican Congressmen Asa Hutchinson and Jay Dickey, each of whom voted for impeachment. As governor, Clinton had once appointed Dickey as a special justice of the Arkansas Supreme Court. Hutchinson, himself a future Arkansas governor, also served with me as one of the lead prosecutors in Clinton's Senate trial.

ton's salty expression of dismay toward two Arkansans whom he felt had betrayed their hometown boy.

Carter pointed to the vintage 1976 campaign button pinned to my lapel. "What's that badge you're wearing?" he asked.

"I wore this in honor of your birthday," I told him. The badge depicted Mrs. Carter and bore the legend, "Rosalynn for First Lady. " I handed it to him, and he passed it to his wife.

"Oh, my!" she exclaimed. "I've seen Jimmy on many campaign buttons before, but I've never seen *my* face on one!"

"Mrs. Carter," I replied, "they made these buttons because the campaign knew it would help win votes for your husband." She handed it back, but I asked her to keep it. I had brought it to give to her. Thanking me, she told me that her son Chip was the collector in the family. "I can't wait to show it to him," she added.

I introduced Carter to my friend David Azbell, who once had served as press spokesman for former Alabama Governor George Wallace. Running four times for the presidency (1964 as a Democrat, 1968 as a third-party candidate, and 1972 and 1976 as a Democrat), Wallace had challenged Carter for their party's nomination in that final race. David's father, Joe Azbell, had managed Wallace's last two presidential campaigns. Carter told us that Wallace had called him after Carter beat him in the 1976 North Carolina primary: "Wallace told me that he was dropping out to endorse me. He pledged his delegates to me because he said he wanted to live to see a Southerner elected president."

I told Carter that I had always felt that Wallace's candidacy that year had given Carter's chances significant help: "Because nobody took your candidacy seriously in the beginning, and because Wallace's earlier populist appeal terrified the Democrat establishment, in many early primaries the anti-Wallace voters threw in with you as a way to 'stop Wallace' in the South and split his base. Of course, by the time you stopped Wallace, nobody could catch up to stop you." I told Carter that another of his rivals for the 1976 nomination, former Senator Birch Bayh (D-IN), had been my law partner before I returned to the bench, and that I had once chided Birch about his *Meet the Press* appearance on the eve of the critical 1976 Florida Democratic primary. During this interview, Birch (who was not on that state's ballot) asked all of his Florida supporters to vote for Jimmy Carter in their primary to help stop Wallace. Carter guffawed when I shared with him Birch's reply after I reminded him of his failed campaign strategy: "That was the absolute dumbest thing I ever said in my entire political life!"

Over dessert, Carter reminisced about the national campaign that preceded his first presidential run, which was the battle for the 1972 Democratic presidential nomination won by Senator George McGovern (D-SD). He shared this recollection of McGovern's doomed race that year: "Most of us Democratic governors that year didn't support McGovern for president in the primaries, but we all wanted to be his vice-presidential running mate at the convention. I was hoping he'd pick me, even though I supported Scoop Jackson[2] over him, and I had placed Scoop's name in nomination. Given how McGovern's campaign ended up in a landslide defeat, it was probably a good thing he didn't choose me!"

I replied that if McGovern had selected him as his running mate, it wouldn't have hurt Carter's later prospects: "McGovern's disastrous convention was run so poorly that the presidential and vice-presidential nominees didn't deliver their acceptance speeches until around three in the morning. Had he picked you, it wouldn't have hurt you in the long run, because nobody would have been awake to know that you were on the ticket with him!"

I told him about the day I had spent campaigning with his former rival for the White House, Gerald Ford (see the previous

---

2   U.S. Senator Henry M. "Scoop" Jackson of Washington (1912–1983) ran unsuccessfully for the 1972 Democratic presidential nomination. Four years later, he ran again and lost the nomination race to Carter.

chapter, "Cold Shoulder"), and how, when I asked him whether press reports of a close bond between him and Carter were exaggerated, Ford quickly disabused me of that suggestion. "As he talked about you," I told Carter, "he spoke with a personal affection in a very heartfelt and moving way. I came away from our discussion believing he viewed you not only as a friend but as a brother."

Carter nodded. "That feeling is reciprocated," he replied. "We did have a pretty bitter race in 1976. After I won, and during the transition, Jerry was very helpful to me, and he did all he could to make it as smooth as possible. I think the ice really began to thaw when I opened my inaugural address [in 1977] by paying tribute to him. That started it."

"Later that year," Carter continued, "President Reagan asked Richard Nixon, Jerry, and me to represent the United States at Egyptian President Anwar Sadat's funeral.[3] On our way to Egypt aboard Air Force One, the three of us got a chance to talk. When Nixon retired to his cabin, Jerry and I sat up all night talking. That started our friendship. Over the years since, whenever we asked Jerry to do a program at the Carter Center, he always came to help. We became very close personal friends, and we were like brothers. In fact, Rosalynn and Betty [Mrs. Gerald Ford] became very close friends, too. So yes, we're very close to the Fords."

When Carter finished his tribute to Ford, he flashed a broad smile and added. "I'll tell you another story from that race against Ford that I'll bet you've never heard. After I won, and during the transition, a member of Ford's team came to Plains and pleaded with me to allow him to remain in his position as head of the CIA during my upcoming term. I met with him and listened to his plea,

---

3   Anwar el-Sadat (1918–1981) served as Egypt's third president. In 1978, Carter hosted Sadat and Israeli Prime Minister Menachem Begin at a Camp David meeting that resulted in a peace treaty between Egypt and Israel, and for which Sadat and Begin later shared the Nobel Peace Prize. In 1981, Islamic fundamentalists assassinated Sadat for making peace with the Jewish state.

but then I turned him down and replaced him. His name was—"
Here Carter paused and stretched out the punchline to heighten
the impact of the answer:

"—George Bush!"

After we shared a laugh over that irony, I replied, "That's strange.
I don't remember hearing Bush brag about that in 1980 when he
ran against Reagan in the Republican primaries!"

Still laughing, Carter replied, "No, I don't think he did!"

Carter asked if I had a favorite for the 2016 Republican presidential nomination. I didn't. As a sitting judge, the canons of ethics
precluded me from engaging in partisan activities. He speculated
that defeated 2012 GOP nominee Mitt Romney would run again,
and then he told me that he credited his own grandson, James
Earl Carter IV, for derailing Romney's previous White House bid.
"James wanted to help President Obama's reelection campaign," he
explained, "and so he started scouring the Internet for Romney
quotes and speeches. He uncovered the video with Romney's '47
percent' quote. That's what killed Romney." The video that Carter
IV unearthed came from a Romney campaign reception where the
presidential candidate told a group of his major donors assembled
at a Florida mansion, "There are 47 percent of the people who
will vote for [Obama] no matter what... who are dependent upon
government, who believe that they are victims.... These are people
who pay no income tax.... And so, my job is not to worry about
those people. I'll never convince them that they should take personal
responsibility and care for their lives. What I have to do is convince
the 5 to 10 percent in the center that are independents." Carter's
grandson turned over the video to a magazine, and the ensuing press
coverage brutalized Romney as someone indifferent to the needs
of 47 percent of Americans. Romney spent the rest of his losing
campaign trying to assure voters that he really did care about all
Americans, but that self-inflicted wound never healed.

"I think Obama owes his reelection to my grandson James,"

Carter told me. "The video proved to be pivotal in the campaign. That '47 percent' quote stuck to Romney for the rest of the race, and he couldn't shake it off no matter how much he tried to explain it away or apologize for it. It was a turning point."

• • •

The emcee interrupted our conversation when he started the program. After welcoming remarks and head table introductions, I stepped to the lectern to begin my speech. Feeling more relaxed and less nervous after the very pleasant time I had just spent with Carter before and during dinner, I took a chance and opened with a story from the enemy camp:

> As we gather to celebrate President Carter's ninetieth birthday, I remember some years ago when the 1936 Republican presidential nominee, former Kansas Governor Alf Landon, turned ninety. The citizens of Topeka held a large celebration for him, and they invited as the guest speaker [Here I turned to Carter and shot him a grin]—if you'll pardon the expression—Ronald Reagan.
>
> After Reagan praised Landon for his lifetime of public service, Reagan closed his remarks by saying, "And so, Governor Landon, I'm honored to be here to salute you on your ninetieth birthday. And I look forward to joining you ten years from today to wish you a happy one hundredth birthday!" As the audience applause faded, Landon looked Reagan up and down, and then he told Reagan, "Well, young fella, you look pretty healthy—you just might make it!"

When this opener drew a big laugh, even from Carter, by telling a story centered on the man who defeated him for reelection, I knew I was almost home free.

While in the White House, Carter had told reporters that his favorite president, and the one that he most admired, was

Harry Truman. As a special ninetieth birthday gift, all of tonight's attendees contributed to purchase a vintage signed copy of Truman's book *Mr. Citizen* to present to Carter at the end of the banquet. Knowing Carter's affinity for the man from Missouri, next I shared the story of how, as a schoolboy, Harry Truman helped me with my homework assignment:

When I was in the seventh grade in 1969, I spent untold hours at the Daly City Public Library looking up the addresses of retired government leaders so I could write them for both autographs and advice on entering politics. Getting former President Harry Truman's address came in handy for one particular middle-school project, although not without causing heartburn along the way.

That year my teacher, Mr. Puhr, assigned us to write a biography of a famous person. This was my first long-term homework assignment. Our paper had to be researched, single-space typed, and at least seven pages long. In the pre–personal computer era, very few twelve-year-olds were keyboard literate or in possession of typing skills beyond the clumsy use of two index fingers, so he gave us three months to complete this monumental task. "But you'd better have it ready to turn in on the due date," he warned ominously, "or there will be consequences."

For my subject, I picked the eighty-six-year-old Truman. Instead of spending three months on it, I finished it in three days. With so much time to spare and having once read that the ex-president answered personally every letter written to him by young people, I decided to mail him my report and get his opinion of it. Long before the ubiquity of copying machines and hard drives, I retained no duplicate of my typed report when I mailed the original to his home at 219 North Delaware Street in Independence, Missouri. It never dawned on me that he wouldn't return it.

Three months elapsed. On the project's due date, I remained empty-handed. Mr. Puhr rejected my explanation, called me a liar in front of the class, and he accused me of never doing the report. "Besides," he announced, "Truman's dead. I watched his funeral on television twenty years ago."

"Actually, Mr. Puhr, he's not dead. He's alive, he has my paper, and when he gives it back to me, I'll be happy to turn it in."

My class project grade: F.

More months went by, and I forgot about the incident. Then one afternoon I returned home from school and found a large white envelope bearing Truman's return address and his bold franking signature in the upper right corner.[4] The envelope contained my report, an autographed portrait of the great man, and a personal letter to me that read as follows:

April 29, 1970

Dear Jim:

I was very pleased to have your letter and manuscript. I am sorry I cannot help you with it, because I have a rule against working on another author's paper. It is clear, however, that you did your homework well.

With best wishes for success in your life.

Sincerely,

Harry S Truman

---

4   A former president of the United States may send free mail (without using postage stamps) by placing his signature in the upper right corner of the envelope. See U.S. Postal Regulation Special Eligibility Standards E050, https://pe.usps.com/Archive/HTML/DMMArchive20030810/E050.htm (accessed August 23, 2020).

At the beginning of history class the next day, I walked up to Mr. Puhr's desk and placed my proof in front of him. His face reddened as he surveyed the documents in silence. When he finished, he handed them back. "Take your seat," he ordered.

"Is that all you have to say to me, Mr. Puhr?"

"I said to take your seat." After humiliating me earlier and calling me a liar, he refused to acknowledge his mistake.

I fumed over this injustice for the rest of class. When the recess bell rang, I jumped from my desk, rushed to the classroom door and blocked the exit. Holding aloft my treasures, I yelled to my classmates, "Hey, if anybody wants to see the letter and autographed picture I got yesterday from the 'late' President Harry Truman, I'll show it to you on the playground."

Despite my protests, Mr. Puhr wouldn't accept my paper. I went to the principal, Mrs. Zenovich, and presented my case. Marching me back to class, she confronted Mr. Puhr and cajoled him into accepting it.

Later, Mr. Puhr handed back my paper in front of the entire class and announced that he marked me down for "repeated punctuation errors" because I kept failing to put a period after Truman's middle initial "S." I told him the omission was intentional: the "S" didn't get a period because "S" was his middle name. He grabbed Volume T of the Encyclopedia Britannica, turned to Truman's entry, and pronounced, "Aha! The encyclopedia lists him as Harry S-With-A-Period Truman! What do you say to that, Mr. Rogan?"

"The encyclopedia's wrong."

"So!" he chortled, "the encyclopedia is wrong, and Mr. Rogan is right! My, aren't we lucky to have such a brilliant student in our midst!" Students laughed as he mocked me for the rest of class. For days afterward, he called on me to "confirm" facts such as George Washington was our first president ("Or was it Benjamin Franklin, Mr. Rogan?") or that Columbus discovered America in 1492 ("Or was it in 1493, Mr. Rogan?").

Growing tired of the ridicule, I took matters into my own hands: "Dear President Truman," my new letter began, "You won't believe this teacher of mine." I told him the story and asked him to settle the issue.

The school year ended without a reply, and again I forgot about it. One day near the end of summer vacation another envelope with the black signature and no postage stamps arrived:

August 19, 1970

Dear Jim Rogan:

The "S" in my middle name stands for the first letter of the first name of each of my grandfathers. In order to be strictly impartial in naming me for one or the other, I was given the letter "S" as a middle name. It can be used with or without a period after it.

I appreciate your very kind comments and send you best wishes.

Sincerely yours,

Harry S Truman

Now, for the first time, I noticed Truman's engraved letterhead: it bore the name "Harry S Truman" with no period after the middle initial. The proof had been in my hands all along.

On the first day of eighth grade, I arrived at school early and tracked down my seventh-grade teacher. Mr. Puhr looked baffled—as if I had made another mistake—when I entered his classroom. I walked to his desk and showed him the second Truman letter. Again, he refused to re-grade my report, but he changed his mind when I threatened him with more Mrs. Zenovich therapy.

As I walked away, he called to me.

"Yes, Mr. Puhr?"

He scowled. "Rogan," he snapped, "I'm very glad you won't be in my class this year."

The story has a postscript: Almost twenty-five years later, in the early 1990s, American Heritage magazine published my story of how Harry Truman helped me with my homework. A few years after that, Readers Digest picked up the story for publication in its April 1995 issue to commemorate the fiftieth anniversary of Truman's presidential inauguration.

When I served in Congress, I attended a weekend retreat with fellow House members. The guest speaker was one of my generation's preeminent historians, David McCullough, who wrote a Pulitzer Prize–winning biography of Truman. When I asked him to autograph my copy of his book, I told him, with tongue in cheek, that I was pleased to meet a fellow Truman scholar. He asked if I had written a Truman book, too. I laughed and said no, and then I explained about my correspondence with old Harry and my story about it.

McCullough's eyes brightened. "The 'homework' story in American Heritage!" he said. "Truman wrote to you and explained about the S in his middle name! I not only read it, but it helped me win a bet on that issue!"

In the end, when Harry Truman took the time to assist a young schoolboy with his research assignment long ago, both David McCullough and I came out as winners.

• • •

When I finished the Truman yarn to a receptive audience, I said that since I talked about Jimmy's favorite president, I must now reciprocate for Rosalynn and tell a story about her favorite president—who, I presumed, was her spouse. For that offering, I shared this recollection of attending Jimmy's Sunday school class during my first visit to Plains in 1988:[5]

> When Jimmy Carter first announced his presidential candidacy, the press took great interest in his confession of faith as a born-again Christian. I didn't really understand what that meant until I met my future wife, who was also a born-again believer. While dating her, I came to know Christ as my Savior, so by the time I visited Plains for the first time in 1988, I was a newly minted Christian.
>
> After I arrived at this charming town, Hugh Carter told me that his cousin Jimmy's Sunday school class the next day was open to all and that I must attend. "But bring your Bible!" he insisted. I didn't think to pack a Bible in my luggage, but thanks to the Gideons, my motel room had one I could use to fill the gap.
>
> The next morning, along with my fellow tourists and some Plains residents, we settled into the small sanctuary at Maranatha Baptist Church to await Jimmy's class. A very hefty middle-aged lady with a lovely Southern accent sat in the pew next to me. We exchanged greetings and struck up a friendly conversation. She proved the height of Southern hospitality, and within a few minutes I felt as though I was speaking with an old friend. As these pleasantries continued, she noticed the Good Book resting on my lap. "Oh!" she exclaimed. "I see you brought your Bible!

---

5   I rarely deliver a prepared speech. My usual practice is to jot down notes on an envelope or a pocket card. Since I did not speak from a text at the Carter banquet, and because there is no known recording from that night, I have reconstructed my remarks delivered that evening both from memory and from my original note card that I used.

How lovely." I nodded. Then she asked, "What kind of Bible is it?"

Today, after decades in the faith, I would know how to answer that question—for example, the NIV, the King James, the New King James, Scofield, and so forth. But back then, I didn't know that different varieties of the Bible existed, so I didn't know how to respond beyond giving her a blank look.

"I said," she repeated, "what kind of Bible is it?"

"What kind of Bible? What does that mean?" I wondered silently. "Is this some sort of Christian-ese code?" I started turning the book over in my hands while scanning the front and back hoping that the answer might leap from the cover. Gratefully, I saw on the Bible's spine what must be the solution. I looked up and, in confidence, I pointed with my finger the answer to her question. I told her, "It's the *HOLY* Bible!"

The woman shook her head. "No, no. That's not—" She cut short her explanation when a sudden buzz permeated the room. Jimmy and Rosalynn had arrived. Jimmy took his place at the small lectern in the front of the sanctuary, and Rosalynn sat in the pew directly behind me. My inquisitive seatmate turned and greeted Mrs. Carter with friendly familiarity.

After Jimmy went around the room asking from where everyone came, he put on his reading glasses and began the lesson that he entitled, "Maintaining Confidence in God" from the book of Exodus. Jimmy began class with a question: "Does anyone here ever worry? Sometimes we do more than worry. Sometimes we panic." Jimmy then said that he planned to quiz us on our knowledge of the previously announced selected reading. "I hope all of you did your homework," he said with a big smile.

Homework? Cousin Hugh didn't say anything about homework. I looked around the room. Everyone else nodded their heads in an expression of inner confidence over their class preparation. "If there's homework," I said to myself, "then Jimmy's right. As of now, I'm panicked."

Continuing with his lesson, Jimmy said that people are afraid to trust Jesus today just as in Bible times, when slavery or death came to those who trusted in the God of Israel. "Even the Israelites turned against Moses because they did not want to put their faith in God," he added. Then, after discussing Moses' trials in dealing with the backsliding Israelites, Jimmy posed this question to the class: "Who are we more like: Moses or the Israelites?"

Silence enveloped the room. When nobody raised their hand, Jimmy repeated the question. Again, stillness. He waited for a volunteer in a sanctuary now filled with people staring at their shoelaces.

As an aside, I'm an adjunct law professor. Whenever I pose questions to my students, I always appreciate it when some brave soul in their ranks breaks the uncomfortable hush by raising a hand and volunteering an answer. It gets the conversation going. Knowing how Jimmy must have felt with a question hanging out there and with no takers, I decided to help him. I raised my hand. He nodded to me as he repeated the question that I heard: "Who are we more like: Moses or the Israelites?"

I answered, "The Israelites."

I must digress again. In teaching young law students, when a law professor asks a question, the correct answer is never "yes" or "no." The correct answer is always, "It depends." To accentuate this, after the student gives me what he or she thinks is a logical legal answer to my question, I start throwing additional hypothetical facts into the mix to create stumbling blocks to their answer: "But what if A happens?" That might change the answer they give. Once they express confidence in their new solution, I'll toss in, "Well, what if B happens?" Oops. Now we have another unforeseen consequence to the answer. Once they try and untangle that knot, I'll ask, "What if A and B happens?" A good law professor can keep twisting their students up by bending the facts until everyone in the classroom is exhausted and confused. That is teaching what we call "Thinking Like a Lawyer." After three years of sorting through these perplexities in law school, a good attorney knows that the right answer to any legal problem is almost always, "It depends."

Unlike me, Jimmy didn't go to law school. He's an engineer. In engineering school, precision counts. In engineering school, when the professor asks the student a question, the answer is either right or wrong. That's why, when I answered Jimmy's question that we are more like the Israelites, his engineer's reply to me was very non–law school-ery:

"No." he told me. "You're wrong. We need to be more like Moses."

People in the audience (none of whom had braved raising their hands) murmured and nodded their vigorous agreement with him, and then they turned toward me and frowned while Jimmy explained my biblical ignorance in detail. To make matters worse, when I answered (or thought that I had answered) "the Israelites," apparently I didn't call them "the Israelites." Accidentally I had called them "the Israelis."

"Oh, and by the way," Jimmy added at the conclusion of his correction. "They weren't the 'Israelis.' They were the 'Israelites.'"

"HEY!" I wanted to say to him, "I'm trying to help you here!" Instead, I kept my mouth shut and sulked.

It grew worse. By now I realized that I had misheard his question. I thought he had asked, "Who **are** we more like: Moses or the Israelites?" instead of what he actually had asked: "Who **should** we be more like: Moses or the Israelites?" That subtlety made a big difference. Before I raised my hand to answer, Jimmy had spoken at length about the Israelites turning their backs on God and rejecting Moses' plea to return to the arms of Jehovah. When Jimmy asked his question, because I misheard it, my answer proclaimed to all in the sanctuary that we should be more like the backsliding idol worshippers instead of like God's chosen leader.

It was at this point in Jimmy's Sunday school lesson that I learned something about Southern culture. No people in the world are more friendly, welcoming, hospitable, loving, and kindly than Southerners—until they think you espouse apostate views. That's where their hospitality streak crashes and burns. After mistakenly urging that we model ourselves after the god-less infidels, I noticed that my matronly seatmate who had been so welcoming only minutes earlier now stiffened. "Well," she intoned as she frowned at me, "it sure is wonderful to have a godly man like President Carter teaching this class. He knows the Bible because he's a Christian."

"What does that mean?" I asked indignantly.

"I'm not going to say," she said as she scooched away from me in the pew. "But I think you understand."

Jimmy moved on with his lesson by asking if anyone knew what the Israelites carried with them during their trek across the desert. Once again, crickets from the class. No hands raised. Finally, Mrs. Carter, seated directly behind me, volunteered the answer:

"The bones of Joseph," she said.

Jimmy nodded in affirmation. "That's correct, Rosalynn. They carried the bones of Joseph."

"Teacher's pet," I mumbled.

My now-surly seatmate's face contorted as she shushed me, and then she added, "As you can see, Miss Rosalynn sure knows her Bible, too. It's so nice to hear from spirit-led people when they answer questions in church."

By now I had grown weary of this fair-weather friend. "Hey, listen, lady," I told her sarcastically. "I don't know if you're aware of this." I pointed to Jimmy in front of me, and then, with my thumb, to Rosalynn behind me. "Uh, hello!" I told her. "Guess what? They're married! He probably gave her the answers before class."

"Well, that's just ridiculous," she snorted, and once again she scooted further away.

As Jimmy's lesson wound to a close, I felt a growing urge to redeem myself and correct the record, or else I knew I'd be haunted by the misunderstanding. I waited until Jimmy asked another question. When he did and (once again) nobody volunteered, my hand went up. Through the corner of his eye, Jimmy saw mine was the only hand raised. Instead of calling on me, he tried pretending that he didn't notice me by looking away. "Uh, anybody over here have an answer?" he asked as he pointed to the opposite side of the church. No hands. Now I started bouncing up and down in my seat just like the character Arnold Horshack from the 1970s TV sitcom, Welcome Back, Kotter.

"Ooh! Ooh!" I called out as I raised my hand higher.

When Jimmy could no longer ignore me, his shoulders slumped a bit. Clearing his throat, he pointed to me, and then he repeated the question.

"That's not the question I want to answer," I told him. "I want to go back to the question you asked me earlier." The crowd squirmed, Jimmy sighed, and I could swear that I saw him roll his eyes heavenward. The fellow seated on the other side of me put his hand on my shoulder and whispered to me that I might do well and shut up rather than embarrass myself again. I ignored this new heckler while Jimmy, with obvious reluctance, told me to go ahead.

"When I said earlier that we are more like the Israelites—" At this point I dropped my voice and added under my breath "a.k.a. the Israelis" before continuing: "When I said that we are more like the Israelites, I meant that we constantly lack faith in God, just as they did, whenever we are faced with a crisis despite the many manifestations of His presence and love. I agree with you that we should strive to be like Moses, but in our flesh, we respond more like the Israelites. That's why I said that we are more like the Israelites. This is our great challenge as Christians— to be more like Moses."

During the interminable silence that followed my new contribution, I looked around the room seeking any sign of affirmation. None materialized. Then, to my great relief, Jimmy said that he agreed with me. Faces in the sanctuary chiseled in chagrin moments earlier now smiled with approval and nodded at me. This last-minute clarification canceled my appointment with the Baptist Dunce Cap fitter.

"That was a very fine answer," my oversized seatmate volunteered as she reverted to her earlier syrupy voice. "Of course, I assumed that's what you meant the first time."

"Oh, save it, lady—where were you when I needed you? You're LLPOF."

"What does that mean?"

"LLPOF—Liar, Liar, Pants on Fire."

In conclusion, ladies and gentlemen, since that first visit to Plains long ago, I've spent all of these intervening years studying the Bible in preparation for this weekend's return visit to President Carter's Sunday school class. And so, Mr. President, whatever topic you choose for tomorrow's lesson, if you call on me, I'm confident that I'll be prepared with the correct answer no matter the question. And if you do call on me, I promise I won't say, 'It depends.' I'll give a tested answer that passes muster with every member of the Maranatha Baptist Church—

"—the bones of Joseph!"

• • •

All of my pre-speech nerves proved unwarranted. Throughout my talk, the banquet's guests of honor, along with the audience, laughed and applauded. When I returned to my seat, Jimmy was still laughing as he patted me on my back and thanked me.

After the dinner wrapped up, and as I said goodnight to the Carters, he gripped my hand. "You'll be at church tomorrow morning for my Sunday school class, right?"

"I'll be there—but only if you don't call on me."

"Well," he grinned, "if I do call on you, I'll be kind—just as kind to you as you were to me tonight!"

"Mr. President, now I'm scared."

• • •

If, in 2014, Plains had remained essentially unchanged in the twenty-six years since I had visited, one significant difference became apparent. Carter's Sunday school classes that I had attended back then were informal to the point of mild chaos. From the moment Jimmy arrived until he concluded his class, flashbulbs fired, people in pews stood up and moved around while taking pictures, others changed seats constantly to get a different view, and the rude or ignorant chatted among themselves while disregarding his efforts to present the Gospel. After the service, when the Carters stood outside posing for photos with visitors, people jostled their way into the line. Once reaching the former first couple, they pawed at them for autographs (after he had made clear his "no autographs at church" policy). They shoved at him news articles or manifestos that they felt he needed to read. They held up the line by monopolizing their moment with babbled commentaries, or they did all of the above.

When I settled into my pew this Sunday morning for the return engagement, I learned that a new sheriff had arrived to bring order to the Wild West.

Her name was Jan Williams.

I first took notice of her as we waited outside the church for the Secret Service metal detector inspection. She stood next to an agent and joined him in studying the faces of the visitors in line. Someone behind me asked her if she was a Secret Service agent. "No," she replied. "They won't let me carry a gun. I'm far too dangerous."

"Then who are you?"

"I'm the person in charge."

Indeed, she was.

Before Carter's class began, "Miss Jan" (as everyone called her) stepped to the front of the sanctuary, smiled, and welcomed everyone to Plains. "Uh oh," I overheard one Carter class repeater whisper to another. "Here it comes."

Her companion replied, "Yeah. Miss Jan. She frightens me."

For the next twenty minutes, Miss Jan offered a charming mix of Southern hospitality, patient and loving teacher, and no-nonsense drill instructor outlining a strict list of dos and don'ts. As long as everyone followed her rules, she promised a cherished memory from attending President Carter's class. I also absorbed the impression that, if required, she would steeplechase the pews and eject rule-breakers by the seat of their britches.

Among Miss Jan's firm rules:

- No applause when President Carter arrives and leaves. "He doesn't like that. He wants your focus to be on the Lord and the message."

- Photographs are allowed while President Carter greets the congregation and asks from where everyone hails. "But once he starts the class with a prayer, every camera is to be down and in your lap. Do not raise it to take pictures during his lesson. If you do, I'll have the Secret Service confiscate it."

- No talking during class.

- No unnecessary moving around the sanctuary.

- No autograph requests at any time while at church.

- At the end of services, President and Mrs. Carter will pose for pictures with visitors. The line will form outside and in an orderly fashion. When you meet President Carter, do no try to shake his hand or touch him in any way. "He's turning ninety in two days," she warned. "We don't want President Carter to get sick from your germs. Hand-to-hand contact is how germs get passed along. We'll use your camera to take a picture of you with the Carters. Then you will collect your camera and move out of line. Do not delay the line with chatter or try to hand anything to the Carters."

- If the line is long, stay in line if you want a picture. If you leave the line prematurely, you'll not be permitted to rejoin it.

By the time Miss Jan ended her presentation, she had frightened me, too.

The author with the incomparable Miss Jan outside Maranatha Baptist Church, September 28, 2014

Wearing a business suit, an open-neck shirt, and a bolo tie with a turquoise clasp, Carter entered the sanctuary as Miss Jan finished leading us in prayer. I noticed a few people raised their hands to clap instinctively, but Miss Jan's stony gaze suppressed that impulse. Carter greeted everyone, asked the tourists to tell from where they came, and he invited a visiting pastor to lead the class in prayer.

Then came an unexpected development.

"Is Jim Rogan here this morning?" he asked. Caught by surprise, I looked up from my church bulletin as several people pointed to where I sat. I tossed him a salute and nodded. Carter smiled at me, and then he continued with this introduction:

"Well, Jim Rogan is a very distinguished person. He's a former congressman from California. He's a judge now, but when he was in Congress he was involved in the impeachment of Bill Clinton, and he wrote a book about it. He told us last night at our dinner that he attended my Sunday school class here twenty-six years ago, and that I had asked him a question during class that he couldn't answer." The audience laughed while watching my fidgety reaction. I wasn't sure where this was going, but I suspected that Jimmy was about to even the score for my roasting him last night. My instincts proved correct:

"Because Jim couldn't answer my question back then," he continued, "he's spent the last twenty-six years studying the Bible, and he became a very distinguished Bible scholar—he says!" Once again, the sanctuary filled with laughter. He waited for it to subside before he pulled the snapper. Saying that he had planned to teach this morning from the book of Hezekiah, he added, "Since Jim's learned so much about the Bible, I want to ask him this morning to come up here and give us the historical context in which Hezekiah lived, and then we'll have him teach us all about Hezekiah's life."

For a moment, fellow guests in the sanctuary thought this a serious invitation. They smiled and nodded approvingly at me— until I pulled out my white handkerchief, raised it over my head, and waved it to indicate my surrender. With the audience now in on his joke, and suppressing his own laugh, Jimmy continued, "Well, as you can see, Jim's a very modest person. He doesn't want to show off his expert knowledge. So, I'll take over that job, Jim, with your permission. But you be sure and correct me if I'm wrong in my presentation."

Jimmy Carter had fun turning the tables on his roaster. I assure the reader that nobody appreciated it more, nor felt more honored by the joke, than its victim.

• • •

For the next fifty minutes, Carter taught from the book of Hezekiah. Amazingly, and with only hours separating him from his ninetieth birthday, he did so without notes. His message was profound and his delivery flawless. He amazed everyone with both biblical knowledge, depth, and ability.

"The lesson that I'd like us to take away," he said in conclusion, "is to live our lives in a way that's more pleasing to God. This reassures us that when difficulties come, we can face them with courage and equanimity. We have a partner available to us who knows everything. We can form an alliance with God to have a full-time partnership."

When the class concluded, and after a brief break, Jimmy joined Rosalynn in her pew for the regular church service. When it finished, the Carters left the sanctuary and positioned themselves outside on the lawn for the photo line while Miss Jan stood guard nearby. Under her supervision, nobody dared violate any rules, especially the no-handshake directive.

When my turn came, Jimmy beamed. "Okay, Mr. President," I said as I approached. "You got me!" He stuck out his hand to me. I started reaching reflexively, and then I pulled back sharply. "Are you kidding?" I said to him. "Do you want Miss Jan to slap me?"

"This is our one exception," Miss Jan called from the sideline.

As Jimmy and I shook hands, I told him how much I enjoyed

his class and my return visit to Plains. "But I have a question for you," I added:

"Are we even now?"

Beaming that infectious and famous smile, the former president replied, "Well, just about!"

I've never been so afraid to shake a hand. With former President and Mrs. Carter, Maranatha Baptist Church, Plains, Georgia, September 28, 2014. (Author's collection)

• • •

Two days later, on Jimmy's official ninetieth birthday, I wrote and told him how much I enjoyed having the honor of sharing with him and Rosalynn his celebration weekend in Plains. Per his request during our dinner, I sent him copies of my three books that had been published at the time: *Rough Edges, Catching Our Flag,* and *And Then I Met.*

A week later, he replied in his trademark fashion: a brief handwritten note in the upper margin of my letter to him. That was how he had replied to my very first letter to him over forty years earlier when he was Georgia's former governor, and I was a high school student. On my latest letter he wrote, "Jim, Thanks for your memorable visit and for the books. Come back and see us soon. Jimmy Carter."

Despite this invitation to return, Jimmy Carter's ninetieth birthday party celebration in 2014 marked my last visit to Plains. It was just as well. I never could have improved upon the very fond memories of America's thirty-ninth president that I brought home from that trip.

Chapter 17

41

If ever this country produced a man whose resume commended him to the presidency, it was George Herbert Walker Bush. This son of a wealthy U.S. senator became a decorated World War II naval combat pilot who returned home and captained Yale's college baseball team. After achieving success as a Texas oil executive, he enjoyed a breathtakingly distinguished political career: congressman, chairman of the Republican National Committee, ambassador to the United Nations, U.S. envoy to China (before the days of formal diplomatic recognition), director of the Central Intelligence Agency, and two-term vice president of the United States before winning the presidency in a 1988 landslide.

Despite these impressive predictors, his administration produced mixed results. During his single term, he appointed one of the best Supreme Court justices of my lifetime (Clarence Thomas) and one of the worst (David Souter). He enjoyed multiple foreign policy successes (the Berlin Wall and the Soviet Union both collapsed on his watch, and he led the coalition that drove back Iraq's invasion of Kuwait), but he caved to congressional Democrat pressure and abandoned his sacrosanct "Read my lips—No new taxes!" campaign pledge. Signing a Democrat-driven tax-and-spend budget, he spun the roaring Reagan economy that he had inherited into a recession. The president who enjoyed one of the highest incumbent favorability ratings in the Gallup poll's history (89 percent in 1991) took a drubbing when he sought reelection a year later. Family matters occupied his post-White House years when he campaigned for his two sons, George W. and Jeb, in their respective gubernatorial and presidential races. In 2001, he joined John Adams as the only other American president whose son succeeded him as chief executive.

I first met "41" (George W.'s nickname for his father)[1] when, as a teenager, I attended the 1972 Republican National Convention that renominated Richard Nixon for the presidency. An invitation from the Nixon campaign to join California's Young Voters for the President (YVP) delegation brought me to the Miami convention with a couple thousand other youths from around the country. Each morning the YVPs met at our holding center, which was a large tent on the athletic field of a public middle school. During the convention down time, we assembled there each morning to paint rally signs and meet a parade of dignitaries dropping by to thank us for our help.[2]

On the second day of the convention, my fellow YVPs and I prepared banners at our holding center when I noticed a sedan pull onto the athletic field and drop off a lone man wearing slacks, an open-neck shirt, and a security pass hanging from a chain around

---

1   George H. W. Bush served as America's forty-first president (1989–1993). His son, George W. Bush, became the forty-third president (2001–2009). Among family, friends, and supporters, they became known as "41" and "43" respectively.

2   Miami's Nautilus Middle School may be the only school in America that enjoys this historical footnote: Over a twenty-four-hour period during the 1972 Republican National Convention (August 21–22, 1972), three future presidents of the United States visited this small junior high: Ambassador George Bush, Congressman Gerald Ford, and Governor Ronald Reagan. This story, along with others surrounding my 1972 GOP convention experience, is detailed in my book *And Then I Met*.

his neck that was similar to the ones we wore. U.N. Ambassador George Bush walked over, introduced himself, and thanked me and the others for helping Nixon's reelection effort. Since nobody recognized the obscure diplomat, I helped coax people to the center of the tent for his impromptu pep talk, and I collected an autograph from him before he departed.

I took this snapshot of U.N. Ambassador George Bush signing autographs at Nautilus Middle School, Miami, during the 1972 Republican National Convention. (Author's collection)

In later years I attended a few Bush events during his vice presidency and presidency. In 1995, while serving in the state legislature, I brought my family for a brief visit with the ex-president,[3] but our personal acquaintance really didn't begin until I served in Congress and had secured his unexpected notice.

3   See James Rogan, *And Then I Met.*

•••

A few weeks after winning a tight congressional reelection battle in 1998 with barely 50 percent of the vote in a Los Angeles-based and heavily Democrat district, I voted to impeach President Bill Clinton—a man who then enjoyed a 75 percent approval rating from my constituents. From the moment I cast that vote, my reelection prospects for 2000 looked grim. The national and statewide Democratic Party, along with their formidable allies in the unions and mainstream media, undertook a sustained two-year retribution campaign against me. I battled back in what became the most expensive and toughest House race in history. Although I lost my bid for a third term, my defeat was not for lack of support from a sympathetic and special fan.

In late November 1999, I received a phone call from Sig Rogich, 41's former U.S. ambassador to Iceland. He told me, "The president and Barbara [former First Lady Barbara Bush] love you. They think you showed real courage during impeachment. They watched all of the proceedings and thought that you were superb. The president knows that you're in political trouble back home because of Clinton. He wants to help you." He related to me that Bush, now seventy-five, had received over three hundred requests to appear at political fundraisers in the upcoming 2000 election cycle: "He doesn't want to do them anymore, but he wants to find a way to do one for you without everyone else bitching that he didn't help them." Sig assured me that Bush was firm in his desire, but for the time being I needed to keep quiet about it so that Bush wouldn't get inundated with complaints about his selective help.

"We'll figure something out," Sig promised.

A few weeks later I received a Christmas card from George and Barbara Bush. Under the pre-printed greeting the former president had penned a longhand note: "Dear Jim: All the Bush family is in your corner. Your courage *must* be rewarded at the polls. On to victory! A big hug to Dana, Claire, and Christine. Love from all the Bushes, George Bush." These back-to-back messages from the former president boosted our campaign team's spirits, but when we tried repeatedly to follow up with his office to set a date, we couldn't breach the protective wall erected by his scheduler. What to do?

• • •

In January 2000, the Richard Nixon Library Foundation invited me to a gala dinner in Southern California honoring Bush and his former national security advisor, General Brent Scowcroft. After accepting the invitation, I vetoed my campaign staff's pleas to lobby Bush personally to do an event for me if I met him there. If I did encounter him, I hoped that my presence might remind him of my tough race and the earlier offer of help relayed by Ambassador Rogich.

After arriving at the library, an escort led me to the private cocktail reception held in a large downstairs meeting room. People there crowded around to thank me for my work in the impeachment trial. I still grimace when I remember the elegant and lovely woman waiting in line to shake my hand. When we met, she said, "Congressman Rogan, I'm so honored to meet you. You're a hero to my family and me. May I have my picture taken with you?" We found a photographer to accommodate us. Before parting, I asked her name. "Julie," she replied. "Julie Nixon Eisenhower." I hadn't recognized the daughter of the man in whose library we had gathered that night. I felt like a dimwit.

When Bush and Scowcroft arrived, I joined their long receiving line to meet the evening's honorees. I was still about a dozen people away from reaching them when Bush glanced down the line and spotted me. "Hey, Jim Rogan!" he called out. He darted from his mark and strode toward me with his hand extended. Everyone watched as he rushed to greet me as though we were old friends. This unexpected display of favor caught me off guard.

Holding up his own receiving line, Bush pulled me aside for a private chat. He said he knew that in my upcoming race Bill Clinton was coming after me "with both barrels." Then, with no prompting, he spoke the words that I had hoped to hear: "Jim, I'm not doing any events for anyone. I just don't do them anymore. But I'm going to do one for you. You *have* to win. We can't let them beat you. All the Bushes love you and we're for you." I told him that I felt overwhelmed with gratitude by this offer, but in fairness I suggested that he had better run it by his son's campaign team, because they might expect his undivided attention in George W.'s current presidential race.

"Don't worry about George," he responded. "He'll be okay. I'll be there for you."

A library official gave me a frantic signal that we needed to get the line moving. I suggested to Bush that the organizers might eject me if he didn't get back to his receiving line. He waved off the staffer who urged him to resume the formalities. Taking me by the arm, Bush led me to the photo station and introduced me to Scowcroft. "This fellow's a hero, Brent," he told his former aide.

To Jim Rogan with best wishes, and man of conviction n courage. All the best. G Bush

"If we don't get this moving, they'll kick me out!" With former President George H. W. Bush, The Richard Nixon Library, January 15, 2000. (Author's collection)

Once the photo line resumed and my unintended monopolization of the honored guest had ended, I headed to the dinner area. There another library official intercepted me. "President Bush sent me to bring you back," he said. "He wants you entering the dinner with him." He led me to the foyer where I rejoined Bush and Scowcroft, and then an announcer introduced each of us individually. My name brought cheers from this Orange County Republican audience. "Lots of impeachment fans here," my escort whispered to me.

"I can tell," I replied. "Too bad none of them vote in my district."

Following dinner, Julie Eisenhower presented Bush with the Nixon Library's Victory of Freedom award. In his acceptance speech, he departed from his prepared text to tell the audience of his personal affection and respect for me, and he entreated the well-heeled audience to support my upcoming reelection effort. I rose to acknowledge the applause and to salute the former commander-in-chief. As I resumed my seat, someone at my table remarked, "Boy, he sure seems to love you!"

"Not nearly as much as I love him right now."

• • •

A few weeks after the Nixon Library event, I visited with Ron Kaufman, a friend and a Washington lobbyist who had been Bush's longtime political director. I told him about Sig Rogich's message, the Christmas card, and my recent encounter with 41. "There's a reason the Old Man feels that way about you," Ron told me. "He believes that you avenged him when you took on Clinton. He knows that Clinton's coming after you for it, and he wants to stand with you."

• • •

Commitments to help a struggling political candidate are easier to get than firm dates on the calendar. Bush's pledges proved no different, although he had a valid excuse: that summer his son had won the Republican presidential nomination after a contentious primary season. As the number of months, and then weeks, before Election Day 2000 narrowed, the polls tightened between Governor George W. Bush and his Democrat opponent, Vice President Al Gore. His son's campaign monopolized 41's schedule, which in turn depressed our fading hopes of getting the former president out to California for an event.

In a last-ditch effort, my district campaign manager, Jason Roe, told the Bush people that we would be willing to do our event with him in Houston (where Bush lived) rather than ask him to travel to the West Coast. This strategy removed the last scheduling obstacle. When Bush's office gave us his only available date, we had less than two weeks to pull together the fundraiser. Since I knew nobody in Houston, my Texas colleagues Tom DeLay (House Majority Whip) and Bill Archer (chairman of the House Ways and Means Committee) graciously loaned us their major donor lists, which we used to drum up donors for our general reception with Bush ($500), and our private VIP reception and photo op with him ($1,000). As I had done two years earlier when former President Gerald Ford attended a campaign event for me, I designed a commemorative badge and program for this special reception.

Serial numbered campaign button and program (autographed by George Bush and James Rogan) from the Bush-Rogan fundraiser, Houston, September 26, 2000. (Author's collection)

• • •

The House of Representatives remained in session on the day of my Bush fundraiser. I made as many votes as I could before catching an early afternoon plane from Washington to Houston. My campaign staff picked me up at the airport, and at 6:15 p.m. we pulled into the circular driveway of L. E. and Ginny Simmons' home, who had agreed to host the event. I went inside and met with our donors until a Secret Service agent told me that President Bush was two minutes away. I followed the agent outside to the front porch and awaited the arrival of our guest of honor.

A large van with tinted windows pulled into the driveway. Bush exited and greeted me warmly. As he asked about my flight out to Houston, he slipped a folded piece of paper into my shirt pocket. "This is a little something for the kitty," he whispered. "Open it later."

"Hey, I almost forgot!" he exclaimed as he spun toward the van. "I brought a surprise. She's a big fan of yours, too." On cue, former First Lady Barbara Bush exited. Flattered and surprised by her unexpected appearance, I thanked her for coming and told her that my wife would be doubly disappointed to have missed the event since she had long admired Mrs. Bush.

"Give Chris our love and tell her not to worry," she replied warmly. "We know you're going to win."

The three of us spent a few minutes on the porch talking about their son's current presidential campaign. When Bush asked for my assessment of how George W. was doing on the West Coast, Barbara raised her hands in the air. "Oh, I can't hear any of this!" she exclaimed. "It's too hard on me."

"She doesn't listen to any campaign news about George," he told me. "It's too rough on her as a mother to hear about the polls, or to watch the news shows, the talking heads, and the rest. I take it all in, but she leaves the room when it comes on TV." Barbara stepped away and engaged our hostess in conversation while Bush and I discussed his son's challenges in several western states. Soon Mrs. Bush drifted back to our conversation, and then she changed her mind. "Oh, I just can't listen!" she said again.

"Then let me share some good news with you, Mrs. Bush." I told her that in the Southern California Hispanic communities, George W. had garnered positive reviews. During his recent walking tour of East Los Angeles, people leaned out of their windows shouting *Viva Bush*. I said that a veteran reporter covering the event told me he hadn't seen anything like her son's reception in that neighborhood since Robert F. Kennedy campaigned there in 1968.

Bush leaned toward me, cupped his hand to my ear, and in a stage whisper asked, "Are you sure they didn't think he was the *other* Bush?" in reference to his half-Hispanic grandson, George P. Bush, whose youth and dark good looks had made him a star at the recent Republican National Convention that had nominated his uncle for the presidency.

The Simmons' escorted us into their lovely home. They had reserved the small den off the entryway for Bush and me to spend time alone before we joined the formal reception. Barbara mingled with guests while Bush and I relaxed for a few minutes. He signed for my family and staff some of the badges and programs that we had created for the event, and he liked them so much that he took some with him for his presidential library.

"This is really something!" he exclaimed as he looked inside the program and pointed to a copy of the photograph that he had signed for me almost three decades earlier when I was only fourteen and he was Republican National Committee chairman. "Look at that wide tie and striped shirt I was wearing! I guess that was high fashion back then," he added.

"High fashion back then!" The photograph George Bush signed for me in 1973 when he chaired the Republican National Committee. (Author's collection)

Mentioning that I had once seen a photograph of him with Babe Ruth during Bush's baseball playing years at Yale, I asked what it was like for him meeting the Sultan of Swat. "Meeting the Babe was a thrill," he said. "He was battling throat cancer at the time. He died shortly afterward. The Babe came out on the field and joined me for a presentation. He looked terrible." Bush then pushed his fingers against his larynx and dropped his voice into a growl to imitate how Ruth sounded: *"I'm so glad to be here today* was about all Ruth could say and still be understood clearly," he reminisced.

He asked when I needed to return to Washington; I told him that I had to fly back that night for votes. "You must be keeping a killer schedule these days," he said. "I remember what that was like in spades. But no travel for me tonight. Bar and I are going home after this to watch George and Laura [Mrs. George W. Bush]. They're on *Larry King* this evening."[4]

At the appointed time Bush and I entered the living room and greeted guests as we made our way to the start of the photo line where Mrs. Bush awaited us. After Bill LaChasse (our photographer) snapped the three of us, she begged off from posing for pictures with donors. "She's having surgery this week for some back problems," Bush told me. "She's not comfortable standing for any lengthy period."

I turned to Barbara. "You're excused," I told her, "because this will save Bill [our photographer] the trouble of asking the lady in the blue dress to get out of the picture." She gave me a puzzled look, and then she laughed when she recognized my reference was to a line that she had used during an interview when her memoirs were published in 1994. Back then she said that she had considered naming her book *Will the Lady in the Blue Dress Please Get Out of the Picture?* because that's what photographers often yelled at her when her husband began his political career.

"Well," she replied, "at least I don't have to hear *that* too often anymore!"

---

4 "*Larry King Live* was an American television talk show hosted by Larry King on CNN from 1985 to 2010. It was the channel's most watched and longest-running program, with over one million viewers nightly." https://en.wikipedia.org/wiki/Larry_King_Live (accessed June 18, 2022).

To: Our esteemed friend, Tim Rojo. A man of principle, who never faltered. G Bush + Barbara Bush

With George and Barbara Bush, Houston, September 26, 2000. (Photo by Bill LaChasse)

I enjoyed watching the old pro handle photo line guests. With each donor's turn, the photographer's assistant removed their press-apply name tag and placed it on their rear shoulder so it would not show in the picture. When the donors posed alongside Bush, he rested his hand on their shoulder. Once Bill clicked the shutter, Bush slid his hand down the person's back, lifted the name tag, and in one quick wrist flick he reapplied it to their lapel for them. He did it with such subtlety that most never noticed his sleight of hand.

During the photo procession, Bush took occasional sips from a vodka highball, and the more he sipped, the more unreserved and chattier he became with donors. When two beautiful young women reached us for their turn, the former president (drink in hand) gushed at them, "What lovely ladies! How charming! You're both so beautiful!" Then, with a chuckle, he nodded his head toward me while telling them, "Jim can't say that. You might call it sexual harassment if he said it! But I'm seventy-six years old. What the hell can anyone do to me?!"

We finished the photo line and joined the general reception. After mingling with guests for half an hour, Bush gripped my arm: "We need to make sure you don't miss your flight out," he told me. "Maybe it's time for us to sing for our supper." With Bush standing next to me, and Barbara seated nearby nursing a glass of wine, I thanked everyone for attending and made a brief campaign pitch before introducing our honored guest.

"Life is so unfair," he began. "First I lost my reelection in 1992, and now I have to follow a speaker like Jim Rogan!" After calling my House race the most important one of the year, he reflected on his own White House tenure when the voters saddled him with a Democrat-majority Congress: "No Republican president has had a Republican Congress in almost fifty years," he said. "I am the only modern president not to have at least one chamber of the legislative branch in the control of my own party during any period of their administration. It's enough to depress you. When in control, the Democrats won't call hearings on your bills. They won't take up any legislation dealing with the issues you campaigned for. They use all their force to do evil things." After delivering that last phrase, he caught himself, chuckled, and then he said, "Okay, I take back the evil part!"

"No!" Barbara called from her seat. "Evil!" Everyone laughed at her ad lib.

"On November 7," he continued, "it will be the first time since Ike won in '52 that we can have a Republican president and a Republican Congress. That will make all the difference in the world. So, our boy, our child—" His references to "our boy" and "our child" brought cheers from the guests. Earlier in the year, liberal pundits had lampooned George W. Bush after his father referred to him in a speech as "that boy of mine." Since then, the elder Bush had avoided such phrases, but this night he resurrected the paternal terms playfully.

"Yes," he continued. "Our boy, our child, our man—"

Barbara catcalled a correction: "Oh George, for goodness sakes! He's our governor!" The room filled with Texas Republicans roared their approval of her modification.

"She's right," he continued. "And our governor—and our beloved son—will make a great president. He will restore dignity to the office and respect to the presidency of the United States."

Throughout his remarks, Bush and his wife engaged in continual extemporaneous banter. While discussing Governor Bush's current presidential campaign, he said, "I listen to everything: news, talk shows, radio, and so on." Pointing at Barbara with his thumb, he added, "But she won't listen to anything!" Mrs. Bush put down her wine glass and crossed her arms in mock irritation as he continued: "Bar just won't listen. She says it's too painful. Imagine that? So, I bought headphones with a long cord. Now I can lie in bed and watch all the news channels and listen to what everyone has to say about George. I can listen all night and Bar can't hear."

"You're so deaf that you turn up the volume so loud that I can hear it anyway!" she retorted.

Turning his body away from his wife, he pretended to share a secret: "As you can see, this is creating a real strain on our marriage. But after fifty-six years together I think we might endure it. We *might* make it!"

Barbara jutted out her chin: "Okay, George," she said. "Go ahead! Keep going! Keep it up!"

Everyone applauded as he walked over and kissed his wife on the forehead. Then he mentioned how George W.'s opponent, Democrat nominee Al Gore, gave his wife Tipper a passionate kiss at their national convention a month earlier: "Can you imagine Al Gore going up in the polls just because he kissed his wife? Bar and I really wanted to help George, so I had her come outside our house in Kennebunkport and I kissed her for twenty minutes. I kissed her that long just to show everyone that we Bushes know how to do it, too. We kissed so long that a neighbor yelled out from behind the breakers, 'Hey, get a room!' "

With this last comical straw, Mrs. Bush threw up her hands in mock exasperation, and then she downed her glass of wine in a single gulp as laughter rocked the house.

I had a front-row seat to the George & Barbara vaudeville comedy act, Houston, September 26, 2000. (Photo by Bill LaChasse)

Before wrapping up, Bush grew serious when discussing my role in the impeachment of the man who had deprived him of a second term. He called my effort exceptional and courageous, and he reminded everyone that I had risked my political career by holding Clinton accountable while representing a Democrat district where the impeached president remained very popular: "Bill Clinton has vowed revenge on Jim Rogan. That means Clinton is coming after a very good and decent man. It angers and sickens me. This is not sour grapes against Clinton. I lost my 1992 race to him fair and square. On my last day in office, I told Clinton, 'Look, you don't have to worry about me. I won't be out there criticizing you every day. It's a very tough job that you are about to inherit. I know. I've been there.' But perjury is perjury, and obstruction of justice is obstruction of justice. You can't act that way and expect no consequences. Clinton disgraced the office of the presidency, and he has disgraced our country. Jim had the courage to stand up to him and all his wrongdoing. It would be a tragedy for Jim not to be returned to Congress in November. All the Bushes are for him. We admire him and we respect him, and we love the guy. This is the most important congressional race in the country. I believe it, and I thank all of you for helping him."

• • •

When the event adjourned, the Bushes and I made our way through the crowd and out to their car. When they reached their van, Barbara looked at her watch, and then she told her husband, "George, we need to get home to watch George and Laura on *Larry King*."

"Bar!" he replied. "After all I said in there, *now* you want to go home and watch George on TV?" He slapped me on the back as he shook his head:

"Go figure!" he said.

• • •

On the flight back to Washington that night, I reached into my shirt pocket and retrieved the piece of paper Bush had put there earlier. It was his personal handwritten check for $1,000 to my campaign committee, which was that era's maximum legal individual contribution. I couldn't believe his generosity.

The next day I sent flowers to Barbara, along with a note of profound thanks to Bush in which I told him that I planned to frame, rather than cash, his check, and that he should adjust his account balance accordingly. A few days later he called and told me that if I wouldn't cash it, then he'd send me a second one to deposit for my campaign account.

"If you do that, Mr. President," I replied, "I'll just frame that one, too. You and Mrs. Bush have done far too much already. Besides, if I can't win my election on our six-million-dollar budget, then I'm not going to win it with an extra thousand. Use that money to buy Barbara a nice set of earplugs for when you're watching George W. on all of those cable news shows."

Suitable for framing: the handwritten $1,000 personal check given me for my campaign by former President George Bush—still uncashed. (Author's collection)

• • •

Six weeks later, in the early hours of Tuesday, November 7, 2000, Americans began the task of selecting the next president of the United States. Judgment day had also arrived in my district: would my constituents stand by me or turn me out? Both sides in the most watched congressional race in the country trucked in thousands of volunteers for the largest get-out-the-vote drive in House of Representatives history.

By 7:00 a.m., I was already three hours into the final day's grueling schedule. My campaign office that morning bustled with scores of workers when the telephone rang. A young volunteer answered it.

The conversation, as was later related to me, went like this:

"Good morning. Rogan for Congress."

"Good morning," said the caller. "Is Jim Rogan available? If he's busy, I don't want to disturb him. I just wanted to call and wish him luck today and let him know my whole family is praying for him."

"I'm sorry, but Congressman Rogan is out. He got a very early start this morning. I'll give him the message when he returns. May I get your name and number?"

"Oh, I don't want him to have to take the time to call back. Just tell him that George Bush called to tell him good luck and to win big."

"Who's this?"

"George Bush."

"Very funny, Monty. Knock it off. I know your voice."

"This isn't Monty. It's George Bush."

"Fuck off, Monty."

Seated nearby, and having overheard the volunteer's side of this conversation, my political director Jason Roe asked the kid to whom he was speaking. "It's Monty," replied the volunteer, "imitating George Bush."

"Give me the phone." Taking the handset, he said, "This is Jason Roe. Who's calling?"

Imagine yourself a seventeen-year-old high school kid volunteering in a campaign office swirling with excitement on Election Day and answering a ringing telephone. You've just called the person on the other end of the line *Monty* a couple of times, you've told him to buzz off (in the most indelicate manner imaginable), and then you hear this end of your boss' conversation with the caller:

"Yes, Mr. President. It's good to speak to you again, too.... I'm so sorry. It was a stupid-ass teenage kid who answered the phone.... No, no, he's not in trouble—don't worry. But this will be a mistake that he'll never forget. I'll make sure of it.... Monty? He's one of our campaign guys.... Yes, sir, I'll tell Jim. Thank you, sir. Please tell Mrs. Bush that we're all working hard down here for Governor

Bush, too—just as hard as we're working for Jim…. Thank you again, sir. He'll be delighted to know that you called. Good luck tonight. Please pass along Jim's love to Mrs. Bush…. Thank you, Mr. President."

After hanging up the receiver, Jason looked into the eyes of the stunned and grief-stricken young volunteer. Jason rose, shook his head, and then he left the room without uttering a word.

On a day that George Bush hoped would end with his son's election to the presidency of the United States—an unimaginable proposition for any father on the planet—he put aside that momentous pressure to pick up the phone and call an embattled junior congressman to wish him luck and let him know that he was pulling for him. I repeat what I said earlier:

I loved that man.

• • •

During Arkansas Governor Bill Clinton's 1992 presidential campaign, he and his team brutalized President George Bush. After defeating Bush, Clinton disgraced his presidency and faced impeachment over it. Throughout the 2000 campaign, Clinton unleashed a barrage of *ad hominem* assaults on GOP presidential nominee George W. Bush. Near the end of that campaign, when former President Bush attended my Houston fundraiser, he did not hide his disdain for his successor.

Five years later, when I next visited with 41, that dynamic had changed in the intervening years. Reports surfaced that Bush's and Clinton's relationship had developed into an almost father-son bond. If true, I suspected Clinton of exploiting the respected elder statesman's sentimentality in a crass effort to rehabilitate his own sullied image. I remained skeptical.

In the spring of 2005, along with my former chief of staff Wayne Paugh, I flew to Austin for a speech and book signing before the Texas Federation of Republican Women. Former President

Bush had arranged for us a private tour of his presidential library, following which he invited us to visit him in his Houston office.[5]

After touring the Bush Library, Wayne and I made the two-hour drive to Houston and arrived at Bush's secure fifth-floor suite shortly before our 2:00 p.m. scheduled meeting. A Secret Service agent led us to the reception room, where a black and white presidential seal etched in glass adorned the wall, along with paintings of the U.S. Capitol and other patriotic scenes.

Tom Freschette, Bush's young chief of staff, welcomed us with an apology: "President Bush is so sorry. He's running late from his luncheon at a nearby club. He'll be here shortly." Bush's delayed arrival gave me a chance to ask Tom about the supposed lovefest between Bush and the man who had deposed him. "It's true," Tom replied, "and it's sincere. At least it is on President Bush's part. Their bond has become so close that President Bush teases that he's the father figure President Clinton always wanted but never had." Tom said the tension broke between the two onetime rivals during their recent joint trip to the Philippines to raise money for tsunami victims. On the flight there, Clinton deferred to the elder Bush and insisted that he take the only bedroom on Air Force One, while Clinton slept in an adjoining conference room. By the end of their trip, Bush had a much softer outlook on the man he had described at my fundraiser five years earlier as having "disgraced the presidency and disgraced our country."

Tom told us that following Clinton's recent open-heart surgery, a rattled Bush telephoned Clinton in the recovery room and asked, "Bill, what the hell happened to you? You're still a young man." Clinton told him that prior to his diagnosis he felt fine other than experiencing constant fatigue after exercise or exertion.

---

5   Former President George H. W. Bush maintained his suite of post-presidency offices on the fifth floor of Park Laureate, a nine-story office building located at 10,000 Memorial Drive in Houston.

"Well," Tom laughed, "that was all President Bush needed to hear. The next thing we knew, every time President Bush felt tired, he grew worried that his heart was failing, and he had the Secret Service check his blood pressure!" Tom said that after a couple months of continuing false alarms, his agents grew weary of them. Tom told us that last week Bush had returned home from an afternoon of deep-sea fishing and felt fatigued. "Quick," he called to an agent, "I suddenly feel dog-tired. Take my blood pressure. Maybe we should call the doctor." The agent told Bush not to worry. His color looked fine, and he had a normal pulse. Bush insisted that the agent check his blood pressure, which registered (again) normal. When Bush pressed the idea of summoning a doctor anyway, the agent grew exasperated:

"Mr. President," the agent sputtered, "this morning you played eighteen holes of golf. After that, you played two sets of tennis. Now you've been deep sea fishing for four hours. For goodness sakes, sir, you're eighty-one years old. Your heart is fine. You're just tired. Now forget about it!"

Tom said that he had accompanied Bush to Little Rock the previous year for the dedication of Clinton's presidential library. Just before the ceremony the three former presidents attending (Jimmy Carter, Bush, and Clinton) had joined President George W. Bush in an upstairs holding room. As usual, Clinton failed to keep anywhere close to the scheduled time. While Carter and the two Bushes waited with growing impatience, Clinton continued chatting with all comers and delayed the schedule. Finally, Carter opened the door and called out, "Listen Bill, we're going downstairs right now to open this library for you. You can do what you want." A sheepish Clinton dislodged himself from admirers and joined his distinguished guests.

Tom had just finished this story when former President Bush arrived. He greeted Wayne and me with apologies for being a few minutes late, and then he grinned and pointed to Tom. "It's all my chief of staff's fault!" he said.

Turning to my former chief of staff, I nodded toward Wayne and said, "Mr. President, I understand completely. Accepting the blame is why God invented chiefs of staff."

Bush led us into his small but comfortable private office at the end of the hallway. In one corner rested a modest-sized desk upon which sat a laptop computer surrounded by stacked books and file folders. Posted alongside his desk were the American and presidential flags, and facing it were Bush's presidential and vice-presidential chairs from the White House's Cabinet Room. Pictures on the walls included a signed photograph of the five presidents attending the Reagan Library dedication (Nixon, Ford, Carter, Reagan, and Bush), an engraved portrait of Martin Van Buren (the last vice president before Bush to succeed by election to the presidency), and a framed 1917 Yale University program depicting Yale's a cappella singing group, the Whiffenpoofs, which included Bush's father as a member that year.

During our leisurely half hour chat, Bush spoke and moved more slowly than the last time I had seen him, although his mind remained sharp as he peppered Wayne and me with questions: How did we like his library? Did the curator give us a guided tour? What did we really think of President George W. Bush's job performance? How was my new book *Rough Edges* selling? When I handed him a signed copy as a gift, he told me, "I already have a copy at home!"

"Well, since this one's signed," I replied, "take the one you have at home and return it to the bookstore for a refund. You can put the money toward your new library wing."

My former chief of staff, Wayne Paugh took this—one of my favorite photographs: former President George Bush reading my first book, *Rough Edges*, April 15, 2005.

Despite his advancing age, Bush told us that he still enjoyed athletics. He spoke of his love for both tennis and golf. Although a recent bout of arthritis had curtailed his tennis game, it hadn't affected his golf swing. When talking about his arthritic condition, he laughed and said, "I guess I'm really battling old fart-ism!" He told us that he wanted to do a parachute jump on his eighty-fifth birthday to match the ones he did to celebrate his seventy-fifth and eightieth. I told him that I saw Barbara's interview before his last jump. When the reporter asked how she felt about it, she replied, "Well, I guess there's no fool like an old fool!"

Bush laughed over his wife's retort, and then he added, "She also told the reporter, 'This is gonna be his last jump—one way or another!' Oh, well, I guess I need to be more sensitive to Barbara's demand that I stop such craziness. After all, she's already mad at me for letting the library archivist put on display a picture of me standing behind her and holding up two fingers behind her head to make it look like she was growing horns!"

"Speaking of golf," he said with a smile, "I played with my son Neil recently. After Neil hit a nasty shank off his tee shot, a big black guy playing in a foursome on the nearby hole started back toward Neil. As he got closer, Neil looked a bit alarmed. Finally, the guy stopped, pointed at Neil, and shouted at him, 'Next time yell *fore*, motherfucker!'" Bush laughed as he delivered his punchline, and we laughed over the unexpected ending of this blue story coming from a former president.

Wanting to get the true story on the supposed Bush-Clinton "bro-mance," I asked him about it. He confirmed the friendship. "In fact," he replied, "Bill's coming out soon to play a round of golf with me at my summer home in Kennebunkport."

I shook my head in mock disappointment. "Your Republican base might have forgiven you for raising taxes in 1990," I replied, "but they'll never forgive this."

Wayne and I had to catch a plane, so we said our goodbyes. Bush rummaged through his desk drawer and retrieved two boxed sets of presidential cufflinks. He gave a pair to each of us. "Oh, you probably have lots of these things," he told me almost apologetically.

"Remember, Mr. President," I reminded him, "I wasn't in Congress long enough to collect much swag like this."

He escorted us through the reception area where we waited together for the elevator. When the doors opened, he put his hand on my shoulder. "The Bush family will never forget what you did," he told me. "You were *very* courageous. I'll never forget you for it."

"Mr. President, those feelings are mutual, and I'll never forget you, either."

And, of course, I never have.

. . .

Although we corresponded occasionally thereafter, my 2005 visit to Houston was the last time I saw President George Bush. When he died of advanced vascular disease at age ninety-four on November 30, 2018, he had outlived every former president of the United States up to that time. His delightful and irreverent wife, Barbara's, passing preceded his by seven months: she died of congestive heart failure at age ninety-two on April 17, 2018.

GEORGE BUSH

March 14, 2001

When I think of Jim Rogan, I think about one of the finest public servants I have ever known. I think about honor, decency, and integrity. He served with distinction in the United States Congress, always making his constituents proud.

Jim Rogan's dedicated service to his community, his State, and his country is well documented and rightly acclaimed. All that remains for Barbara and me is to get in the long line of Rogan friends and admirers to thank him for all he has done for the United States of America.

All the best, Jim. We Bushes send you and your family our warmest personal regards.

Former President Bush sent this letter to be read during a tribute dinner held for me after I returned home from Congress, March 14, 2001. (Author's collection)

Chapter 18

Le Rapprochement

Before President Clinton's impeachment, my various meetings with him during my early congressional service were pleasant. Later, those cordial relations grew understandably frosty. Since I wrote previously about some of our pre- and post-impeachment encounters in my earlier book, *Catching Our Flag*, I won't repeat them here. Let's just say that once I (in Emerson's famous phrase) struck but failed to kill the proverbial king, Clinton targeted me for defeat in the next election. The other House impeachment prosecutors represented safe Republican districts, so Clinton and his team trained their retribution guns on the sole vulnerable GOP congressman representing a Democrat district. Such is politics. I didn't take it personally. Had our roles been reversed, I would have done the same thing to him—and with comparable gusto.

I helped impeach him, and he helped in my defeat for reelection—both valid grounds for mutual dislike. And yet, thanks to Lanny Davis, a rapprochement, to the extent that it lasted, occurred between the former antagonists.

Lanny had served as Clinton's White House special counsel during the lead-up to impeachment, and then he became the embattled president's most visible media defender. During that era, Lanny and I crossed swords so many times in televised duels that one D.C. columnist described us as greenroom buddies from the cable TV news circuit.[1]

Soon after Clinton survived our Republican impeachment efforts, Lanny (then in private law practice) was scheduled to testify before the House Judiciary Committee as a witness on behalf of a client. Suspecting that he might anticipate a roughing up from some of us as payback, during the hearing I passed along a note telling him that I thought he had done a great job for Clinton. I attached to it a gift from my campaign button collection: a 1976 badge produced in Maryland supporting Jimmy Carter for president, Paul Sarbanes for U.S. Senate, and a very young Lanny Davis for Congress.

That note began a friendship that lasts to this day.

Our newly minted bond raised eyebrows among some of my Republican colleagues (I imagine it did likewise to various White House eyebrows). When Lanny joined me for lunch in the House Members Dining Room, word spread quickly around the Capitol about this odd couple breaking bread under the dome. Later that evening, Judiciary Committee Chairman Henry Hyde summoned me to his office and asked if the lunch rumor that he had heard was true. Confirming it, I told him that Lanny and I had become friends. Henry's face scrunched in exasperation and disgust. The normally charming and elegant chairman snorted, "Friends with Lanny Fucking Davis!" Then, with a silent wave of his hand, he dismissed me.

• • •

As I mentioned in chapter 16, after losing my reelection battle in November 2000, I returned to Washington for the "lame duck"

1   Mary Ann Akers, "Bill Clinton's Secret Pen Pal," *The Washington Post*, November 29, 2007, http://voices.washingtonpost.com/sleuth/2007/11/bill_clintons_secret_pen_pal.html.

congressional session.[2] I visited Lanny's law firm, where he and his partners wanted me to come aboard when my term expired. When I asked Lanny what his former boss might say about his recruitment effort, he told me that he had already broached the matter with Clinton recently at their White House farewell party. Instead of Clinton having a visceral reaction against me, he said the outgoing president spoke highly of me and in a respectful way. That was unexpected but appreciated news.

Two months later, with my congressional tenure having just expired, I attended the January 20, 2001, inauguration of President-elect George W. Bush. At the Capitol, I joined my former colleagues, along with the senators, Supreme Court justices, governors, and the new president's cabinet, family, and friends in the procession onto the platform. The U.S. Marine Band played "Hail to the Chief" a final time for the outgoing president as Bill Clinton arrived and descended the red-carpeted steps. The formal program opened with prayers, musical selections, and the swearing-in of the vice president-elect. After a final patriotic song, Chief Justice William Rehnquist stepped forward to administer the oath to the new president.

With all eyes focused on Bush, I raised my camera to take his picture, and then on impulse I turned my lens away from the incoming leader and on Clinton. Through the viewfinder I saw Clinton turn away from the main event and look back for one last gaze, as president, at the Capitol dome. My finger clicked the shutter in time to capture this swift moment before he returned his attention to the ceremony. Since all other photographers had trained their cameras on Bush during the oath, it dawned on me that

---

2   "A lame-duck session of Congress in the United States occurs whenever one Congress meets after its successor is elected, but before the successor's term begins. The expression is now used… for any portion of a regular session that falls after an election. In current practice, any meeting of Congress after Election Day, but before the next Congress convenes the following January, is a lame-duck session." See Lame Duck Session, https://en.wikipedia.org/wiki/Lame-duck_session (accessed November 25, 2022).

I might have been the only one to capture Clinton's poignant last presidential moment. Given his recent generous comments about me to Lanny, I wanted to reciprocate the kindness and send Clinton a print of the photo that I had snapped of him. Before doing so, I ran the idea by Lanny. He urged me to do it, and he said that if I had any qualms, I should tell Clinton that I was following Lanny's suggestion. He added that the Big Guy (his nickname for Clinton) would appreciate it.

In my letter to Clinton, I wrote, "As you can see from the attached, I am about as good a photographer as I am an impeacher of presidents." I explained the story behind the photo and that our mutual friend Lanny had suggested that I mail it to him, adding, "I hope that describing Lanny as our *mutual* friend doesn't hereafter make him my *exclusive* friend!"

A last look back: Bill Clinton at George W. Bush's inauguration, January 20, 2001. (Photo by the author)

Clinton replied with a handwritten letter in which he told me how much he appreciated the photograph, and that he had not received any others from Inauguration Day. Then he added an unexpected idea. He wrote that he came to Washington frequently to see his wife, Hillary (a newly elected U.S. senator representing New York). He suggested that on a future D.C. visit he and I should get together for a talk, and that it would be interesting to do so.

I called Lanny and told him about both the note and Clinton's mention of a get-together. Lanny urged me to do it, adding that it would prove interesting for both of us. He told me one question still bothered Clinton that he would ask me if we ever talked: Was there anything he could have done to stop the impeachment train?

I told Lanny that if he wanted to ask me that question, then I had better not meet with him because Clinton wouldn't like the answer. There *was* a way for him to sidestep impeachment at a critical moment, but someone close to him prevented it. I then shared the full story with Lanny:

> Over the nine months preceding Clinton's impeachment by the House of Representatives, and at the request of Speaker Gingrich and Chairman Hyde, I had engaged in backroom discussions with Clinton's two designated White House liaisons, former Congressmen Butler Derrick (D-SC) and Tom Downey (D-NY). Both Gingrich and Hyde had directed me to keep open this confidential White House channel in the event our mutual interests at some point warranted a compromise short of impeachment. Team Clinton had agreed to these unofficial and secret discussions, and they designated Butler and Tom as their representatives. Throughout the spring, summer, and fall of 1998, the three of us met or spoke on the telephone intermittently to discuss hypothetical options or compromises both sides might accept if and when the time proved ripe.
>
> Convinced that Clinton's scandals would cause a backlash against the Democrats, throughout 1998 Gingrich had proclaimed both publicly and privately that we would gain upwards

of thirty new GOP seats. Accepting Gingrich's prognosis, House Republicans expected to hold the whip hand in dealing with the White House after the midterms. In late October 1998, just as Congress prepared to adjourn for the final recess before the November midterms, Tom and I had agreed to meet for lunch immediately after the elections to assess the situation and see if we could reach a resolution.

Things didn't work out as expected. On Election Day, the Democrats shellacked us. We not only failed to pick up any new House seats, but we also suffered a net loss of five and barely clung to a slender GOP majority.

After surviving a very tight reelection myself, I returned to Washington and huddled with Gingrich, Hyde, and then later with our new Republican Speaker-designate Bob Livingston (R-LA).[3] They felt that the specter of the upcoming impeachment hearings (scheduled to begin a couple of weeks after the midterms) had contributed mightily to the fallout. Our three dejected leaders wanted to ring down the curtain and dump the scheduled Judiciary Committee hearings. They directed me to meet with my White House counterparts and negotiate a non-impeachment exit strategy.

With these marching orders, I called Tom Downey to confirm our upcoming scheduled lunch. Tom apologized and said that he needed to cancel it. I suggested an alternative date. He then told me that he was *canceling* our meeting, not rescheduling it. He said that his White House "principal" had instructed him to end negotiations. When I asked why, he told me that his principal stated that the Republicans "wouldn't dare impeach Clinton" after our thrashing at the polls.

---

3 Given the worst midterm performance of a party out of power since 1822, Gingrich announced that he would not stand for Speaker in the newly elected Congress and would resign from the House. The Republican Conference chose Appropriations Chairman Bob Livingston as Gingrich's designated replacement.

"I understand that sentiment," I replied, "but remember that before the House adjourned last month, we passed a resolution *ordering* the Judiciary Committee to return to Washington after the midterms to begin impeachment hearings. Despite the election results, those hearings will launch in two weeks unless we can come to terms."

"Yes, I know."

"Tom, once those hearings start, we might not be able to put the genie back into the bottle."

"I understand, but I have been directed by my principal to cut off all negotiations. I'm sorry, Jim."

Before ending the call, I said, "Tom, I've got to know. Who gave you this order?" I assumed that it had come from some hubris-filled mid-level staffer subject to being overruled by a more sensible superior. Tom's answer stunned me:

Hillary Clinton.

Of all the "what ifs" from the Clinton impeachment saga, this one remains the most ironic. When I called Tom Downey that day after the midterms, the dejected House Republican leadership wanted to cut their losses and head for the exits. A window of opportunity had opened for Bill Clinton to avoid impeachment. Per Tom Downey, the president's wife had slammed it shut.[4]

---

4   After completing this chapter in late 2022 (almost twenty-five years after Tom Downey had canceled our meeting and told me why), I emailed a draft of the chapter to Lanny Davis for his review. In his reply, he insisted without equivocation that Mrs. Clinton never opposed an impeachment compromise, although he conceded that Tom Downey might have caught her "in a bad moment" on that particular day. I suspect that is precisely what occurred. Per Lanny, Mrs. Clinton had remained open to a compromise generally. When Tom approached her about our final scheduled meeting, he did so within hours of the Republicans near-catastrophic midterm election showings, and when the House GOP leadership was splitting apart at the seams and in full cut-and-run mode. Under that scenario, why would the Clinton White House negotiate a truce with an enemy in disarray and in full retreat? When she told Tom to cancel the meeting, her instincts were sound politically. In the end, however, the expected retreat scenario didn't play out the way that favored the odds at that moment. The history books are filled with such ironic "What ifs".

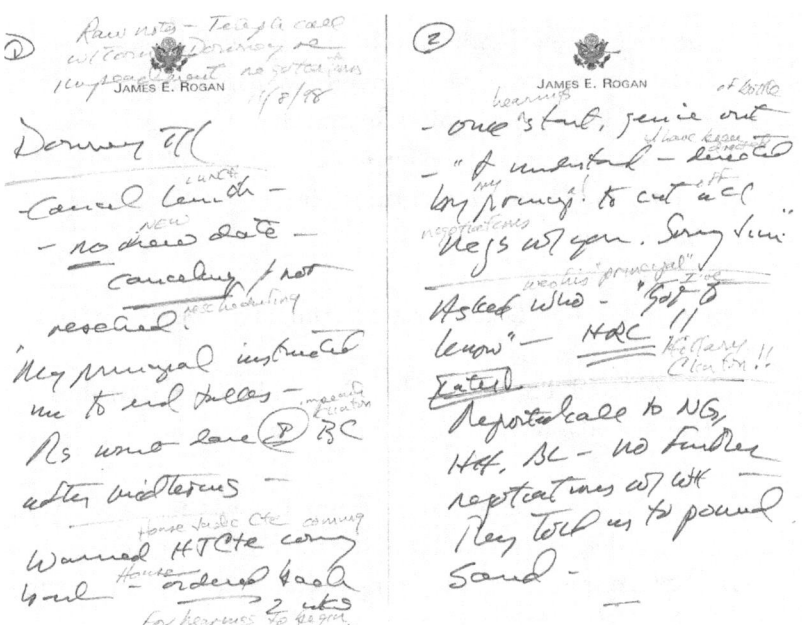

Notes from my telephone call with Tom Downey, November 8, 1998. The blue ink notes are what I scribbled as we spoke; I went back later and interpreted in pencil what my hurried hieroglyphics represented. (Author's collection)

In fairness to Mrs. Clinton, she assessed the political situation correctly. The Republican leadership *did* want to scuttle impeachment. Still, her instincts regarding the GOP's unwillingness to press forward on impeachment, no matter how well-founded in probabilities, proved wrong. It turned into a miscalculation that resulted in her husband's legacy forever bearing the impeachment tattoo.

In any event, the meeting President Clinton suggested to talk over impeachment with me never occurred. It's just as well. If he had asked me whether he missed any opportunity to avoid it, I didn't want to be the one breaking this news to him.

• • •

Although our post-presidency meeting never materialized, those first letters began an infrequent but pleasant, and even mildly playful, correspondence between Clinton and me over the next few years. Once again, Lanny facilitated it. The *Washington Post* reported that after I sent Clinton the inauguration photo, he told Lanny, "Your friend Jim Rogan reached out to me." Lanny asked the former president what he did about it. Clinton replied, "I reached back."[5]

• • •

A year or so after I sent Clinton the photograph, I read a news story that he was seeking items from his early campaigns for Congress, state attorney general, and governor for his presidential library under construction. I had a few such treasures in my political memorabilia collection, so I began sorting through it to set some aside for him. During this process my younger brother Pat called me. Then serving as operations manager at Pacific Bell Park[6] (home stadium for the San Francisco Giants), Pat told me that he had just spent the day with Clinton, who visited Pac Bell to watch a Giants game with Hall of Famer Willie Mays. As the ballpark's supervisor, Pat inherited the job of greeting Clinton upon his arrival, giving him a private tour of the stadium, escorting him to his skybox, and sticking around during the game to ensure his comfort. "I was so worried about upsetting him if he found out that I was your brother that I removed my nametag so he wouldn't see the name Rogan anywhere!" Pat told me.

When I shipped the campaign mementos to Clinton, I wrote a note and told him about Pat's experience with him and how Pat had removed his nametag to avoid ruining his guest's day. Soon

---

5   Akers, "Bill Clinton's Secret Pen Pal,".

6   In 2022, the baseball stadium was known as Oracle Park.

a letter from Clinton arrived thanking me for the memorabilia. In a handwritten postscript, he reminisced about his time at Pac Bell, and he said that Pat needn't have worried since he had now reached the age where he couldn't remember at whom he was still supposed to be mad. In reply, I wrote that I was delighted to know he had reached such an age, but I added that if he *really* couldn't remember with whom he was still supposed to be mad, I could send him a box of videotapes stored in my garage that would refresh his recollection very quickly.

• • •

During the summer of 2004, and by coincidence, Clinton's and my publishers released our first books simultaneously. Both were memoirs: *My Life* by him and *Rough Edges* by me. Mine sold with modest success; Clinton's became a runaway international bestseller. The hosts of a national cable news show invited Lanny and me to appear together to discuss these literary releases. While on the air, the liberal host asked me, with a hint of sarcasm, "Oh, I suppose *you* won't be reading Clinton's book, will you?"

"Actually, I look forward to reading it," I replied. I said that despite our differences, Clinton's life represented a perfect example of the Great American Story: he grew up as the son of a widowed mother in rural Arkansas, obtained his education, and then rose through hard work and determination to the greatest position that Americans can offer one of their own. When the interviewer asked if I thought his book would outsell mine, I shrugged off further comparisons: "My book is about three hundred pages. His is over a thousand pages. His book will sell infinitely more copies, but at least you won't get a hernia when lifting mine!"

Clinton watched the interview and told Lanny (who told me) that the former president enjoyed my remarks, and that he wanted a signed copy of my book. Before I could comply with Clinton's request, doctors had hospitalized him and ordered emergency quadruple heart bypass surgery on the former president. After he returned home to recuperate, I sent him my book and inscribed it, "Dear Mr. President, I hope you find this book 'interesting'—but not so 'interesting' that it gives your cardiologist angst!"

Clinton responded with a nice note thanking me for sending flowers during his recovery. In a handwritten postscript, he told me that he found my book not only interesting, but also good. He urged me to write another—and also to keep praying about my right-wing politics.

• • •

Alas, our cordial exchanges ended after a few years because of circumstances for which neither of us were responsible. To explain requires some background.

In 2006, President George W. Bush nominated me for a seat on the federal bench. Along with other Bush judicial nominees, my paperwork languished in a Democrat-controlled Senate. That same year, reporters learned that Clinton had dined with an unlikely companion: Richard Mellon Scaife, the owner of the *Pittsburgh Tribune-Review* and the funding source behind many efforts to investigate and maintain public focus on Clinton administration scandals. More unlikely than their peacemaking lunch was the later revelation that Scaife had donated $100,000 to the Clinton Foundation.

Soon thereafter, the columnist who had reported the friendship between this unlikely duo lunched with her friend (and my former political director) Jason Roe. During their conversation, the Clinton-Scaife story came up. "Scaife isn't the only one of Clinton's former enemies that he communicates with," Jason told her.

"Who else?" she asked.

"My old boss Rogan. They've shared some notes back and forth."

The columnist called me. I confirmed that Clinton and I had exchanged occasional friendly notes, but I turned down her repeated requests to provide her with copies of the letters. Perhaps in retaliation for my lack of cooperation, in her story she suggested that I had chummed up to Clinton in an ongoing effort to apologize for impeaching him as well as to advance my current judicial nomination prospects.[7] Both insinuations were unfounded. Clinton and I had started corresponding almost six years before Bush had nominated me, and impeachment never arose as a subject between us beyond playful jesting. The intimation that I had been apologizing for my impeachment vote is unworthy of reply. Indeed, my judicial nomination, made late into Bush's second and final term, languished and died eventually in the Democrat-controlled Senate, but it died alongside a staggering 52 other doomed Bush judicial nominees.[8] The Senate Democrats simply refused to confirm the vast bulk of Bush's late-game federal judge picks with a new presidential election in the offing.

Standing alone, that *Washington Post* column probably would have meant nothing. But at the same time, Senator Hillary Clinton was campaigning for the 2008 Democratic presidential nomination. A reporter on the campaign had read the column and asked Mrs. Clinton's deputy press secretary to comment on a report that Clinton and I had corresponded. The deputy, unaware of the former president's and my private communications, issued a sweeping denial that it had ever occurred, and then she parroted the columnist's insinuation by accusing me of making up the story to soften Democrat opposition to my judicial nomination. The campaign's denial became its own story. Reporters called and hounded me to release copies of the letters. Again, I refused. One pushy journalist told me, "Well, if you won't give us copies, we won't believe you."

---

7   Akers, "Bill Clinton's Secret Pen Pal,".

8   President George W. Bush made fifty-three federal judicial nominations that the Democrat-controlled Senate failed to confirm. See, e.g., https://en.wikipedia.org/wiki/George_W._Bush_judicial_appointment_controversies (accessed November 10, 2022).

I let him know, in the language of the longshoreman grandfather who had raised me, what he could do with his credibility assessment.

After a day or so, someone must have shared the truth with the campaign press aide, because she stopped issuing denials and declined further comment, but the damage was done. The existence of our private correspondence had created a mild embarrassment to his wife's campaign. I waited a while, and then I wrote to Clinton and expressed regret that the press had made an issue out of something so innocuous. I didn't hear back from him.

In the ensuing years, I dropped Clinton an occasional note about something of interest. Other than a brief acknowledgment for a book that I had sent him at Lanny's request, there were no further replies. In late 2021, doctors hospitalized him for an infection. I sent flowers and a get-well message to his hospital room (coincidentally, just a few miles from the Southern California state courthouse where I was then serving as the supervising judge). Neither were acknowledged, so I don't know whether he ever received them.

• • •

To those wondering why I bothered corresponding with a man whose presidency I sought to terminate, and who succeeded in crushing my cherished congressional service, I share two reasons. First, on a personal level, I always liked Bill Clinton, and I enjoyed our infrequent but good-natured ribbing.

There is a second reason that explains my soft spot for him. Growing up with a love of history, government, and politics, my goals from boyhood were to become a lawyer and one day serve in Congress. In late 1978, during my final college semester, I had submitted law school applications and was still awaiting replies. During that period, I attended a national Democratic Party workshop in Memphis. Although many famous luminaries spoke at the forum, the only person whom I met on the panel was the unknown thirty-one-year-old lawyer who had moderated it. When the workshop closed at the end of a long day of presentations, and as the moderator collected his notes, I walked over and introduced myself.

While we talked, I mentioned my pending school applications, and I asked his advice about whether he felt a legal career was the best path for my future goals. He put down his notes and launched into a ten-minute pep talk. After sharing how he had parlayed his law degree into his own now-budding political career, he urged me to pursue my ambitions and keep him posted on my progress. We shook hands and said goodnight. The kindness shown to me while a young college student is something I have never forgotten.

On that Memphis evening nearly a half century ago, the young moderator who had taken the time to encourage me was the attorney general of Arkansas.

His name was Bill Clinton.

Chapter 19

Easy Come, Easy Go

Time for a Politics 101 pop quiz:

Question: What happens to a congressman when he votes to impeach a president enjoying a three-to-one approval rating in his district?

Answer: He gets clobbered at the next election.

In November 2000, Democrat State Senator Adam Schiff beat me in my reelection effort by a pretty wide spread. Schiff was a tough competitor. I know. I had run against him successfully twice for the state legislature before our congressional battle royale. No offense to Schiff, but after my impeachment role, the Democrats could have run Uncle Fester against me that year and walked off with a victory.

I saw the writing on the wall almost two years before my loss. In my closing argument to the Senate in Clinton's impeachment trial— twenty-one months before the election—I predicted that my role as a House prosecutor would result in my defeat.[1] What a dichotomy: Clinton and I devoted our lives trying to get to Washington. After committing perjury and obstructing justice, he kept his job. Because I helped call him to account for violating the law and his constitutional oath, I lost mine. In politics, easy come and easy go.

Shortly before the vote to impeach Clinton, my campaign consultant ran a poll in my district. The results confirmed that if I sided against the president, a whopping 75 percent of high propensity voters reported that they would never vote for me again. A particularly discouraging aspect of the survey showed that this hostile percentage included a significant chunk of Republican voters. Upon receiving these results, I showed the poll to Judiciary Committee Chairman Henry Hyde. He reviewed it, and then he put his hand on my shoulder. "Jim," he said to me in a fatherly way, "I've been in politics a long time. I'm here to tell you that this poll means nothing. Here's what I want you to do. Vote your conscience, do your job honorably, and then go home and explain to your constituents why you impeached Clinton. If you do that, I promise you'll find that any poll telling you that 75 percent of your constituents will never again vote for you is a meaningless poll."

Some months after my defeat, I spoke at a dinner honoring Henry. I recounted the story of that poll and Henry's advice to me. "Mr. Chairman," I told him as I concluded my tribute speech, "I did exactly as you said. I voted my conscience, I did my job honorably, and then I went home and explained to my constituents why

---

1   Near the conclusion of my closing argument before the United States Senate in the Clinton impeachment trial (February 8, 1999), I said, "From the time I was a little boy, it was my dream one day to serve in the Congress of the United States. My dream was fulfilled two years ago. I am a Republican in a district that is heavily Democrat. The pundits keep telling me that my stand on this issue puts my political fortunes in jeopardy. So be it. That revelation produces from me no flinching. There is a simple reason why. I know that in life dreams come and dreams go, but conscience is forever. I can live with the idea of leaving Congress. I cannot live with the idea of remaining in Congress at the expense of doing what I know to be right."

I voted to impeach Clinton. And you were absolutely right. The poll claiming that 75 percent of my constituents would never vote for me again *was* meaningless—

Only 60 percent of them never voted for me again!"

• • •

During that final campaign, one of my heartiest supporters wasn't even a voter in my district. Melanie Morgan, the conservative firebrand host of a San Francisco (of all places) talk radio show, exhorted her listeners throughout my race against Schiff to send checks to my campaign. Thanks to her, thousands of Northern California dollars rolled into our Southern California coffers.

Throughout the campaign, Melanie interviewed me often on her drive-time morning show. With Election Day nearing and impeachment passions sizzling, I joined her on air once again. As our interview wrapped up, she elicited sympathy for me by commenting, "I'll bet you've encountered some very nasty people because you impeached Clinton."

"Melanie," I replied, "I've met some people who are so nasty, so vicious, and so bitter toward me that I've come up with my own name for them."

Melanie hesitated before asking the obvious follow-up question. No doubt she feared my recitation of the term might require her engineer, under FCC regulations, to bleep out my answer. After a momentary pause, she took a chance: "What *do* you call these nasty, vicious, and bitter people?" she asked.

"Melanie, I call them . . . *constituents*."

• • •

Representing a district with a substantial majority of voters holding contrary views strips away much of the glamour and perks that might otherwise attach to the job of congressman. As my third year in the House of Representatives drew to a close, and with the

2000 election cycle looming, I entered the new year as America's number-one-targeted-for-defeat Republican incumbent.

In the House chamber one night in late 1999, my friend Dana Rohrabacher (R-CA) struck up a conversation with me. Unlike my heavily Democrat district, which made my ongoing political survival tenuous even in the best of times, Dana (a Libertarian-leaning conservative Republican and former speechwriter for President Ronald Reagan) had first won his seat in deep-red Orange County in 1988. For the next thirty years, he won reelection every two years without breaking a sweat.[2]

"Congratulate me," Dana said as he sidled alongside me.

"For what?"

"I just topped the $1 million mark in my fundraising."

"Dana, that's great. Raising that kind of money in an off-election year while representing a safe district is quite a feat. You must have worked the telephones very hard."

Dana gave me a funny look. "No," he corrected me. "Not *this* year. I mean I just hit the $1 million mark altogether since I first came to Congress."

I gasped. "Are you telling me that in the eleven years that you've been here, you've raised a paltry $1 million while representing one of the wealthiest counties in America? Dana, I have to raise $6 or $7 million next year alone for the coming cycle, and I'll probably lose anyway. I can't imagine what it's like to represent a district where you can cruise to reelection every two years by making the barest effort."

Intrigued by Dana's anemic fundraising either for himself or for party building, I asked him, "Tell me what you like about being a congressman?" For the next few minutes, he rattled off all sorts of fun things he did while on the job: military flights on high tech

---

2   In time, Rohrabacher's Southern California district changed from deep red to purple. He lost his reelection in 2018 after serving fifteen terms.

fighter jets; a recent VIP inspection weekend aboard the U.S.S. *Enterprise* while it patrolled the Middle East; around the world fact-finding trips; surfing in exotic locales while on government travel; and a bevy of other exciting activities and experiences.

When he finished, I shared with him a glimpse of *my* life in Congress: untold hours holed up in a cramped cubicle making thousands of fundraising calls; reviewing truckloads of angry constituent letters; a 24-7 bashing from my district press and community activists; an average of seven death threats a day; weekly home-grown protests that occasionally ended with the crowd burning me in effigy; and the need to return to a hostile district most weekends (after putting in long hours at the Capitol during the work week) to engage in ongoing thermonuclear warfare to defend my seat.

Our conversation produced a stunning revelation for me. "I've been here for three years," I told Dana, "and now, for the first time, I realize something. You and I have the same title. We don't have the same job. I get my ass kicked every day trying to hold this seat to help maintain our slim Republican majority—a majority that lets guys like you hold committee chairmanships, travel the world, and enjoy yourselves. I won my seat in 1996 with 50.1 percent when Bob Dole [the Republican presidential nominee] lost my county by over twenty points. I won reelection in 1998 with 50.6 percent when Dan Lungren [California's GOP gubernatorial nominee] lost my county by over twenty-five points. Next year, I'll have to run alongside a Republican presidential nominee who'll probably lose my county by thirty points.[3] We don't have the same job, Dana. We have the same title. I don't think you'd like my job."

Dana stared at me for a moment before commenting on my plight: "Hmm, you're right," he told me. "Your job sucks."

---

3   In 2000, when Adam Schiff beat me for reelection by nine points, Texas Governor George W. Bush, the Republican presidential nominee, ended up losing my county by thirty-two points.

Your job sucks. In three little words, Dana Rohrabacher summarized the entirety of my district's job description for any conservative Republican representative.

No wonder the guy wrote speeches for the Great Communicator.

• • •

It always helps a congressman's reelection prospects if he shares his constituents' ideology or, if he doesn't, he fakes it. I struck out on both counts. Impeachment wasn't the only issue that put me out of step with my Los Angeles County constituents. I ran twice for the state legislature and three times for Congress, and I refused to backpedal on first principles: I ran as a pro-life, pro-Second Amendment, pro-tax cut, pro-law enforcement conservative seeking to return power to the states and localities from the bureaucracy blobs of Sacramento and Washington. Amazingly, I won five out of six elections in a district where defeat appeared likely in all six contests. Polling showed consistently that my constituents didn't agree with me on most issues, but because they admired my spunk and candor, they overlooked policy differences. Impeaching President Clinton changed that dynamic. My vote to dispossess him from the White House angered those once-tolerating crossover voters. They weren't in a forgiving mood when Adam Schiff teed up against me in my final race.

Even without the impeachment elephant in the room, at times my blunt style almost dared constituents to turn me out of office. I recall an appearance in Burbank (a city that I always lost) where I held one of my district town hall meetings. A hundred or so constituents filled the auditorium. After I made preliminary remarks and gave an update from Washington, I opened the forum for questions. About thirty minutes into it a man in his mid-twenties sporting a ponytail, a graphic tee shirt, torn jeans, and sandals approached the microphone. "Congressman," he said, "I lost my job two months ago. A congressman is like a father to his constituents. I need a new job. As my elected "father," what are you going to do for me?"

When I heard his question, a smirk crept over my face. I looked at the audience expecting others to join my display of eye-rolling disdain. Their response caught me off guard. They looked back at me in anticipation of hearing what I planned to do about this guy's plight.

"Wow," I told him. "You lost your job two months ago? Why didn't you call me right away when this happened? Well, better late than never." I directed my chief of staff Dan Revetto (watching from the back of the room) to get his address and phone number. Dan walked over to him and took down the information.

As people in the audience nodded approvingly at my apparent interest in Mr. Ponytail's predicament, I addressed my needy constituent: "Did you give your information to Dan? You did? Fine. Now, here's what we'll do. When you go to bed tonight, leave the key to your apartment under the mat. I presume that you have a coffee pot. You do? Great. I'll pick up a newspaper on my way to your apartment tomorrow morning. I'll get there at 5:30 and let myself in. I'll wake you gently, and you can shower while I put on a pot of coffee and cook you some eggs. While you're getting dressed, I'll sit at your kitchen table and read the want ads for you. I'll circle the ones that are looking to hire people. After you've had your breakfast, we'll get in my car, and I'll drive you to the first place circled in the want ads. We'll go in and meet the manager, and I'll tell him that you need a job. If that doesn't work out, we'll go on to the next circled place. We'll keep doing that until someone hires you or until we run out of circles. If you don't have a job by the end of the day, we'll start all over the next morning. I'll come over early, let myself in, fix your breakfast, read the want ads for you, and then I'll drive you around to the circled businesses."

The idiots among the audience members nodded approvingly as the questioner's eyes brightened. "You're really gonna do this for me?" he asked.

I didn't leave him or the crowd in suspense long: "Actually, no. I'm not doing any of that for you."

"Let me tell you something, buddy," I continued. "My wife and I adopted twin girls eight years ago. I didn't adopt you. I'm not your father. I'm your elected representative. Since my early teens I held about two dozen jobs before I came to Congress. Some of those jobs I quit; at some I was fired, and at others I was laid off. Yet in all those periods of unemployment, it never dawned on me to show up at my congressman's town hall meeting, call him daddy, and then ask him, 'What are you going to do for me?'

"What am I going to do for you?" I concluded. "I'm going to give you some good advice. Get off your ass and go look for a job."

A smattering of people in the audience laughed and applauded. Most huffed or murmured. Dan Revetto stepped forward and declared the town hall adjourned. As we exited the building, I turned to the district office intern accompanying us that day and said, "You have just witnessed yet another reason why I probably won't win reelection in this district."

• • •

Not long after that town hall encounter, I attended a local middle school awards ceremony in (where else?) Burbank. Upon arrival I learned that the students had been asked to draw and paint posters celebrating the theme "Peace." At the ceremony, the principal introduced the student finalists, each of whom came forward and explained the significance of their creations. After distributing the awards, the principal asked me to say a few words.

I congratulated the students on their efforts, paid compliments to their various artistic abilities, and then I closed with this thought: "Although *Peace* is a worthy topic for a poster, when your school holds this contest next year, might I make a suggestion? Next year your theme should be *Liberty*. Liberty is far more important than peace. A prisoner can have peace in his jail cell, but he's still a prisoner. A slave might find peace in submitting to his bondage, but he's still a slave. Liberty can never be preserved without the willingness to defend it, which is the opposite of utopian notions of 'peace.' Defense of liberty, and not peace at any price, is the debt owed to our Republic by every American. I hope that all of you young people will keep that in mind as you leave here today."

Of course, the school never invited me back to speak at another awards ceremony. And I'm sure the peacenik parents of all those future National Endowment for the Arts grant awardees signed up to walk precincts for my opponent.

• • •

My good friend Mike Dukakis, the former Massachusetts governor and 1988 Democratic presidential nominee, once described his unsuccessful White House bid with two words: "Losing stinks." When I lost reelection in 2000, I remembered Mike's assessment, as well as my late colleague Sonny Bono's observation: Washington, he told me, is just like the entertainment community. When you have a hit show in Hollywood, or when you win a seat in Congress, everyone around you is your best friend. But when the Hollywood execs cancel your show, or if you lose reelection, your best friends in either town "wouldn't piss on you if you were on fire."

After my defeat, I returned to Washington for the lame duck congressional session. Sonny's warning proved true. People with whom I had served and developed what I thought were close bonds during my four years there suddenly averted their eyes when passing me in the hallways. Very few called or dropped by to express condolences. Most were too busy cultivating the new class of incoming freshmen who might help them advance their ambitions. When the voters turn a congressman out of office, he becomes yesterday's news in multiple ways.

Because I never allowed my personal sense of identity to get wrapped too tightly in temporary titles conferred by public office, I took the "ghosting" treatment that accompanied defeat philosophically. However, in the ensuing years, I knew many vanquished incumbents who took it hard. Defeat drives some of them into deep depression, shame, or both. For many cycles following my congressional eviction, after each election I wrote or called every defeated House incumbent to thank them for their service and assure them that life goes on. In a small way, this outreach became my biennial ministry.

One to whom I turned my sympathies was George Gekas (R-PA). George had represented his district from 1983 until 2003, and he was among our thirteen House managers prosecuting the Clinton impeachment trial. When the Democrat-controlled Pennsylvania legislature redistricted George into a Democrat-majority district, they defeated him for reelection in November 2002. I heard through the grapevine that the loss had left George devastated. He refused to return to the Capitol for lame duck session votes, return calls to his staff, or even go to his office to pack his personal belongings.

When I learned of George's plight, I called him daily for a couple of weeks until he finally answered the phone. He told me that he didn't go back because he felt too ashamed over being kicked from office after twenty years of faithful service. In a breaking voice he lamented that very few of his so-called close friends in Congress had even bothered to call him. Knowing from personal experience how he felt, I tried cheering him up.

"Listen, George," I told him, "you won ten consecutive congressional elections with ease because your constituents knew you and loved you. You had a close bond with them, and because of it they wanted you as their voice in Washington. The only way the Democrats could beat you, George, was to push you into a new district where people *didn't* know you. Had you run in your old district, you'd be back for another term."

Sensing that my words brought him no relief, I pushed the envelope further: "Now, George, take my case. For seventeen years I was my constituents' deputy DA, trial court judge, state representative, Assembly majority leader, and their congressman. The Democrats didn't need to redistrict me to beat me. My voters *knew* me when they threw me out. The only way they could beat you was to move you to an area where people *didn't* know you. That's a huge difference between us that you should appreciate."

George brightened. "By God, you're right!" he told me. "I hadn't thought about it that way. Thanks, Jim. I feel much better now."

"You're welcome, George. I'm glad you feel better. But now I have a question for you."

"What?"

"How come all of the sudden I feel like shit?"

• • •

A couple of weeks before my defeat, I ran into my old family friend, former Congressman John Burton (D-CA). John and I had served together in the state legislature. More than that, in his younger days he had worked as a bartender at a San Francisco night spot alongside another bartender (my father) and a cocktail waitress (my mother).

When I encountered John outside the Rayburn Building, he asked how my campaign was going. After I shared the uphill road that I faced, he asked me a pointed question: "Why the hell do you want a job where you have to kill yourself every day for two years just for the privilege of hanging on to it by your fingernails?"

I had never thought about it in those terms. After pausing to reflect on his question, I replied, "Johnny, I guess it's like the janitor whose job was to shovel up behind the circus elephants. For twenty years, all he did was shovel and gripe, shovel and gripe, shovel and gripe. Finally, after hearing the janitor complain every day for two decades, the circus manager approached him and asked, 'If you hate your job so much, then why don't you quit?'

" 'What!' replied the shocked janitor at the radical suggestion, 'And give up show business?' "

On January 3, 2001, at the invitation (or, more correctly, the insistence) of California's twenty-seventh congressional district voters, I gave up show business.

• • •

There you have it. As for my time in Congress, I came, I saw, and then I left. I didn't get to exit on my own terms, but I try avoiding quarrels with God when His timetable doesn't comport with those of His creations. In the near quarter century that has elapsed since I said goodbye to the United States House of Representatives, and as I count the bountiful blessings enjoyed since, I find that this approach helps avoid the separation anxiety suffered by others.

If she were still alive, I'd be tempted to tell Alice Rogan, "Look, Mom, I'm an *ex*-congressman!" And, trusting in the Lord's promise that though I stumble I shall never fall—

—I wouldn't have it any other way.

Acknowledgments

While writing this book, I imposed on keen-eyed proofreaders who have done me the same favor for my previous works. Once again, deepest thanks to my former chiefs of staff Jason Roe and Wayne Paugh, and to Jon H. Jacobs—my buddy since Mrs. Firpo's fifth grade class.

Appreciation flows to my literary agent, the inestimable Sealy Yates, who did his best to sell this book to traditional publishers. If Sealy can't get a writer a contract, nobody can. Sealy sent me the responses he received from mainstream publishers who reviewed the manuscript. The consensus was that they enjoyed the stories, they thought the book was a fun read, but because I no longer haunted the cable news shows with regularity or had a massive social media following, they felt that I couldn't market the book sufficiently to interest them in publication. In the old days, a writer just needed to ink a good book, and then the publishing houses promoted sales by setting up interviews and book tours, running ads in the trades, getting books reviewed, etc. Today, unless a writer has a widely circulated television, radio, or podcast presence; a major literary following; or has some other means of mass self-promotion, publishers usually take a pass. That is why God invented independent publishing. You hold this volume in your hands thanks to Plan B.

With this book I am again reunited with two great friends who have worked with me on all my previous books: editorial director Geoff Stone and creative director Mark Karis. They brought polish and elegance to this final product, and I am grateful for their gifts. I also want to thank Idekunik, the freelance illustrator who did the caricatures for the book jacket. I never looked this good in real life! Thanks also to my old friend and colleague Jeff Ferguson for his graphic artist assists when I needed them.

Love and hugs to my wife, Christine, and my twin daughters, Dana and Claire, and to my granddaughters, Ellie, Ava, and Olivia. Keep Jesus in your hearts.

Since this is a book about some of my experiences as a member of the United States House of Representatives, a word of appreciation is due to my former constituents of California's (then) twenty-seventh Congressional District. Whether you loved or hated me, it was my privilege to represent you, and I remain grateful that you twice chose me to be your voice in Washington before sending me to the showers in November 2000. Thanks to you, I can say that I once served in Congress, but not so long as to let it cause any permanent psychological damage.

If you read this or any of my other books, I'd love to hear what you thought of it/them. Feel free to contact me through my website: www.jamesrogan.org. I do my best to answer all emails personally (if they contain a modicum of civility).

God bless you all.

MAY 2024

Index

Index

Index

Also by James Rogan

www.jamesrogan.org

ISBN: 9781735131757

ISBN: 9781735131771

ISBN: 9781736933435

ISBN: 9781735131771

ISBN: 9781956033014

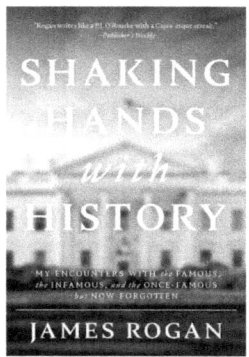

ISBN: 9781734638592

www.ingramcontent.com/pod-product-compliance
Lightning Source LLC
Chambersburg PA
CBHW061137120626
46546CB00005B/1827